CW00765321

Routledge Guides to t

The Routledge Guidebook to Smith's *Wealth of Nations*

Adam Smith (1723–1790) is famous around the world as the founding father of economics, and his ideas are regularly quoted and invoked by politicians, business leaders, economists, and philosophers. However, considering his fame, few people have actually read the whole of his magnum opus *The Wealth of Nations* – the first book to describe and lay out many of the concepts that are crucial to modern economic thinking. *The Routledge Guidebook to Smith's* Wealth of Nations provides an accessible, clear, and concise introduction to the arguments of this most notorious and influential of economic texts. The *Guidebook* examines:

- the historical context of Smith's thought and the background to this seminal work
- the key arguments and ideas developed throughout *The Wealth of Nations*
- the enduring legacy of Smith's work

The Routledge Guidebook to Smith's Wealth of Nations is essential reading for students of philosophy, economics, politics, and sociology who are approaching the Smith's work for the first time.

Maria Pia Paganelli is Professor of Economics at Trinity University in San Antonio, Texas. She is an editor of *The Oxford Handbook on Adam Smith* (with Christopher Berry and Craig Smith) and *Adam Smith and Rousseau: Ethics, Politics, Economics* (with Dennis C. Rasmussen and Craig Smith). She is the President of the International Adam Smith Society.

Routledge Guides to the Great Books

The Routledge Guidebook to Smith's *Wealth of Nations*

Maria Pia Paganelli

Routledge
Taylor & Francis Group

LONDON AND NEW YORK

First published 2020
by Routledge
2 Park Square, Milton Park, Abingdon, Oxon OX14 4RN

and by Routledge
52 Vanderbilt Avenue, New York, NY 10017

Routledge is an imprint of the Taylor & Francis Group, an informa business

British Library Cataloguing-in-Publication Data
A catalogue record for this book is available from the British Library

Library of Congress Cataloging-in-Publication Data
A catalog record has been requested for this book

ISBN: 978-1-138-68614-4 (hbk)
ISBN: 978-1-138-68615-1 (pbk)
ISBN: 978-0-367-82420-4 (ebk)

Typeset in Times New Roman
by Newgen Publishing UK

To my father and my mother

CONTENTS

Acknowledgments   viii

1   **Adam Smith and the Scotland of his days**   1

2   **Introduction and Book I, Chapters I–III**   13

3   **Book I, Chapters IV–VII**   27

4   **Book I, Chapters VIII–X**   48

5   **Book I, Chapter XI**   70

6   **Book II**   95

7   **Book III**   123

8   **Book IV, Chapters I–VI**   139

9   **Book IV, Chapters VII–IX**   166

10   **Book V, Chapter I**   189

11   **Book V, Chapters II–III**   221

12   **Legacy**   252

Index   260

Acknowledgments

Thanks to Trinity University, Universitade Federal de Minas Gerais, Hokkaido University, Institute for Humane Studies, and Liberty Fund for their support and encouragement during this project.

Thanks to the participants of the several readings groups on *The Wealth of Nations* I held over time. Thanks in particular to Nicole Gordon, David Harper, Mario Rizzo, Will Compernolle, Julia Anderson, Thomas Sargent, Hugo da Gama Cerqueira, and Tsutomu Hashimoto.

Thanks to Tyler Cowen, Andrew Farrant, Asgeir Berg Matthiasson, Shinji Nohara, Reinhard Schumacher, Craig Smith, and Anthony Waterman for commenting on the manuscript.

1

ADAM SMITH AND
THE SCOTLAND OF HIS DAYS

Adam Smith was born in Kirkcaldy, Scotland, in June 1723. His father, also Adam Smith, died before little Adam was born. His mother, Margaret Douglas, died in 1788, not long before her son Adam's death in 1790.

Smith was educated in the parish school and was fluent in Latin and Greek. He went to the University of Glasgow where he studied moral philosophy under Francis Hutcheson; mathematics under one of the leading scholars on Euclid, Robert Simson; and natural philosophy or experimental philosophy, including astronomy, under Robert Dick, who used the most modern instruments to study Sir Isaac Newton's new theories. He then won a Snell Scholarship to study at the University of Oxford, at Balliol College. The scholarship was intended for those who would be ordained in the Church of England and serve in the Episcopal Church in Scotland. Smith moved to Oxford where he spent several miserable years, studying mostly on his own, given that "our only business here [is] to go to prayers twice a day, and to lecture twice a week" as he wrote home (Letter to William Smith dated August 24, 1740. Correspondence, p. 1). This experience affected his view of education, as his criticisms of the endowed universities, such as Oxford, in the *Wealth of Nations* testified. He asked for, and managed to obtain, an exemption from taking holy orders, and went back to Scotland to live with his mother.

His first job was to offer public lectures on rhetoric in Edinburgh in 1748. They were a great success. He was paid with fees, a system that he will endorse in his analysis of education in the *Wealth of Nations*. His lectures were so successful that when an opening at the University of Glasgow came up, he was invited to move there. He took the Chair of Logic at the University of Glasgow in 1751 and then in 1752 that of Moral Philosophy. He taught Jurisprudence as well as Moral Philosophy. He continued his career as an administrator and was in charge of new acquisitions for the library. In his correspondence, he described his days at Glasgow as the happiest and best of his life.

In 1759, he published his first book, which turned out to be a best seller: *The Theory of Moral Sentiments*. Smith kept working on it throughout his life, with five additional editions, the last one of which came out soon before his death in 1790.

His success as a teacher and as a scholar was such that he was hired to be the private tutor of the Duke of Buccleuch, a great landowner in Scotland. As was then the custom, he accompanied the young duke on a Grand Tour of Europe. Smith and the duke left for the continent and spent time in France and Switzerland where they met many of the intellectual and aristocratic elite, including the leading economists of the time: the physiocrats. But Smith was bored in France. So he started to write the book that eventually became *The Wealth of Nations*. Because the brother of the young duke got sick and died, the Grand Tour had to be cut short, and Smith and his pupil went back to Scotland. Smith received a very generous pension as a compensation for his tutoring services, as well as a lifelong friendship with the duke and his family.

Back in Scotland, Smith moved back in with his beloved mother in Kirkcaldy and continued his writing of the *Wealth of Nations*. Being a meticulous writer, Smith took his time in finishing the book. So much so that both his publisher and his friends kept putting pressure on him to deliver the manuscript. The first printing of the *Wealth of Nations* dated March 1776. Given increasing tensions with the North American colonies, which culminated in the declaration of independence in July of that same year, everybody had their eyes on Smith, eager to read his thoughts on the health of the British Empire.

This book was also an immediate best seller. The 3,500 copies of the first print run sold out immediately. It went through five editions during Smith's life and it has been in print ever since. It was translated into German the very same year as its British publication; into French and Italian within three years; and by the beginning of the new century it was also in print in Portuguese, Spanish, Danish, and Russian. The *Wealth of Nations* was also cited in British Parliamentary discussions on several occasions – 37 times between 1773 and 1800 alone, to be precise. Napoleon allegedly took it with him when he was sent into exile in Saint Helena. After Smith's death, it was the book from which everyone learned economics.

Despite his pension and royalties from the two books, which alone would have provided for a comfortable life, Smith and his mother moved to Edinburgh in 1777 so he could start working as a Customs Commissioner. He took his job so seriously that he told a friend never to read the actual trade restrictions Scotland had, or he would find himself in violation of most of them. Smith did: he read the trade restrictions and found himself in violation of most of them. To set a good example, he burnt all that he was not supposed to have: most of his wardrobe!

He lived in Edinburgh until he died on July 17, 1790. He asked his executors, the chemist Joseph Black (1728–1799) and the geologist James Hutton (1726–1797), to burn all his manuscripts, at least 18 volumes. But because he did not believe they would really do it, he ended up doing it himself a few days before he died. Possibly in those pages there was also a third book, on the theory of jurisprudence, which he promised in the last paragraph of the first edition of *The Theory of Moral Sentiments*, and which he claimed to be still working on in the advertisement of the last edition of *The Theory of Moral Sentiments*. While we were able to have copies of the notes of his lectures on jurisprudence because two sets of students' notes have been discovered, one in 1890s and one in 1958, there is still no trace of a surviving copy of this third book, which most likely would have been based on those jurisprudence lectures.

The house he owned in Edinburgh, now property of the Edinburgh Business School and a center for the promotion of Adam Smith's legacy, was used for his extensive entertaining. Smith hosted dinners for famous visitors to Edinburgh and some of the many clubs he belonged to, as well as a regular Sunday evening dinner for friends.

THE SCOTTISH ECONOMY

The clubs and societies Smith belonged to were typical of the time in which he lived. Clubs were groups of intellectuals who met on a regular basis to discuss topics of interests and recent scientific discoveries. France had an equivalent in the form of salons. But differently from France, where ladies attended and sometimes hosted the salons, Scottish clubs were all male. Participants came from all walks of life: they included businessmen, chemists, botanists, poets, astronomers, physicians, physicists, clergymen, lawyers, moral philosophers, inventors, geologists, architects, academics, and bureaucrats. Almost all intellectuals now associated with the Scottish Enlightenment belonged to some of these clubs.

The intellectual excitement of eighteenth-century Scotland took place in a small developing country growing at a very fast rate. Since the Union with England in 1707 and the formation of Great Britain, Scotland may have lost its political independence, but it gained access to large overseas markets, including the English colonies. The colonial trade was now fully available to Scottish merchants and Scottish ports. The total tonnage of oceanic vessels passing through Scotland ports rose from 54,407 in 1759 to 109,895 tons in 1771, and costal vessels from 150,995 to 257,494. Glasgow soon became the largest port for tobacco trade in the world. Scottish linen manufacturing ballooned. Iron manufacturing and coal output increased by more than a factor of 10. Sugar refining, rope and sailcloth manufacturing, tanning, kelp and soap production, and fishery, all experienced very rapid growth. Agricultural production improved too, driven by high demand. In few decades, the price of Highland cattle tripled.

This rapid and significant growth required and was sustained through investment in infrastructure: dikes and fen draining, roads, harbors, bridges, canals, including the construction of the Forth and Clyde Canal connecting the two coasts of Scotland, and the Monklands canal linking Glasgow to the coalfields of Coatbridge. Scotland developed an extremely competitive and sophisticated banking system able to finance all these activities and to provide the financial stability needed during this rapid growth. Scotland went from being a peripheral country to a commercial and intellectual center.

SCOTTISH POLITICS

The 1707 Union with England opened Scotland to new markets but also caused some tensions. Especially in the Highlands of Scotland, there was still support for the dethroned Stuart monarchy. This led to armed rebellions aiming at restoring the crown to the Stuarts. The most formidable of these rebellions was in 1745, while Adam Smith was at Oxford. Charles Edward Stuart, nicknamed "Bonnie Prince Charlie", and his Jacobite militia marched without much resistance into England to remove the Hanoverian "usurper" George II. They got as far as Derby – 130 miles from London. They then retreated into Scotland followed by the Hanoverian armies. The complete defeat of the Highlanders eventually took place in Culloden, in the Highlands, on April 16, 1746.

This episode was embarrassing for some Scots, including Adam Smith, who was made fun of because of his Scottish origins by his English classmates at Oxford. Scotland was considered a backward country, far from the more developed and "superior" England, inhabited with, in the words of David Hume – another prominent Scottish philosopher and eventually Smith's best friend, – "bare-arsed Highlanders". But this rebellion was also a warning that a few thousand of those "naked unarmed Highlanders" (in Smith's words this time) could arrive unscathed at the door of the capital of the largest empire in the world – a concern that Smith would generalize in his treatment of national defense in the *Wealth of Nations*.

To prevent further insurrection, in part under the pretext of, or simply in conjunction with, agricultural reforms, the clan system in the Highland was outlawed and many forced to leave their land, either to the lowlands or to the colonies: the so-called Highland Clearances. The feudal power of life and death of Highland chiefs was abolished in 1746, weapons were forbidden, and the tartan outlawed. The chiefs could no longer have private armies, thus finding it more profitable to use their land for sheep.

There were thus two Scotlands until after Culloden: the prosperous, Anglophone Lowland corridor from Glasgow to Edinburgh, Whig in politics and Protestant in religion; and the tribal, Gaelic-speaking Highlands far from government and the rule of law, a "no-go" area for peaceable Lowlanders; Tory in politics and either Catholic or Episcopalian in religion; which the Enlightened Scots wanted to "improve".

THE HIGHLANDS AND THE STAGES OF DEVELOPMENT

The relationship between Scotland and its Highlands remained ambiguous. On the one hand, the Highlands represented a backward part of the country, especially compared to the booming Lowlands. On the other hand, it represented a set of admirable values to contrast against the corruptions that this fast economic growth was bringing.

All this trade Scotland was experiencing was transforming Lowland Scotland into a commercial society. A commercial society differed from other kinds of societies: hunter-gatherer, pastoral, and agricultural. The common belief was that each kind of society had its own set of values; its material conditions and material incentives; and its legal, political, social, and moral characteristics. Hunter-gatherers were "savages", with little property and little government. Women were subjected to men, there was slavery, and age and physical strength were marks of distinction. Shepherds were "barbarians" who began to recognize property, but only in a limited way. Tribal chiefs ruled with personal power and justice was generally arbitrary. Property in land developed with agricultural societies and with it chivalry too. These were "civilized" societies. "Civilized" meant urban, organized in urban communities – from the Latin *civis*, or city. Commercial societies were the apex of "refinement" and "politeness". Here we see fully developed courts and legal systems, and evolved forms of government that rely on impersonal rule of law. Opulence was, therefore, linked with good governance, the presence of the rule of law, and of a good administration of justice. The Scottish thinkers generally believed that commerce and thus commercial societies brought about the "two greatest blessings that man can possess" – "opulence and freedom" (LJ p. 185) – not just for a few but for all.

Note that the language used here, inappropriate by today's standards, was not meant to be offensive at the time. These are all specific terms of art to indicate specific characteristics of different kinds of societies. *Civil* is in contrast to *rude*, as opposed to, say, the contemporary Swiss philosopher Jean-Jacques Rousseau who would contrast *civil* with *natural*. The rudeness of the savage hunter-gatherer and barbaric nomadic shepherd is contrasted to the civilized agricultural and refined commercial society in a way that is mostly descriptive rather than judgmental.

Associated with these different stages of development, the Scots observed and appreciated different virtues. Agricultural societies valued stability and "masculine" virtues. The enlargement of society, which commerce brought about, implied increasing interactions with others, and with the other sex as well, which induced people to be more sociable and more likely to develop sociable virtues. Historical development was perceived as a process of civilization and "feminization". Societies developed from rude savagery and barbarism, from masculine stages, where aggression, strength, and courage are valued, to more civil and feminine stages, where sociability, kindness, and desire to emulate are valued – to a world of conversation and commerce.

Feminization could slip into "effeminacy", though. While feminization is generally a positive thing for the Scots, effeminacy is not. This was a derogatory term. Effeminacy was dangerous and reproachable. Commercial societies, with their wealth and luxuries, more than any other kinds of society, may lead to effeminacy, potentially distracting individuals from the public sphere and weakening the traditional masculine virtues. Andrew Fletcher of Saltoun (1655–1716), Adam Ferguson (1723–1816), and Robert Wallace (1697–1771), in particular, saw the cost of the increased sociability as a decrease in martial spirit that could become a problem if the country needed to be defended. This was an issue that Adam Smith also understood, though he developed his own response to it.

Agriculture and agricultural values were seen as counter to this commercial laxity. Home gardening was promoted and became fashionable at this time: a small piece of land to cultivate in an urban or semi-urban environment was a way to mitigate the effeminacy tendencies of commerce and to keep alive the more masculine virtues of agricultural societies.

James Macpherson (1736–1796) claimed to have collected oral Gaelic stories of ancient origins and then translated them for publication. Many doubted the authenticity of Macpherson's account, attributing the entirety of the poems to him. Nevertheless his "translation" of Ossian's poetry between 1760 and 1763 solidified the ideals of traditional agricultural values of sobriety, as opposed to commercial laxity, and the martial spirit of the Highlanders.

The Caledonians, the local Gaelic-speaking Celtic tribes of the Highlands, became an idealized type that was able to combine the politeness and civility of a commercial society, in which there is no slavery and women are treated with respect and gallantry, with agricultural values of martial masculinity.

The reception of this image of Scotland was not always successful, especially among its southern neighbors, but it became influential in Europe, especially Germany, sowing the seeds of what would become the Romantic movement.

IMPROVEMENTS AND ENLIGHTENMENT

The booming economic growth and the booming intellectual life were linked with an "ideology of improvement" and experimentation. A large variety of experiments were tried with a large variance in their success rates, especially in agriculture. For example, spade husbandry and potato cultivation were introduced and were immediate successes. There were attempts to introduce different kinds of sheep to develop sheep farming, the success of which was evident after 1790s. There were also attempts to improve the climate by planting palm trees throughout Scotland. Palm trees, after all, grew with good weather. So, if palm trees were brought to Scotland, the theory went, then they would have brought good weather with them. It did not take long to learn the direction of causation.

Studies and improvements in botany brought medical, commercial, and aesthetic improvements, as well as political conflicts. In the eighteenth century, botanical gardens grew in number, size, and importance. There were attempts to domestically cultivate products to be offered as alternatives to produce made with slave labor: Silesian milkweed was to replace cotton, sugar beets to substitute for sugar cane. Tobacco was successfully produced in Scotland to cut imports from Virginia, but it was successfully stopped by the powerful lobby of tobacco merchants, as Adam Smith would tell us. Sir Alexander Dick (1703–1785), president of the Royal College of Physicians of Edinburgh, grew rhubarb, from seeds brought from St. Petersburg, in the attempt to break into the Russian monopoly. Rhubarb was thought to be a remedy for indigestion, itself a side-effect of luxury. He succeeded but eventually the production was moved to the possessions of the East India Company, a British monopoly. To limit China's dominance in the tea market, John Hope (1725–1786), also president of the Royal College of Physicians of Edinburgh and Regius Keeper of the Royal Botanic Garden and King's Botanist, as well as Professor of Botany and Materia Medica at the University of Edinburgh, tried, and failed, to produce Chinese tea in the Highlands of Scotland. Joseph Banks (1743–1820), a naturalist and botanist as well as an explorer not only made the Royal Botanic Gardens of Kew in England the world's leading botanical gardens, but also introduced Chinese tea cultivation in India, with better results than in Scotland.

The experimentation that brought both failures and improvements in all fields was a result of the systematic application of a new method of enquiry – the experimental method. In Scotland, the experimental method was practiced both inside and outside the universities. Men of ability with expansive views and innovative ideas were to be found inside or around universities, and their ideas spread among the intellectual elites through the different clubs.

Edinburgh University was the first to teach Newtonianism, even before Cambridge, where Newton was a professor. Newton's *Principia* was published in 1687 and it was in Edinburgh's library as early as 1690. In Glasgow it appeared in 1695 and a bit later in Aberdeen and St. Andrews. The University of Glasgow had Adam Smith, Joseph Black, James Hutton, and James Watt; the University of Aberdeen had Colin Maclaurin who wrote the textbook on Newton's *Principia* used in Scotland and at Cambridge, John Gregory, and Alexander Gerard; the University of Edinburgh had William Cullen, John Hope, and John Sinclair. David Hume, though, did not have an academic position.

The main idea of the Scottish Enlightenment was that humankind was part of nature just like the plants and the planets in the sky. A method similar to the one used to study rocks or the sky could be used to study the rest of nature – humankind included. Humankind was now a proper object of study by natural sciences. And the empirical and scientific investigation of humans looked for deeper understanding of human nature, institutions, politics, religion, law, and the economy. David Hume called it the "science of man".

When the experimental method was used, history was made into the source of observations. The more observations, the better off the formulation of laws concerning human nature would be. In eighteenth-century Scotland, the study of history became a way of extending the powers of observation. Adam Smith's writing blooms with historical examples. In his library we can count a large collection of history books. Not surprisingly, the number and popularity of histories published multiplied: David Hume's *History of England* and William Robertson's *The History of Scotland*, *The History of the Reign of Charles V*, and *The History of America* were all bestsellers. And history for the Scots was not just the history of a country or of a people over time. It was also the comparison of different populations across different places in the same, and in different, times. Travel diaries also bloomed as a genre contributing to history, and therefore to the "science of man", by describing the newly encountered societies of the new world.

Yet, some differences among humans raised questions as to whether there was more than one nature of man present in nature. In his 1758–1759 edition of *Sistema Naturae* (1735), the Swedish naturalist Carl Linneaus, while placing and classifying humans in the natural system together with flora and fauna, divided humans into homo sapiens and troglodytes (coining the terms), placing humans in the class of mammal and in the order of primates. Humankind was classified in four varieties, depending on their physical and moral characteristics: American, European, Asiatic, and African. These classifications opened the door to two ways of classifying the human species: one in which every human group may derive from a single original stock; the other in which human differences developed from different progenitors. Montesquieu, Adam Smith, John Millar, Thomas Reid, James Beattie, and the Wise Club of Aberdeen are usually associated with the first group, while David Hume, Lord Kames, and William Robertson with the second, though this is controversial.

Regardless of how many kinds of human natures there are, for most of the Scottish intellectuals an individual's character was formed through the "mirror of society". Character was a product of society, thus the appropriateness of its characteristics changed with different social environments. But the fact that character may change did not imply that human nature was thought to change. With the idea of developing a science of man, or science of human nature, most of the intellectuals associated with the Scottish Enlightenment implied that the fixed human nature had laws, similar to the laws we found in physical nature, which can be discovered through observation. The challenge was to understand what is "constant" and what is "accidental" to use two ideas Adam Smith used in his *History of Metaphysics*, an essay that survived the flames. This challenge was an underlying constant in Smith's works, *Wealth of Nations* included, as we will see throughout this *Guidebook*.

It was thanks to this method, to discover what is fixed and what changes, that the thinkers usually associated with the Scottish Enlightenment studied and discovered natural laws. It is through this method of discovering what was constant and what was accidental that wealth formation can be studied in a scientific way, understanding its nature and its causes. It is in this context that *An Inquiry into the Nature and Causes of the Wealth of Nations* was generated.

Note that from the title Smith embeds the spirit of questioning and discovering of his time. The *Wealth of Nations* is not a *Treaty*, it is not a *Theory*, it is not a *Principles*, it is not even a *System*. It is an *Inquiry*.

The reading of the *Wealth of Nations* that I suggest in this *Guidebook* is twofolded. In my view, Smith offers a moral justification of wealth, and prioritizes morality over efficiency in his justification of wealth. Smith's analysis of wealth is nevertheless scientific and empirical: Smith identifies human nature as fixed, and the environment in which people live as variable, implying thus that characters and behaviors would vary as a consequence of these variations. In my view, he emphasizes that what we commonly see is not necessarily what is; precise empirical observations and reason allow us to extract patterns that form theories to be tested using history. Applying these ideas to the understanding of wealth, we learn that even if money seems like wealth, it is not, and policies that seem to be beneficial to a nation may not be.

FURTHER READINGS

Berry, Christopher J. 1997. *Social Theory of the Scottish Enlightenment*. Edinburgh: Edinburgh University Press.

Broadie, Alexander. [2007] 2011. *Scottish Enlightenment*. Edinburgh: Birlinn.

Jonsson, Fredrik Albritton. 2013. *Enlightenment's Frontier: The Scottish Highlands and the Origins of Environmentalism*. New Haven, CT, and London: Yale University Press.

Paganelli, Maria Pia. 2015. "Recent Engagements with Adam Smith and the Scottish Enlightenment". *History of Political Economy* 43.3: 363–394. (On which this chapter is based.)

Phillipson, Nicholas. 2012. *Adam Smith: An Enlightened Life*. New Haven, CT, and London: Yale University Press.

Ross, Ian. 1995. *Life of Adam Smith*. Oxford: Oxford University Press.

Sebastiani, Silvia. 2013. *The Scottish Enlightenment: Race, Gender, and the Limits of Progress*. New York: Palgrave Macmillan.

2

INTRODUCTION AND BOOK I, CHAPTERS I–III

INTRODUCTION

Adam Smith published his most famous book, *An Inquiry into the Nature and Causes of the Wealth of Nations*, in 1776. In his title (and in most of his text as well) Smith avoids mentioning the words "political economy". Just a few years earlier, in 1767, the term *political economy* had been used for the first time as part of a title of a book in English, in James Steuart's (1707–1780) work: An *Inquiry into the Principles of Political Economy*. Smith consciously ignored Steuart's wording and work, with which he did not agree. The inquiry Smith wants to engage with is about the nature and causes, not the principles, possibly implying his willingness to focus on an open-ended scientific and empirical account of wealth.

Smith's work opens with his own introduction. He summarizes about 1,000 pages in a couple of pages, telling his readers what to expect from his work. We need to pay a great deal of attention to this short introduction because Smith is telling us on what to focus.

In the opening sentence Smith declares that labor is "the fund" that supplies "the necessities and conveniences of life" consumed in a nation. There are at least three key points here: labor, conveniences, and consumption.

The main source of wealth is labor. It is labor that supplies what we need and want. It is labor, not gold, not land. We can read this claim as Smith already telling us against whom he is going to argue, and the alternative he is offering. The so-called mercantilists, for Smith, claimed that wealth came from gold and silver, from money that is, and what mattered for a country was their accumulation. Smith is saying that it is the fund of labor that matters instead. And the so-called physiocrats claimed that land was the most important factor in creating wealth. Again, land is not mentioned, just the fund of labor. We can read Smith as implicitly telling us that he is providing an alternative way to understand wealth and wealth creation, a way based on labor, not on money or on land. Note also that labor will appear in the first paragraphs of each chapter of the first two books of the *Wealth of Nations*.

Smith also tells us that the fund of labor supplies us with "necessities and conveniences". We do not want only what is necessary, we want also what is convenient. And what is convenient and not necessary is usually a luxury. So for Smith we want both necessities and luxuries. For Smith, we do not want just a copper teapot, we want a silver one, as he tells us in his other book, *The Theory of Moral Sentiments*. A shirt is necessary, but a fine shirt is better, when possible. Luxury is almost just as important as necessity for us.

And finally, our production is the means to get to consumption. The ability to consume is what makes a country wealthy, not its production, let alone production for its own sake. The implication seems to be that the accumulation of gold and silver, or of domestic products at home, is not what makes us wealthy. Our ability to consume is what makes us wealthy. This can be read as another indirect criticism of the so-called mercantilists who would promote expensive domestic production and discourage consumption of cheaper foreign imports. If the way to understand wealth is the ability to consume, what reduces consumption for the sake of production is not a way to promote wealth, but a way to diminish it. And this is all encapsulated in the first sentence of the introduction!

But why should consumption be so fundamental in understanding wealth? Because if we cannot consume, we die. In the fourth paragraph, Smith tells us that some societies are "so miserably poor" that the people who cannot produce cannot consume, and therefore they die. The people who cannot produce and therefore cannot consume are the ones who are "too old, or too young, or too infirm". So, in some societies that are so miserably poor, people are forced, "or think themselves reduced", to abandon "their infants, their old people, and those afflicted by lingering diseases, to perish of hunger, or to be devoured by wild beasts". The image of someone being forced to leave their own baby or their own elderly parent to be devoured by wild beasts is chilling today. But if you are so poor that the people who can't work can't consume even the necessities required to survive, you will die.

Not all societies are so miserably poor though. Some societies are richer than others. In these societies not everybody works, and they who do work can produce enough to support themselves and all who do not work as well. In fact, Smith tells us, someone who does not work, not only does not die of starvation, but also can consume even a hundred times more than someone who works! In a rich country there is so much abundance that even one of the poorest workers can consume more than what the richest people in poor country could ever have. Wealth allows you to consume necessities and conveniences; it allows you to live, and to live well too. Poverty, by contrast, kills you. This will be a recurrent theme in the book, so much so that Smith will measure economic growth through the ability of a country to support an increasing number of people.

A conspicuous absence in Smith's introduction may highlight the relevance of labor and consumption even more: markets and prices are not mentioned here. There are just labor, consumption per capita, and production per capita.

A country is wealthy depending on the proportion of what it can consume given the number of consumers (paragraph 2). On what does what we can consume depend? Smith's answer is: the skill of workers, as well as the proportion of people working productively versus not working productively – everything else the same (paragraph 3). But what matters the most are the skills of workers. As we just said, in poor countries everybody works, but little is produced and therefore consumed; while in rich countries not everyone works, but all consume abundantly without much trouble. What matters the most for wealth accumulation is the improvement in the productive power of labor, not the proportion of productive laborers to those who do not labor.

Smith also tells us that he uses Book I to analyze the causes of this improvement in the productive powers of labor. He will also look at the distribution of output among different groups of society. Book II looks at how it is possible to change the proportion of people who work productively and people who do not. His distinction between "productive" and "unproductive" labor was a reaction against the distinctions that the physiocrats made, and it would become central for all the classical economists, including Karl Marx, and their analyses of production and accumulation. Here Smith announces that what makes the difference seems to be "capital stock". So, Book II analyzes the nature of capital stock, its accumulation, and its different uses. Book III is about the accidental circumstances that seem to have unintentionally introduced and established different policies, and that gave different encouragement to wealth creation in different nations and at different times. Book IV presents the different theories of political economy, their effects, and their political influence, such as mercantilism and physiocracy. And finally, the fifth and final book will be about the expenses and the revenue of the sovereign. It deals, in particular, with whether some of the necessary expenses should be funded from general revenue or from local revenue; with the different methods of paying for these expenses, including government debt.

An additional thing to note about the introduction, which is also true for the rest of the book, is, as we saw in Chapter 1 of this *Guidebook*, that the language Smith uses may not be the most appropriate for our days, but it is what was common in his days. The distinction between "savages" and "civilized" people is a technical distinction based mostly on the prevalent means of production of different societies. A society that is based on hunting and gathering was commonly referred to as savage. Pastoral societies were commonly thought of as barbarians. Societies based on agriculture tended to be called civilized and the ones based on commerce were considered refined. Or, in broader terms, what is not based on either agriculture or commerce is considered rude and uncivilized. The contrast between commercial and noncommercial societies will be a regular presence throughout the *Wealth of Nations*. The *Wealth of Nations* can be seen as a defense of commercial society, with the recognition of its limits and defects, but still a defense of it. The "mercantile interests" in Smith's words, or what today we would call crony capitalism or special interest groups, jeopardize the wealth that commerce creates. And theoretical and moral critics, such as Jean-Jacques Rousseau, jeopardize the moral foundation of commerce by claiming that wealth and commerce degrade morals. In the view suggested here instead, Smith wants to show that commercial societies offer the best way to secure both justice and prosperity.

BOOK I, CHAPTER I: OF THE DIVISION OF LABOR

The first sentence of *An Inquiry into the Nature and Causes of the Wealth of Nations* is a terse statement: the greatest improvement in the productive power of labor is the effect of the division of labor. This is something Smith will explain in more details in the next chapter.

In the second paragraph we have a first warning: the common eye makes mistakes, a theme recurrent in the whole book, in my view, possibly one of the most important lessons Smith wishes his readers to learn. How do we correct for those mistakes? He will tell us later (paragraph 5 and 9, as well as in a "juvenile" essay published posthumously titled *The Principles Which Lead and Direct Philosophical Enquiries; Illustrated by the History of Astronomy*) that the philosopher is the person who lets us know about our mistakes and offers to help us to arrive the correct view.

A philosopher is someone who specializes in observing everything. The division of labor applies to knowledge too. And thanks to this specialization, the philosopher is able to combine the most distant things, which a common observer would not be able to do.

For Smith, the mistake we commonly make is to believe our eyes. There is more to the world than our eyes can see at any one time. Our eyes cannot see at once the division of labor in a great manufacturer, but they can see it well in a small one. In a great manufacturer, which provides many things for many people, the division of labor is so large and fragmented in so many different places that we cannot see it all at once. However, a small manufacturer can have all its production in a single small place. So we can easily see how all the labor is divided because all is under our sight at once. Consequently, we think there is more division of labor in a small business than in a large one, while in reality it is the opposite.

Because of this incorrect belief, a common way to describe the division of labor is to describe what goes on in a small business, not in a large one. So Smith tells us he will continue using this common example of division of labor, even if it is not ideal, simply because it is such a common example. The example is the one of the pin factory, which was used also in the French reference work the *Encyclopedie*.

If a person tries to make a pin, he could make perhaps one, or at best 20 pins a day. But if the work is divided into, in the case of the pin, 18 separate tasks, even if only 10 people are employed, each man can make around 12 pounds, or 4,800, pins a day. How does Smith come up with these numbers? We are not sure, but these numbers are consistent in all his works and with the ones reported in the *Encyclopedie*. He may have visited a pin factory himself as he claims, "I have seen".

When we think in terms of the production of goods that are common among even the poor, say a basic woolen coat, Smith also tells us, we have to realize that it is the product of the work of thousands of people. It is not just the wool, but also the dyes that generally come from distant lands, requiring ship building and thus a large network of trade. Leonard Read, with his story "I Pencil" (1958), where he describes the hundreds of activities needed to have an object as simple as a pencil, gave new life to Smith's story of the woolen coat.

It is also worth noting that this simple story is not just descriptive, it is also normative: commerce brings cooperation among thousands because "even the meanest person is in need of the cooperation of thousands". Trade, even if unintentionally as we will see later on, does not divide people, it brings thousands of people together peacefully, and this is a good thing.

If the division of labor is the cause of all improvements of the productive power of labor, why do we observe it more in commercial societies? For Smith, it is because commercial societies rely more on manufacturing than on agriculture, and only manufacturing allows for division of labor to be used extensively. In farming it is difficult to divide labor both because of the nature of the tasks and because of their seasonality. In manufacturing it is much easier. So we observe more division of labor and, as a consequence, more improvement of the productive power of labor where manufacturers are more common. It follows that the "most opulent nations" are the ones with the greatest division of labor, that is, commercial societies. Commercial societies tend to be better than their poorer neighbors in both agriculture and manufacturing, even if more in their manufacturing, because, being wealthier, they are able to dedicate more resources to improve agriculture.

Smith gives us a full theory of productivity. When labor is divided into specific tasks, the worker becomes more productive because he[1] becomes more dexterous in his task, he saves time from not switching from task to task, and he will invent machines to better do his task. This allows for more production, more trade, and more division of labor.

What is interesting to note here (paragraph 7) and to keep in mind as we read through the rest of the book, is a side note in Smith's description of a country laborer and his justification of it. A country laborer is often seen as slothful and lazy, not because he is naturally so, but because day in and day out he is forced to switch work and tools every half an hour or so. This makes him less productive, which is the reason why Smith brings it up here. But that the nature of employment will shape the character of a worker, as opposed to the character of the worker being the determinant of his employment, will come up again soon enough. What is not present here, but will come up later on, is the analysis of the costs of division of labor. Smith's usual style is to provide the costs and benefits of what he describes.

The chapter ends picking up the thread Smith laid out in the introduction. Commercial societies make people, all people, better off, including, or, especially, "the lowest ranks of the people". The division of labor brings opulence to the poor and to the poorest poor in particular. It also brings equality. Smith tells us that the home of a frugal peasant in Europe is not that different from the home of a prince. That same home, though, is much better than the home of an African king. What is poignant is the comment that Smith makes about the African king. The African King is "the absolute master of the lives and liberties of ten thousand naked savages". The European prince is not. The frugal peasant not only is clothed but he is also free. Commerce brings wealth for all, as well as life and liberty for all, and this is especially true for the people at the bottom.

BOOK I, CHAPTER II: OF THE PRINCIPLE THAT GIVES OCCASION TO THE DIVISION OF LABOR

We now know what the benefits of division of labor are. But what are the causes? Smith has a very clear answer: the division of labor is "the necessary ... consequence of [our] propensity to truck, barter, and exchange". The division of labor is not the result of any human wisdom. It is not the result of any action that has the intention of creating wealth. It is not the result of a plan that foresees prosperity or such an extensive utility. We may like to think we are responsible for these great results. But we are not. No human reason is capable of this. No human reason is capable of designing and predicting the consequences of such improvement in the productive powers of labor. It is the unintended and unplanned, but "necessary consequence of our propensity to truck, barter, and exchange". Smith is a very cautious writer. He seldom uses absolutes. But here he does. It is not only a consequence of this propensity. It is a necessary consequence of the propensity to truck, barter, and exchange one thing for another.

If you look in the *Oxford English Dictionary,* you will see that "to truck", in Smith's time, means to bargain, to deal, to exchange something with someone. It may also mean to pay in kind. In this chapter, a substitute Smith uses to indicate to truck is "by treaty" which in Smith's time means by agreement, by contract, by persuasion. To barter is to exchange one thing for another thing, as distinguished from a monetary transaction.

In each of the five paragraphs that compose this chapter Smith refers to these three activities: the "propensity to truck, barter, and exchange" (1), "by treaty, by barter, by purchase" (2 and 3), "trucking disposition" (3), "the disposition to truck, barter, and exchange" (4 and 5). Humans are naturally trading animals, he repeats in each paragraph. The implication we can infer is that what differentiates us from other animals is not that we are created in the image of god, or that we have an immortal soul, as most theological doctrine of his time would claim, but that we exchange. For Smith, this propensity to trade is a human characteristic and ours alone. We are the only species of animals capable of trade. Dogs do not trade; they do not have "fair and deliberate exchange" or any contract. A dog fawns to get the food he wants from a human. People may fawn too, but we can't rely on just fawning to get what we want. We do not have time to do it. In our lifetime we only have time to be friends with very few people. And in a civilized society we need the help of many, as the story of the woolen coat from the previous chapter tells us. This propensity to truck, barter, and exchange is quite handy because humans, for Smith, are one of the few species of animal incapable of surviving alone.

Here we have possibly one of the most cited sentences of the *Wealth of Nations*: it is in vain to expect our dinner only from the benevolence of the butcher, the baker, and the brewer. We are different from dogs because we can appeal to the self-love of the butcher, baker, and brewer to persuade them that it is to their advantage to give us dinner: "it is not from the benevolence of the butcher, the brewer, or the baker, that we expect our dinner, but from their regard to their own interest. We address ourselves, not to their humanity, but to their self-love". Only beggars chose to depend chiefly on the benevolence of others, but even they never do so entirely. They use the money they receive to buy things they like, or they exchange things they receive for things they like more.

Commerce is therefore an equalizer, as it gives equal dignity to all. When I get dinner from the baker, the brewer, and the butcher, I do not have to fawn like a dog, or to be like a beggar. I can simply look at them from the same level they stand and engage their self-love as my equal.

A couple of other things are worth noting here. Smith tells us we engage other people's self-love. Is self-love the same as self-interest, or selfishness? Today we use this Smithian sentence to claim the dominance of self-interest in the economic (and occasionally social) world. But the word Smith uses is *self-love*, a well-understood term in eighteenth-century moral and theological discourse, thanks to Bishop Joseph Butler (and popularized by Josiah Tucker), not self-interest or selfishness.

The other thing to note is that Smith simply says we do not get our dinner by relying exclusively on other people's benevolence. Smith does not say we have no benevolence. We are indeed benevolent, but it is in vain to rely entirely on the benevolence of others to get dinner. As a matter of fact, he starts his *Theory of Moral Sentiments* by observing that, however selfish we might think people are, they also care about other people's happiness.

Now let's go back to our propensity to truck, barter, and exchange. It is through this propensity that we specialize. And our specialization will allow us to develop those skills that make us better than others at what we do. Smith tells us that we are naturally very similar: there are no noticeable natural differences between individuals. We become different, but we are not born different. Our differences are the *effect*, not the cause, of the division of labor. We are hunters. Thanks to our trucking disposition, I give you arrows and bows in exchange for your venison. Before we know it, we realize that we can have more bows and arrows and more venison if I make only bows and arrows and you go catch the deer. We divide our labor. I start to excel in making arrows, you excel in getting deer. We develop different skills thanks to our specialization. We can both consume more than otherwise could. But we started from equal ground. It is our trucking disposition that drove us to specialize and develop different talents.

Similarly, for Smith, a street porter and a philosopher are naturally the same. Their differences are the product of customs, habit, and education. Indeed, Smith goes so far as to claim that all children are so much alike until the age of six to eight that not even their parents can tell them apart: "when they come into the world, and for the first six to eight years of their existence, they were, perhaps, very much alike, and neither their parents nor playfellows could perceive any remarkable difference". What makes the difference is that when they are six or eight years old, children start working (child labor is not an issue yet, but it is the norm in Smith's time). And that work leads them to have different life experiences that will eventually develop into the differences that make the vanity of a philosopher looking down on the porter and acknowledging no resemblance between himself and a street porter. Indeed, if we had no disposition to trade, we would all do more or less the same things, and we would all remain more or less the same even as adults.

By nature, Smith continues, the street porter is much closer to the philosopher than a greyhound is to a shepherd's dog. But while animals cannot take advantage of their differences, humans can and do. Our differences are useful to each other because we can trade with each other.

Smith's argument here is quite radical. And it does not go unnoticed. The champions of the future proslavery debate based their arguments on natural inequalities, so that for them some people are naturally slaves and others naturally masters. They stand ready to accuse Smith and his followers in the science of economics of undermining the stability of the social order. For them, it is a horrible thing, a dismal thing in fact, that the economists, followers of Adam Smith, would consider an African black no less human than a British white. For them, economics is therefore a "dismal science" because our propensity to truck, barter, and exchange makes all humans fundamentally equal, as opposed to differences in our skin colors or size of our head allegedly making some more human than others.

It may be easier to see how strong Smith's position is when we compare it to an alternative theory of division of labor that was already well established in Smith's day. Smith was not the first to realize the gains from division of labor. The ancient Greek philosopher Plato already spelled out quite clearly the benefits of divisions of labor and specialization. But in contrast to Smith, Plato believed that the division of labor is a consequence of our natural differences.

Similarly, in today's principles of economics courses, when we talk about the division of labor we talk about comparative advantage, which is a theory developed by David Ricardo, who wrote after Smith. The idea of comparative advantages is that people or countries should specialize in the production of the things in which they have a comparatively lower cost due to some preexisting differences. So, today our starting point is that people have different talents in production of things. Those people then specialize in the activity in which they have comparative advantage, and then they trade. Smith works the argument in reverse. We are naturally the same. We start trading because of our propensity to truck, barter, and exchange, and as a consequence of our trading, we start to divide labor and to specialize. This specialization brings about differences in skills and talents. Our differences are the consequences of trade, not the cause of it.

BOOK I, CHAPTER III: THAT THE DIVISION OF LABOR IS LIMITED BY THE EXTENT OF THE MARKET

Why, one may ask, as we are all naturally the same and we all have the same propensity to truck, barter, and exchange, don't we experience the same degree of the division of labor everywhere? There are several reasons, as Smith will tell us throughout the book. But for the moment, assuming everything else is the same, the extent of the market is what allows us to divide our labor and produce more.

We need to trade to specialize, which means we need to have access to markets, as we cannot eat pins. The larger the markets we can access, the more we can specialize and benefit from it. The smaller the market, the less specialization and the less division of labor.

Can we test this idea? Smith implicitly asks. Yes. We can look at the world in Smith's day and we can look at earlier times to find out if we can see the expected behavior. History, as we saw in the previous chapter of this *Guidebook*, is Smith's database.

What do we see in Smith's day? That some industries can be found only in great towns, Smith tells us. A street porter would not be able to support himself in a small village in the isolated Highlands of Scotland, or even in general outside London. If a worker specializes in the production of nails and makes something like 300,000 nails a year, to whom would he sell them in the Highlands where at best there is demand for only 1,000 nails a year? So, in the isolation of the Highlands, a villager cannot specialize in the production of nails; everyone needs to be their own baker, their own butcher, their own brewer, and their own pin maker. The division of labor is limited by the limited market.

What do we see in the past? Smith tells us that the first civilized countries developed where there were navigable waters – by the Mediterranean Sea, in Egypt by the Nile, in Bengal, in East India, in East China where there are many rivers and communicating canals. Most of Africa and Tartary (central Asia inhabited mostly by Turko-Mongol people) may have bodies of water, but they are few and too far away from each other, so communication between them is too difficult. Those countries were not as prosperous as the ones closer to navigable and communicating bodies of waters.

Wherever it is possible to use water to transport goods and people, we see larger markets. Water carriage is significantly cheaper and faster than land carriage. So it is there that we first see an increase in industry, division of labor, and improvements. Smith saw this also in his time: the opening of canals in Scotland opened markets and generated wealth.

How much cheaper is water carriage compared to land carriage? According to Smith, to carry 200 tons of weight between London and Edinburgh, it takes either 6 to 8 men and a ship, or 50 broad-wheel wagons, 100 men, and 400 horses. It is much cheaper to transport goods by water. Imagine trade between London and Calcutta only by land. It would be so expensive that only precious goods would travel. But then safety becomes a problem, which would make the cost of those good even more prohibitive. In Smith's day, thanks to water carriage, there was a great deal of trade between London and Calcutta, and this made both places richer. In our days still, 90 percent of consumable goods world-wide are transported via water.

The extent of the market, that is the extent of the market demand, is the first constraint division of labor faces.

NOTE

1   I will follow Smith's language and use the masculine pronoun to refer to a person. I will use the feminine pronoun only when Smith uses it.

FURTHER READINGS

Arrow, Kenneth. 1979. "The Division of Labor in the Economy, the Polity, and Society", in *Adam Smith and Modern Political Economy*, ed. Gerald O'Driscoll, J. R. Ames: Iowa State University Press. 153–164.

Diamond, Jared. 1997. *Guns, Germs, and Steel: The Fates of Human Societies*. New York: W. W. Norton.

Meek, Ronald and Andrew Skinner. 1973. "The Development of Adam Smith's Ideas on the Division of Labour". *Economic Journal* 83: 1094–1116.

Peart, Sandra J. and David M. Levy. 2005. *The "Vanity of the Philosopher": From Equality to Hierarchy in Post-Classical Economics*. Ann Arbor: Michigan University Press.

Read, Leonard E. 1958. *I Pencil: My Family Tree as Told to Leonard E. Reed*. http://oll.libertyfund.org/titles/112

Young, Allyn. 1928. "Increasing Returns and Economic Progress". *The Economic Journal* 38.152: 527–542.

3

BOOK I, CHAPTERS IV–VII

BOOK I, CHAPTER IV: OF THE ORIGIN AND USE OF MONEY

As Smith just showed us, one of the limitations of the division of labor is the extent of the market. Another limitation is the absence of money. But while the extent of the market as described in Chapter III is in part exogenous, meaning it depends on the natural conditions of a country, that is, on the presence or absence of navigable rivers and seas, the presence or absence of money is endogenous, meaning it depends on the stage of evolution of the division of labor. Division of labor and money go hand in hand.

A commercial society is a society in which much of what we consume comes from exchange, where division of labor is fully established, and every man is a merchant. A commercial society exists where transactions are monetarized because, without money, the possibility of trade and thus the division of labor are very much limited.

When division of labor starts to take place, we start to produce more of a particular good than we consume, and we would like to exchange it for something we do not produce but want to consume. Another way of saying what Smith is saying is this is not easy if we rely only on barter because we run into all the difficulties of what today we call double coincidence of wants. If a baker wants to get a beer, he needs to find a brewer who wants bread in exchange for his beer. If the brewer has already enough bread, the baker will not get his beer. With barter there are few incentives to divide labor.

So, Smith says, any prudent person will keep at hand something that he imagines someone else would not refuse in exchange for goods or services.

The choice of words here may not be an accident. I imagine myself as you, and I think: what would I not refuse if I was in your position? The role of imagination is critical here. It is critical, even if not explicitly mentioned, that when I want to appeal to your self-love to get my dinner, I have to imagine what you want and persuade you that I have what you want. Smith is explicit in appealing to the use of imagination to understand what others may want. The use of the imagination is key in Smith's other book, the *Theory of Moral Sentiments*. It is only through our imagination that we can try to relate to each other, and that we can understand each other and help each other grow morally. Here the same imagination helps us develop a solution to the problem of barter: money – what Smith calls the instrument of commerce.

Historically, Smith tells us, what people imagine others would not refuse in exchange for the produce of their industry varies. Different commodities take the role of the instrument of commerce: cattle, salt, shells, dried cod, tobacco, sugar, hides, even nails. But metals take dominance as money in most countries because they are less perishable and more easily divisible than other things previously used as money, such as an ox.

In different countries, we see different metals becoming the most common form of money. This is due mostly to chance and availability.

A simple bar of metal has its limitation, though. It needs to be weighted and assayed (verifying the quality and purity of the metal) every time it is exchanged. So, Smith continues, to decrease these transaction costs and the chances of fraud, metals tend to be stamped in mints. Originally the stamp is only on one side of the bar, to verify the finesse of the metal, and it is exchanged by weight. So the trouble of weighting remains. Eventually, the metal is made into coins, with stamps on both sides. The denominations of this coined money usually reflect the weight and quality of the metal. So the English pound sterling originally contained a pound of silver, just like the penny contained a pennyweight of silver, that is, the twentieth part of an ounce of silver.

Note that Smith is defining money only with regard to its function of medium of exchange, and he disregards its function as a unit of account. This may not be historically accurate. The example he gives of someone who wanted to buy salt and having to exchange a cow for it, so having to get a huge amount of salt, is ludicrous. An ox was indeed a form of money, but mostly as a measure of value not as a medium of exchange. You measure value in oxen but do not exchange the ox, you exchange something else of comparable value or, more likely, you keep track of what you owe with a credit system, the unit of which is oxen. Yet the story Smith tells makes some sense given the priority that Smith gives to exchange.

We can see how Smith's account of the evolution of money is, like the one of the division of labor, spontaneous, linear, and unintentional, in the sense of not having a specific designer. We go from barter to money because barter becomes inconvenient as commerce develops. As the number of transactions increase, we go from using metals as money to coin and we stamp them because it is more convenient to do so. Nobody, in the sense of no specific individual, planned these changes; they emerge spontaneously from the interactions of people. The role of the state is simply to fulfill a need when that need emerges. The state does not create money in Smith's account. This is a very different story from the more constructivist story that associates the introduction of money with an invention of a particular individual or with an imposition by the state, or even with the need for the state to act as a guarantor of money. This view of money is often called the state theory of money, with Georg Knapp (1842–1926) as its most famous exponent, but it dates back to antiquity. Smith, by contrast, ignores this hypothesis and sticks to the idea that great human institutions are unintentional results of human interactions. Just like the division of labor is not the result of any human wisdom able to predict its consequences, similarly money is not the result of any human wisdom but the unintentional consequence of human actions.

In this account, the government fulfills a positive role by stamping the coins with their weight and purity of metals. But before you know it, Smith twists it, claiming that, basically everywhere in the known world, the avarice and injustice of princes and sovereigns led them to diminish the real quantity of metal in coins, while the stamp did not change. So, for example, Smith tells us that the English pound in his days had about a third of the metal it originally had.

Smith explains that the reason why princes and sovereigns decrease the quantity of metals in coins, while leaving the coin names the same, is to defraud their creditors, paying their debts with a lower real amount of metal, thus abusing the confidence of their subjects. They fulfill their nominal obligations by ruining their creditors. This avarice and injustice, for Smith, causes private fortunes to change hands in a more dramatic way than public calamities.

So we can see that money, as useful as it is, is immediately presented as problematic. It causes fraud when it is not stamped and coined. It causes fraud even when it is stamped and coined. It causes fraud when it is left in private hands as well as when it is put in government hands. In saying this, Smith seems to be starting his criticism of the incorrect idea that money is wealth, one of its major intellectual fights in the *Wealth of Nations*. Money is an indispensable universal instrument of commerce, but it is also a dangerous tool for fraud. It is definitely not wealth.

This chapter is also the start of some problematic economic analysis for Smith. What today we see as a naïve account of the evolution of money is one of the problems that we recognize, while Smith may not have seen it as problematic. But there are also a series of problems that are problems for both us and Smith. He is candid about his unclear understanding of the subject matter of the following three chapters and he apologizes to his readers because he will be tedious and obscure. The problem Smith will run into in the next chapters is the one of trying to understand value and prices without marginal analysis. The so-called marginal revolution took place about a century later when Leon Walras (1834–1910), William Stanley Jevons (1835–1882), and Carl Menger (1840–1921) put forward the theory of subjective and marginal value, which explains that one more unit will have a different value depending on how many units one person already has.[1] Smith, not having the benefit of that insight, struggles in understanding and explaining what he sees as the rules of exchange: that is, the rules that determine the "relative or exchangeable value of goods". Although Paul Samuelson (1915–2009) would eventually vindicate Smith and show that his analysis of relative prices is robust even without marginal analysis, it remains a complicated analysis.

Smith's struggle is evident with the example he chooses to use: the water–diamond paradox, a paradox that disturbed scholars for centuries. Water is necessary for life, yet you can get it for free or buy it very cheaply. Diamonds are basically useless, yet they are very expensive. Lacking a unified theory of value, Smith needs to rely on an *ad hoc* explanation: we have two kinds of values, a value that captures the usefulness of something, the value in use, and a second value that captures the power of purchasing other goods, the value in exchange. The two kinds of values are different and unrelated. Water has low value in exchange and high value in use, and diamonds have low value in use and high value in exchange.

Life would become much easier when the idea of marginal utility is introduced: the value of one more unit depends on how many of those units we have already. On average, the value of water is very high, true, but our willingness to pay does not depend on the average utility of water, but on its marginal utility. If we have a great deal of water, having one more unit of water is not going to increase our utility by much, so we do not value it much, that is why we are not willing to pay much for it. However, having very little water (or having very few diamonds) implies that we will value one more unit of water (or an extra diamond) very highly and we will be willing to pay a high price for it.

Without marginal theory, things get tedious and obscure, especially when one needs to explain "the real measure of this exchangeable value; or, wherein consists the real price of all com-modities" and "what are the different parts of which this real price is composed" and why the market price may different from the natural price of commodities. Note that Smith is here telling us that even if there are two meanings of value, he will not deal at all with value in use, and he will concentrate exclusively on value in exchange.

The next three chapters will deal with this, and although they are problematic in the light of subsequent understanding, they are nonetheless more interesting than Smith gives himself credit.

BOOK I, CHAPTER V: REAL AND NOMINAL PRICE OF COMMODITIES OR OF THEIR PRICE IN LABOR AND THEIR PRICE IN MONEY

If we want to measure this exchangeable value, or value in exchange, how do we do it?

A bit of context with modern terminology may be useful to understand Smith's reasoning. First of all, as for any measure-ment, what we need is a stable unit of measurement. If we meas-ure height in feet (or meters), we do not want a foot (or a meter) to become longer or shorter over time or between different places, otherwise we are no longer able to have a meaningful measure-ment of height because we have no shared understanding of the unit of measurement. So, the first thing we need is to find a stable or fixed unit of measurement. When dealing with value, this is easier said than done.

Generally, money is considered the measurement of value. That is, for example, how Aristotle defines money, as the unit of account used to compare values. The problem is that when this idea of money as a unit of account is directly linked with the idea of money as a medium of exchange, the unit of account may become unstable. If the medium of exchange is a precious metal like gold or silver, and if the value of the gold or silver changes, then the unit of measurement of value risks changing as well.

For Smith, all is well when our monetary transactions are not that frequent and when the number of gold and silver mines known to us is limited. But when most of our "necessities and conveniences" come from market transactions, as in a commercial society, and when we discover several new rich mines, like the ones in the Americas, then measuring things with gold and silver money becomes a problem as their value becomes significantly variable.

We know that the attempt to find a stable measurement of value is a problem that afflicted scholars for centuries. Most of the attempts to stabilize the unit used to measure value involved trying to fix the value of money, of gold and silver coins. But the mint becomes in this way a constant source of instability rather than stability. Smith does not mention this, but we know that even Isaac Newton, who was put in charge of the mint of England, had unconvincing results. Others proposed alternatives to gold and silver money. One thing that does not change in quantity is land. Therefore, its value does not change either. Today we know this is not correct on both fronts, but in the eighteenth century it may not have been so clear. So if land is fixed, then land can be money, meaning land can be the instrument with which we measure value. But land cannot be the medium of exchange, as it cannot circulate. So instead we use paper that represents pieces of land. This ingenious solution to the problem of an unstable measurement of value was implemented, for example, in the form of land banks. One of the most famous was designed by John Law (1671–1729), another Scot, whose bank failed spectacularly, making things even worse.

So here is Smith, also trying to understand what could be a stable measurement of the exchangeable value of things. His answer is just as unconventional as John Law's, perhaps even more so in fact. But Smith's answer at least was not implementable and so it had no disastrous real world consequences. It just caused much of confusion for subsequent economists who tried to understand his theory of value.

In Chapter V of Book I, Smith tells us that the real measure of exchangeable value is labor. This was not something he says while distracted because he repeats it throughout the chapter: labor is the real measure of value in exchange.

His warning that his argument is going to be obscure is most appropriate here.

How can labor be the real measure of value? Equal quantities of labor have equal value to the laborer. A laborer *must always lay down the same proportion of his ease, his liberty and his happiness*, therefore labor alone never varies in its value and *alone it is the ultimate and real standard of value* (paragraph 7). One way to interpret this is that, if we are naturally the same, as he told us in Chapter II, and if we do not know the theory of marginal utility and disutility, then what I give up in an hour of work is the same as what you give up in an hour of work, that hour being our first of the day or our tenth one: we both give up our *ease, our liberty, and our happiness to the same proportion.*

Note that Smith is not saying that my output of an hour's work should be valued the same as yours. Nor that time spent working should be the measure of value. The output of an hour of my work may contain 10 years of training, and therefore more labor than a month worth of work in another activity, Smith tells us. There are variations in hardship and ingenuity that will also make a difference. We do not know how to measure them. What Smith is saying, in my view, is that, given the assumption that we are by nature all equal, what we give up to work an hour is the same for everybody: ease, liberty, and happiness.

It follows that the real price of something is the toil and trouble of getting it. Thus, the real value to a seller is the quantity of labor they can buy with what they receive. And the value to a buyer is the toil and trouble that it can save. Later on, Smith will muddle with these definitions, but so far this is what he proposes.

The consequence of this definition for Smith is that being rich or poor means being able to command the labor of others, that is how much of the necessities, conveniences, and amusements one can afford to buy and enjoy. With an increased division of labor, we depend more and more on the labor of others. So the difference between rich and poor relies more and more on how much labor one can command, or how much one can afford to buy. Wealth is thus purchasing power.

And if it seems that labor varies in value because it can buy different amounts of goods at different times, Smith reminds us that it is the value of those goods that changes, not the value of labor. The value of labor remains fixed, it is the value of everything else that changes instead.

Note that so far in this account of Smith's theory of value, money is not present. Money is not wealth. We use it as an intermediary in exchange, to make exchange easier. Hitting straight at the mercantilists, Smith shows that it is labor that buys wealth, not gold or silver.

We may think, incorrectly, Smith continues, that money matters because we exchange money for commodities, rather than directly exchanging labor for commodities. So we think it is easier to estimate value with money rather than with labor. We exchange bread for money and money for beer, not directly bread for labor needed to brew a beer. So it becomes natural to think of value in terms of money. Additionally, it is easier to grasp the quantity of a concrete thing rather than the abstract quantity of labor. So we think that money is the measure of value, even if it is labor, and only labor, that is the real and unique measurement of exchangeable value.

Smith identifies the problem of using money as a measure of value in that the value of gold and silver money varies and varies a great deal. Commodities that continually vary in value cannot be good measures of value. The value of gold and silver varies for two independent reasons that, when combined, can make things very difficult.

One source of the instability of the value of gold and silver coins is that the quantity of gold and silver in coins that have the same denomination will change over time. The change is usually in one direction and one direction only: down. The reason is, as Smith told us in the previous chapter, that princes like to decrease the quantity of precious metals in coins while leaving their denomination constant because they can more easily pay their debts (by cheating their creditors). This is also why it is impossible to see an increase of the metal content of coins of the same denomination: Who would cheat in such a way as to pay more than what is owed?

The other source of instability of the value of gold and silver coins is that gold and silver are commodities like any others. If new mines are discovered, as they have been with the discovery of the Americas, the value of gold and silver will go down, as it did in Europe. If one is paid a fixed amount of gold and silver over time, even if by weight and not with coins, one would receive less over time. The quantity of gold and silver will be the same, but what they can buy will be less. What seems constant, is not.

Smith notes that this is particularly devastating if one estate has a perpetual rent to be paid in money. Some "ancient rents", once very valuable, are now worthless. If the same rents are paid in corn, rather than money, then the value of rent would remain the same because corn preserves its value over time.

Which leads us to corn. Corn is not maize, or "Indian corn", but is the generic name that Smith uses to include all grains. For Smith, even corn, (that is, grain) is a better (that is, more stable) measurement of value than money. True, the value of corn varies significantly from year to year. From year to year, gold and silver are quite stable instead. But over the centuries, the value of gold and silver varies significantly while the value of corn remains more or less unchanged. So to compare value in different places and in different times, we should use the price of corn, for which there are decent records. Ideally, we should use the price of labor, but records of this are practically nonexistent.

Smith soon enough undermines even this concession that money is more stable than corn on a yearly basis. He does not take a shortcut to do it; he starts from the beginning.

First, Smith describes how different metals became measures of value because they were first used as medium of exchange. Then, he points out that even if we may still count in those metals, we use coins of different metals. Generally gold is used for large payments, silver for medium payments, and copper for small change. But in Rome, copper was the most common metal and estates were denominated in copper. Even silver coins had value in copper.

Then, Smith continues, the coins of the metal used as standard of value were made into legal tender, that is, they were the form of money that could not be refused to extinguish a debt. Other metals were accepted at will and with a flexible exchange rate. Eventually though, by law, the exchange rate for the different metals became fixed. The fixed exchange rate between gold and silver implies that changes in the value of a coin would cause changes of how much of the other metal was needed to pay debts.

As a result of this, the value of metal coins becomes quite volatile. Before the reformation of the gold coins of William III, the price of gold bullion was more than the mint price of gold. That is, the price of uncoined gold (bullion), determined by the market, was more than the price of a gold coin (minted) – the gold coins being old and worn out. But after the reformation, the price of gold bullion became less than the mint price of gold. The price of silver bullion remained more than its mint price. According to Smith, even John Locke misunderstood what was going on. Locke believed that silver bullion was pricier than silver coins because the exports of bullion increased its demand, thus its price. But because silver coins were banned from being exported, their price was lower. Smith notes that, in his day, the same policies apply to gold – gold bullion can be exported, and gold coins cannot – but the bullion price of gold is less than its mint price. The problem for Smith is that there is a fixed exchange rate between gold and silver and that fixed exchange rate is wrong. True, the quality of silver coin is quite poor, especially compared with the excellent quality of gold coins, but reforming the silver coins will not solve the problem. It will make it worse. By restoring the quantity of silver in the old coins, while keeping the exchange rate between the two coins the same, we would encourage people to get silver coins and melt them into bullion because silver is more valuable as bullion than as coin. They would sell the silver bullion for gold coins, and then sell the gold coins for silver coins and bring them to the mint to be melted again. What is needed, for Smith, is to increase the fixed ratio of silver and gold so that the value of silver is higher.

If one looks at the behavior of gold coins, one can learn what to do with the silver coins. Gold coins are more valuable than gold bullion even if there is no seigniorage. Seigniorage is a fee, or a tax, to be paid to the mint to coin a metal. When you bring bullion to the mint to be coined, it takes time. And that long wait is like a fee. So you prefer to keep the coins rather than to have bullion and then wait for it to be coined. So if the value of silver coins is brought to proportion to the one of gold coins, there should be no need to reform the coins. Or, if we add some seigniorage, the coins will be worth more than the bullion, as the coins will increase in value by the same amount of the seigniorage, just like the value of plate (precious metal melted into something other than coin) increases in proportion to the amount of fashion. This would decrease the melting of coins and reduce the exportation of metal. And if the coins would go abroad, they would also come back soon enough. Abroad they sell for their weight. At home they sell for more than their weight.

This is a very long story Smith tells us to indicate that the value of gold and silver is unstable and unsuited to be used as a measure of value. Not only does their value vary like the value of any other commodities, in the sense that the wear and tear of the metal and their nonmonetary uses create a constant demand for them, but also the supply may at times be more, and at times less, than is needed, so the price of the metals will vary accordingly. But there are times in which the price of a metal will be systematically higher or lower than what it should be. That is usually when there is a problem with the coinage. Reading between the lines, Smith seems to be giving us one more reason for being skeptical of considering money as a measure of value or as anything more than what it is: a medium of exchange.

BOOK I, CHAPTER VI: OF THE COMPONENT PARTS OF THE PRICE OF COMMODITIES

If the value of labor embedded in each good does not change, but the value of the good changes, there must be other things that determine its value. That is the subject of the next two chapters.

The first example Smith uses to address the problem is an example in which the problem does not arise. In societies where there is no accumulation of stock (what he later will call capital, or useful resources) and no ownership of land, production depends on labor alone. So the labor embedded in a good (the labor used to make a good) is more or less the same as the labor one good can command (the labor that one good can buy with its sale). The rule of exchange seems simple enough: things exchange in proportion to the amount of labor contained in them, that is, in proportion to the relative cost of production of those things, assuming of course, as Smith does, that producing a unit has the same cost as producing subsequent units. For example, if it takes twice as much labor to kill a beaver than to kill a deer, a beaver will exchange for two deer. Yes, some activities are harder than others, but that is already accounted for by the proportion with which things exchange. And yes, some activities require more dexterity and ingenuity than others, but as we saw in the previous chapter, that simply means that the superior value of their produce is a compensation for the labor spent acquiring that skill. In "advanced societies", when labor is monetized, the more hardship and the more skills are present in a job, the higher is the wage for that job. But in rude "societies", where only labor is required to produce things, only the labor embedded in a good can regulate the labor that good can buy. This is why, in "rude societies", Smith tells us, the whole produce of labor belongs to the worker.

Things become more complex as society becomes more complex. When stock (productive resources other than labor, as mentioned earlier and as Smith will explain later on) can be accumulated, the owner of stock will use it, and not let it sit idly. With the accumulated stock, an undertaker (which is how Smith calls an entrepreneur) will set industrious people to work. He will advance them the materials and what they need to live on until they are able to produce something and able to successfully sell it. The undertaker therefore takes a risk when he advances his stock to these people. Thus, he needs to be compensated for the risk involved with the use of his resources while setting industrious people to work. The compensation for the advance of the stock is profit. If there were no profit, there would be no point in advancing one's resources and taking risks. Profit is, therefore, a necessary condition for the use of the accumulated capital stock and for capital stock accumulation to start.

Smith notes that the profits of stock should not be confused with the wages of labor for inspection and direction. The labor needed to inspect and direct different activities may be the same, but the profits those activities generate may be very different if the risk of the two activities is different.

Under these circumstances, then, when stock is accumulated and advanced to workers, the value that the laborer adds to the materials needs to pay both the wages of the laborer and the profits of the undertaker. In a "ruder state" of society, where stock was not accumulated, whatever proceeds a sale generates belongs to the worker. Here, instead, not all the labor that can be commanded by the sale of a good belongs to the worker because a share of it belongs to the owner of stock too for having anticipated the materials and the subsistence of the laborer.

There is one more layer of complication to consider. In "advanced societies", not only stock is accumulated, but also there is private ownership of land. The production of most goods is now done by using this privately owned land. Landlords ask for a fee to use their land, which is called rent. Smith seems to indicate that the reason for these rents is simply because the landlords can ask for them: they "love to reap when they never sowed and demand rent even for its natural produce". So the labor that a good commands must now cover not only the wage to the worker, but also the profit of the stock owner, and the rent of the landlord.

This also means that we have the three components of price: wages, profits, and rents. All of which are still measured by labor, by the way, because labor measures the value of everything, as Smith reminds us here as well.

There are a few exceptions to this in an "advanced society". Fishing in the ocean does not have any rent, even if fishing salmon in rivers does. And scotch pebbles, small stones collected from river banks and sold for carving, just have labor. But the price of most other things does depend on all three components. Granted, the more "advanced" the society, the less rent plays a role, and the more profit plays a role, but still all three components are present.

How is this possible? How is it possible that in "rude society" a laborer can keep all the produce of his labor, while in an "advanced society" he has to share it with both stock owners and landlords? Smith does not remind us explicitly about it, but the explanation is implied in his argument so far. With the division of labor, stock can be accumulated, and production and productivity increased. A worker gets only part of the labor his own labor commands but can get more of it because the pie got larger. Before, he would get a small pie all by himself. Now he has to share the pie, but the pie is much bigger, so his part may be bigger. Smith does bring up this explanation, explicitly, as he concludes the chapter: in a "civilized society", the labor embedded in a product, that is the labor needed to produce something, is less than the labor that product can command, that is the labor that can be bought with that product, because of the contributions of profit and rent. If a country could put to work the equivalent labor that it can buy, that country would experience a continuous economic boom. But much of the value of what labor can command is used to support idle people. And this is increasingly true in a "civilized society". This is the same argument Smith used in the introduction of the *Wealth of Nations*. Rich countries are rich because they can support the life of people who do not work. Poor countries cannot spare able hands, all have to work, or they may die.

There are a few caveats to keep in mind, Smith tells us.

First, there are distributional implications. Even in the aggregate, we would use the idea of wage as the revenue generated by labor, of profit as the revenue generated by stock, and rent as the one generated by land. This implies that the whole revenue of a country will be distributed among wage, profit, and rent earners.

Second, the profit of stock can come both if the owner uses his own stock and if the owner lends his stock to someone else to use. In this latter case, profit is derivative revenue, and it is called interest. The interest, or use of money, is the compensation that the borrower gives to the lender for the risk the lender takes in giving the opportunity to the borrower to make this profit. So, the profit for lent stock must belong in part to the borrower, who runs the risk and uses it, and in part to the lender, who also runs the risk of lending it.

Third, if we think that some activities require a fourth component of price, the one determined by the cost of replacing worn out materials or animals used in production, we have to remember that even the price of those is composed to wage, profit, and rent. So, at the end, all always boils done to wage, profit, and rent.

Finally, Smith tells us that common language, with its imprecise use of terms, adds to the difficulties of the topic. If a gentleman farms his own land, he gets both profits and rent, but calls all of it profit. A common farmer does the job of both the laborer and his own overseer, earning wages from both activities, but its revenue is often called profit too. An independent manufacturer earns both wage as a journeyman and profit as the master of a journeyman (himself) but calls all of it profit. If a gardener earns rent, profit, and wage, he calls all of it wage.

BOOK I, CHAPTER VII: NATURAL AND MARKET PRICE OF COMMODITIES

Now that we know what constitutes value, we need to figure out what determines how much we end up paying for the goods we buy. What we pay is the market price, which may or may not be the same as the natural price.

For Smith, the natural price is the price that pays for the natural costs of all its components: that is, the price that covers the natural rate of wages, the natural rate of profits, and the natural rate of rents.

What is natural about these rates, you may ask? Smith defines *natural rates* as "the ordinary or average rates"; the typical rates are the natural ones.

The natural rates of wage and of profit depend on the general conditions of society and the kind of employment. The natural rate of rent also depends on the general circumstances of society as well as on the fertility of the land. Smith will go into the details of these claims in the following four chapters.

One thing to note here is that the analysis of this chapter starts with a defense of the earnings of the middleman. Smith describes the middleman as the person who buys goods at their natural prices and brings them to the market to be resold, and for doing this he deserves a profit. Not only does he need to earn enough to live, but he also needs to earn the ordinary rate of profit. If not, he loses out and should use his resources in a different way. He does earn profits from his activities because he advances his wage to himself: without profits he would have no way to recover his costs. So the natural price of a good will include the profit of the middleman too.

The actual selling price, which is the market price, may differ from the natural price, Smith explains. The market price depends on the quantity supplied in the market and the demand of those who want to pay the natural price, that is, on the effectual demand. Note that the willingness to pay for a good (the effectual demand) is different from the absolute demand (the people who want the good). Only the effectual demand is effective in attracting goods to the market. The absolute demand does not bring goods to the market because the buyers are not willing or able to pay the natural price, the price that covers all the costs of production.

Why is the market price not always equal to the natural price? Because suppliers may not know for sure how large or small the effective demand is. So, if the quantity supplied is less than the one demanded, the market price will go up, above the natural price, because of the competition among buyers. Rather than go without the good in question, buyers will be willing to pay more. How much more? It depends on their wealth and on how important the item is to them.

If, however, the quantity supplied is more than the quantity demanded, the market price will go down, below the natural price, because of the competition among sellers. How much lower? It depends on how important it is for the sellers to get rid of the goods for sale. Perishable goods, like oranges, will see a deeper decrease in market price than durable goods, such as iron.

If the quantity demanded and supplied are the same, then the market price will be the same as the natural price. Note that this argument is extremely familiar to our modern ears even if the distinction between natural and market price is not how we commonly think about it. This distinction between natural and market prices make Smith's argument quite peculiar for us today. In Smith's apparatus, the natural price is fixed, and we have adjustments through the supply side. It also seems to imply that the effective demand and the natural rates are somehow known. It is indeed the effective demand to determine the quantity of goods brought to market. Prices help clear the market but do not necessarily convey information about relative scarcities, as we think about them today.

Because it is in the interest of earners of wage, profit, and rent not to bring a quantity of goods that is more than the effective demand, and it is in the interest of everybody else not to have a quantity supplied that is less than the effectual demand, the natural price is the central price around which the market prices gravitate, thanks to adjustments of the quantity supplied.

Indeed, if the quantity of a good brought to market is more than the effective demand, its market price will be less than the natural price. So rent, profit, or wage, or any combination of them, will earn less than their natural rate. Now there are incentives to offer less, so that the quantity supplied will be equal to its effectual demand with the rent, wage, and profits at their natural rates, which means with the market price nearing its natural price.

The same thing is true in reverse. If the quantity supplied is less than the effectual demand, the market price will be more than its natural price, which means that the rate of profit, rent, and wage will be more than ordinary, attracting more people into this activity and therefore producing more. The increased supply will bring the quantity supplied in line with its effectual demand and the rent, profit, and wage close to their natural rate. Here Smith's language is a bit ambiguous for today's standards especially in terms of changes in quantity supplied or demanded versus changes in supply or demand.

So the market price will always naturally gravitate toward its natural price.

Twice in this chapter Smith refers to gravity: market prices gravitate toward their natural prices. The use of the word *gravity* may be an implicit reference to Newton's discovery of physical gravity. In the physical universe there is a force that holds planets together. In the economic universe there is also a force that holds natural and market prices together: market competition. As we saw in Chapter 1 of this *Guidebook*, Smith is quite familiar with the latest developments in astronomy and is also an admirer of Newton's system. Newton has a simple and elegant explanation for the movements of the skies: gravity. Smith possibly has an equally simple and elegant explanation for the movements of the economy: competition. The implicit reference to Newtown may not be accidental, but historically it also led to the recognition of Smith as the "Newton" of social sciences.

That said, Smith notes that the supply of certain goods is much more volatile than that of other goods. For example, the production of corn, as we saw before, is quite volatile from year to year because it depends in part on the weather. The production of linen, however, is quite stable. This implies that the market price of corn has greater variations than the market price of linen because it depends on changes in both demand and supply, while the market price of linen depends mostly just on changes in demand.

These changes in market prices will affect wages and profits, but only marginally affect rent because they depend on whether there is too much or too little of a good or of the labor required to produce it. Smith gives the example of changes in market price of black cloth due to a change in demand. If there is a public mourning, the price of black cloth will increase. But the wages of weavers will stay more or less the same. Only the profits of the merchants will increase. What is missing is black cloth, not weavers. Yet, the wage of tailors will go up in this case because more work needs to be done. At the same time, the price of color cloth will go down with the same but opposite effect.

Finally, Smith concludes this chapter noting that, while the market price will always naturally gravitate toward its natural price, there may be obstacles such as accidents, natural causes, and regulations that prevent the market price from being as close to its natural price as possible.

If there is an increase in effectual demand, the market price will increase. The suppliers will try to hide it to avoid competitors entering their market and eating their profits by lowering the price. Distance helps. But extraordinary profits seldom last long.

For Smith, secrets will last longer in manufacturing than in trade because it is easier to hide new discoveries in ways of productions than in changes in demand. Sometimes with manufactures, the extraordinary gains may be due to very high price of labor, which requires high wages. It may also be by accident, or by a singularity in production such as something very unique about a specific soil, such as the ones of some vineyards in France. In these cases, it is the rent that will capture the higher price, while wages and profits remain normal.

Having a monopoly is similar to having a secret, according to Smith. Monopolies keep the market undersupplied so that the market price remains more than the natural price. Note, Smith tells us, that the monopoly price is the highest possible that it is squeezed from buyers. The competitive price is the lowest possible while staying in business.

Corporations, which in Smith's time were not companies but guilds, tend to put restrictions in the labor market. They are like monopolies, like enlarged monopolies, and they last as long as their regulation lasts.

So, the market price can stay above the natural price for a long time; but it cannot stay below it for long. The group that feels the loss the most will eventually change its employment, if there is the liberty to do so.

Smith reminds us that apprenticeships exclude people from employment, in the sense that they exclude people from one's employment, but they also exclude one from other employments. When the price of labor is kept above its natural rate, things are okay. But when it is kept below its natural rate, there will be problems. Keeping wages below their natural rates can't last for more than a generation. If the price of labor is kept too low, the next generation will not be there.

NOTE

1 I value "one more" slice of pizza a great deal when I am hungry; not so much after I ate a whole pie (marginal value). If you are on a low-carb diet, you value the same slice of pizza less than me (subjective value).

FURTHER READINGS

Aspromourgos, Tony. 2008. *The Science of Wealth: Adam Smith and the Framing of Political Economy*. New York: Routledge.

Buchanan, James. [1969] 1999. *Cost and Choice: An Inquiry in Economic Theory*. Indianapolis, IN: Liberty Fund.

Kennedy, Gavin. 2008. *Adam Smith*. London: Palgrave Macmillan.

Hollander, Samuel. 1973. *The Economics of Adam Smith*. Toronto: Toronto University Press.

Meek, Ronald. 1956. *Studies in the Labor Theory of Value*. New York and London: Monthly Review Press.

Samuelson, Paul. 1977. "A Modern Theorist's Vindication of Adam Smith". *American Economic Review* 67.1: 42–49.

4

BOOK I, CHAPTERS VIII–X

BOOK I, CHAPTER VIII: OF THE WAGES OF LABOR

Smith seems to ask: Why do we need to understand wages and their determination? If this is the implicit question he asks, a possible answer he offers is that wages are linked to population growth, which is an indicator of the well-being of an economy. And the reason for this is that wages are what allow most people to live. If population grows, it means that wages are high, and we have an indication that the economy is growing as it can support an increasing number of people. If population declines, wages must be low, and we have an indication that the economy is also declining because there is not enough in the economy to support the existing population, ergo the decline.

But the determination of wages is not easy. Wages are the natural compensation for the product of labor. If there is no accumulation of productive resources, what Smith calls stock (and we call capital), and no ownership of land, then all the produce of labor goes to the worker. This idea of labor working without or with capital comes from the French economist Turgot and is eventually used by Karl Marx and classical economics.

Following Turgot, Smith sees that labor becomes more productive when capital is used. Furthermore, he claims that when we introduce private ownership of land, the landlord requests rent. Because a land worker is not in the position to support himself before harvesting, the master uses his resources, his stock (capital), to give an advance on the harvest to the land worker. The worker can now subsist until harvesting time. The worker will have to pay the master back for what he advanced him: that is the profit of the stock owner. This means that from the produce of the land, one needs to subtract rent and profit. Whatever is left is the wage of the land worker.

The most common situation is that the laborer uses the materials and things that the master advanced to him. Which means that, in most cases, the produce of labor includes both profit and wage. The proportion between the two is to be determined by contracts between workers and masters. This also means that, for Smith, one of the determinants of wages is bargaining power.

Here Smith's tone is matter of fact. Later on, it will become accusatory. As a matter of fact, the interest of the workers is always different from the interest of the master. Workers want higher wages and masters want lower wages. The bargaining power is uneven, and it is tilted in favor of masters. Following an impeccable logic of what today we call collective action theory, Smith tells us that the masters are few and therefore can combine easily (concentrated interest) and are quite effective in creating what today we call a cartel.

In Smith's time, Smith tells us, masters can combine legally, meaning that the law does not explicitly prohibit it. Workers cannot, because the law explicitly prohibits their combination. Masters can hold out without workers for one to two years. Workers can hold out without masters for less than a week. True, there is interdependence between masters and workers; they need each other to produce. But they do not need each other equally. This can be a problem.

The asymmetry goes further. For Smith, we do not hear about the cartels of masters, but they do cartelize. In fact, masters always combine, but tacitly, to keep wages low. Workers combine with "loudest clamor" and with the "most shocking violence and outrage" – acts of "folly of desperate men". Workers may have the traditional *right to resistance*, but it is not going to do them much good. Masters call, again with clamor, for the laws to be enforced, and workers tend to be punished rather than become any better off.

So, masters are good at keeping the wages low. But how low can wages go? Well, a wage has to be enough to support a worker and his family. If not, Smith reminds us, there will be only one generation of workers.

Are wages always at subsistence level then? No, for Smith in many cases they are more than subsistence. If there is a scarcity of workers, the master will have to bid up the wages to attract workers. This competition among masters increases wages above subsistence.

And when is there a scarcity of hands? Smith tells us wages will be high. Then the economy is growing. High wages are indeed linked to increasing national wealth. Wages are the highest in thriving countries. Look at the North American colonies, Smith tells us. Wages there are high; higher than in Britain. And it is not because the subsistence of workers is higher there. Food is cheaper in North America. Wages are so high because hands are in high demand. A widow with four children remarries in an instant in North America because of her children: they are workers for the fields. In Britain the same widow would not be able to remarry at all because of her children: they are just mouths to feed.

The demand for workers is so high in North America that population is said to double every 20 to 25 years, as opposed to every 500 years in Britain, Smith claims.

Does the relationship between wages and population and the growth of the economy also extend to mediocre wages and low wages? Let's see. For Smith, in a stationary economy there is no scarcity of hand, just the right amount. So wages should not be very high as workers bid against each other to get the job. The wage is, therefore, enough to bring up a family. Is there empirical support for this? Yes, Smith tells us: China. China is a rich country, but it has a stationary economy (Smith will tell us later in

Chapter 9 why that is the case). Smith believes that China has not changed much since Marco Polo traveled there. And the poverty of the lower ranks of people is such that they barely survive, mostly because they eat garbage, putrefying dogs, and drown children whom they cannot support like they drown puppies. Remember what Smith told us in the Introduction of the work: poverty forces us to kill children. Here again we are reminded that poverty forces us to dehumanize some people and to do the most horrendous things.

But if this is the condition of the poor in a stationary economy, what about in a declining one? There, for Smith, the demand for labor is so low that many workers simply starve to death. So we see a population decline. And indeed this is the case in Bengal, where, in Smith's account, despite a fertile land, 300,000 to 400,000 people die of starvation yearly!

So why does the population of the North American colonies double every 20 to 25 years while in Bengal 300,000 to 400,000 people die of hunger every year despite the fertility of the land? Smith is clear on this: institutions. North America is blessed with the genius of the British constitution. Bengal is cursed with the evil of the mercantile companies. Institutions are what make the difference in the competitiveness of wages.

What about Britain? How is Britain doing? For Smith, Britain is not North America, but it is not China either. Britain is doing fine. It is not booming, but it is not stagnant either. How do we know? Look at wages. In Britain the lowest wage is above subsistence. Here is the evidence that Smith gives us.

One: in the winter, wages are lower than in the summer, but in the winter the expenses of a worker are higher than in the summer. If a worker can survive in the winter, there must be some affluence in the summer. Two: wages do not change with changes in prices of food. If one can survive in bad years, it means the wage is more than subsistence in good years. Three: wages vary with location more than the price of food. The price of food is about the same, but wages are about 25 percent higher in cities than in the countryside. If that price difference that labor experience was to be experienced with commodities, those commodities would move across the world. Granted, a man is "of all sorts of luggage the most difficult to transport", yet if a worker can maintain a family where wages are lower, without moving, it means there is affluence where wages are higher. Four: wages tend to move in the opposite direction from food prices. This means that the real price of labor is higher in real terms because things are now cheaper and/or better. For example, the Scots eat worse corn than the English, and they are also paid less than English workers. In which direction is causation? Smith reminds us that it is not that the Scots are poor because they eat bad corn. They eat worse corn because they are poor. How can we tell? Why do rich people use carriages and poor people walk? It is not the carriage that causes wealth, but wealth that allows the purchase of the carriage. The logic is the same.

All this is a demonstration that the poor are better off in Britain than they are in China and Bengal.

Smith then asks something that nowadays sounds like a very provocative question: Is the improvement of the conditions of the laboring poor a good or a bad thing? Smith's answer is unquestionably clear: the improvement of the living conditions of the poor is good. If something is good for the majority of the population, it cannot be bad for the whole. And given that the majority of the population is poor, what is good for the poor is good for society. Indeed, no society can be happy if the majority of the population is miserable. Some later scholars use this passage to suggest that Smith can be thought about in terms of median utilitarianism, as opposed to simple utilitarianism. We can debate the meaning and the appropriateness of the idea of utilitarianism in Smith, but what is relevant here is that whatever that may be, it is based on the median not on a mean. This means that it is not the average well-being or the average happiness that matters, but the well-being or happiness of the majority of the people.

A couple of things to note: Smith talks both about happiness and about fairness (he used the word "equity", which in this context means fairness). A society cannot be happy if the majority of the people are miserable. Happiness, not utility. Then, also because of equity those who feed everybody should also be fed. Equity (read fairness), not utility, not efficiency.

This question may be far from our standards. We generally take for granted that it is good if the poor are better off. But this was not the case in Smith's time. Some people thought that the poor were naturally lazy and prone to vice. The only way to keep them out of trouble was to get them to work. But if paid more than subsistence, they would indulge their natural laziness. As a consequence, wages should be kept at subsistence and *maximum* wage laws for workers should be implemented. Smith is strongly against this claim. Working with the assumption of human homogeneity, the poor are not different from any other group of people. They are not naturally lazy but respond to incentives like everybody else. And wages are an incentive. Higher wages, in addition to giving better subsistence and therefore more strength, give workers more incentives to work as now they can hope to better their condition. Indeed, with higher wages they will work so much that they may risk injuring themselves. This is particularly true when workers are paid by piece: they work so much for four days that they must rest for the other three because of their exhaustion, not because they are lazy.

Thus, Smith notes that productivity increases with increased wages and also with increased rest. If there is no rest, productivity may suffer because the health of the worker will suffer. If the masters would listen to reason and humanity, they would make sure workers work moderately, but constantly. The health of the workers would be preserved, and productivity over time increased. Equity and efficiency work together, not against each other.

Note also that Smith seems to work with the assumption that having children is a good and happy event. His measurement of whether a society is happy – yes happiness again – is therefore based on the number of children raised to maturity. This is a useful measurement for another reason, not just because it picks up happiness and equity: the direction of population growth is also a good proxy for economic growth. The more people a country can support, the wealthier a country is. The fewer people, the more miserable, the poorer. As he told us in the Introduction of his work, the problem with poverty is that poverty is more likely than wealth to kill the innocents. A young woman in the poor Highlands of Scotland may bring to life 20 children, Smith claims, but only a couple of them will survive. In general, child mortality is very high among the poor, more than half will die before they are 10 because their parents cannot support them.

Humans, like animals, multiply according to their means of subsistence, states Smith, especially among the "lowest rank of people". Again Smith tells us, the poor are forced to "destroy" the great part of their children. This may be why Smith calls the conditions of the working poor in a declining economy "miserable" and that state "melancholic".

High wages, however, allow people to have more children, at least in proportion to the growing demand for labor. So Smith tells us that a progressive state, a growing economy, is not just the most comfortable but also the happiest, the most "cheerful and hearty". A stationary state is hard for the working poor and it is "dull".

For Smith, high wages are caused by wealth and are a cause of population growth, which means that high wages are both the cause and the effect of the greatest public prosperity, as well as happiness of the majority of the people. Those who complain about them, complain about the greatest public prosperity! The improvement of the poor is indeed a good thing.

Furthermore, just like an increase in stock (capital) increases the productive powers of labor and the division of labor, which causes the invention of better machines, the larger the number of people in society, the more division of labor, the more inventions of machines, and therefore the more production there will be.

There are a couple of implications of this logic.

Smith explicitly spells out one: it is the demand for men, like the demand of any other commodities, that regulates its production. This is an indicator of Smith's essentially "modern" economic analysis – and also of his understanding of the "Malthusian" theory of populations and wages. That men can be thought of like any other commodities is also present in the description of the "wear and tear" of slaves and free servants. The wear and tear of slaves is an expense for their masters, while the wear and tear of the free servants is an expense they will face themselves. Slave masters are negligent masters when they manage the fund of slaves. While a free servant will manage his own repair fund, thus not negligently. This alone makes slave labor more expensive than the work of the freemen.

The other implication is spelled out two centuries later by another economist, James Buchanan, who claimed the *Wealth of Nations* can be read as a book about a just system that also happens to be efficient. This is an example of it. The liberal reward of labor is not only just because it allows people to be happy and to have many children, but it also makes workers more productive.

In addition, note that Smith's analysis of wages looks quite familiar to contemporary eye because of what seems to be the adjustment of wages to demand and supply changes. It also looks familiar to a Marxian eye: wages depend on bargaining powers and on what is customary. Smith does not give us a definition of subsistence, but usually when he refers to necessities, he also includes conveniences, maybe implying that what we call living wage today may depend on historical circumstances. For him, bargaining power also depends on historical circumstances. It tilts on the side of masters in times of economic decline and it tilts on the side of workers in times of growth.

This chapter also indirectly addresses a question raised centuries later: Is Smith "left-leaning" believing that there is a need to improve the lives of the poor, or is Smith more "right-leaning" believing in the unfettered expansion of industry? Smith may be both and neither at the same time, mostly because it may be that Smith does not see the two as a contradiction, as an either/or. The expansion of industry will improve the lives of the poor. This may indeed be the reason why we want an expansion of industry. Malthus would later disagree with this, criticizing Smith for assuming that economic growth would bring rising wages.

In general, economists consider Chapter VIII of Book I one of the most important chapters in the *Wealth of Nations*, particularly when read in conjunction with Chapter III of Book II. The two together are thought to contain Smith's complete macrodynamic account of a market economy, as understood by today's economists. However, this account may not square with Smith's emphasis on the division of labor and the increasing returns to scale that it implies – which is why his successors (with some notable exceptions) ignored the division of labor in their own analyses.

BOOK, I CHAPTER IX: OF PROFITS OF STOCK

As we just saw, different growth rates of wealth will affect wage rates. But different growth rates of wealth will also affect profit rates. In particular, as capital (which Smith keeps calling stock here) increases, wages increase too, but profits decrease because of the increased competition.

A precise measurement of the ordinary profit rate is impossible for Smith. According to Smith, there are too many things that affect it, so that even a trader cannot tell. But not all is lost: we can get a sense of it by looking at the market rate of interest. The market rate of interest cannot be that far off from the rate of profits, in particular it cannot be more than the rate of profits. If it were, people would not borrow because their returns would not be enough to cover the borrowing costs. So we can infer that the market interest rate will move more or less with profits.

Smith qualifies the interest rate as the market interest rate because not all interest rates may be determined by the market. Some may be determined by law, the so-called usury laws. In Britain, for example, there were usury laws, but they were not binding, as they followed the market rate for people of good credit, rather than trying to alter it.

That said, is there evidence that supports the idea that profits move in the opposite direction to that of wages with changes in capital? Yes, of course. Smith makes this claim by observing that, for example, in the countryside there is less stock (capital, that is) than in a city. And indeed we see that profits are lower in the city than in the country, but wages are higher in the city than in the country. Holland is richer than England. It is not by accident that its profits are lower than England's. Interest is indeed so low in Holland that only very few rich people can live off it. Most people need to be involved in business. So much so that it is fashionable to be so – a point the economic historian Deidre McCloskey emphasized in recent years.

When profits are low, merchants complain that trade is declining because lower prices give them lower profits. Instead, Smith emphasizes, low profits are a symptom of prosperity, not of decline.

Smith explains that when profits are low, it means that there is more capital employed than before. By contrast, when profits are high, prices are generally high too. And prices tend to be much higher when there are high profits than when there are higher wages. Meaning, most likely, that, when there are high profits, there may be a markup on price because of the monopolization or lack of competition in the market. When wages are high, however, prices do not rise that much, most likely because the high wages are the result of the competition for workers. This high price due to high wages is, therefore, a more competitive price, which merchants cannot control, and it is, therefore, more likely that it erodes their high profits.

And what do merchants do when profits are low? Not surprisingly, they complain. But merchants complain only about high wages as the cause of higher prices. They remain perfectly silent on their high profits being the cause of high prices, Smith asserts.

There are few exceptions to the inverse relation of profits and wages, in Smith's account. Only the colonies experience simultaneously high profits and high wages because they are both understocked and underpopulated. But as they become richer, and more and more improvements take place, population will increase and capital will accumulate, so that interest and profits will decrease while wages will increase.

It is also possible that profits increase with the acquisition of new territories. Profits may increase because capital goes to new trades, decreasing the amount available for the maintenance of the existing industry in the homeland. This also will come to an end with economic growth and new capital accumulation.

Yet, Smith claims, there is a way to obtain and maintain high profits: monopoly. Let's look at China as an example, Smith says. China is a rich even if stationary economy. Profits should be low. But they are high. Why? Because of bad laws and institutions. They neglect foreign commerce, and they do not use all the capital available. Why? Because there is security for the rich but not for the poor. The poor can be plundered at any time under the pretense of justice, so they have no incentives to accumulate and to use capital. Smith identifies the monopolistic use of capital by the rich to keep profits high as the cause of this oppression of the poor.

For Smith, bad laws and bad institutions can also affect profits in a different way: whenever there are problems with enforcing laws, this is particularly true when it comes to contract laws. Poor enforcement of the laws increases the risk of lack of contract enforcement. Interest rates increase with risk. Borrowers are thus likely to be treated as if they were going to go bankrupt because of the high uncertainty of repayment.

A final consideration. Smith tells us that risk also increases when there is a prohibition of interest. Prohibiting interest does not mean that there is no interest. If there were no interest on a loan, there would be no loan. So there will still be borrowing, but the interest will now be higher to compensate the risk of being caught breaking the law.

BOOK I, CHAPTER X: OF WAGES AND PROFITS IN DIFFERENT EMPLOYMENTS OF LABOR

Given the assumption of human homogeneity, and the assumptions that the value of each unit of labor is the same and unchangeable, and that competition attracts prices to their natural rates, like gravity, this chapter has a challenging goal: to show that price of labor is equal across different employments. The advantages and disadvantages of different employments need to end up being the same, or, in an environment with perfect liberty and movement, there will be movement among different employments to reach that equality. Smith succeeded in his task, even if using tools quite different from the ones we use today. He manages to do everything with a cost-based theory: wages depend on costs, not on willingness to pay based on how valuable the service provided is considered by consumers. An impressive task.

The first thing to note, tells us Smith, is that we need to be careful about what we look at. We need to look at total compensation of labor, not just at monetary wages. There is indeed inequality in the monetary wages, but they are balanced out with other forms of nonmonetary compensation based on the characteristics and on the nature of the employment. There are also differences in wages that are independent from the nature of the job and are not compensated by anything else. They are generated by policies and are destined to create real inequality – and injustices.

This chapter is, therefore, also interesting because of its focus on the causes of wage inequality. Smith offers a possible explanation (and condemnation) of at least some forms of the income inequality he sees in his day. He also offers a possible solution. We already saw that in a growing and competitive economy profit rates tend to decrease and wage rates to increase, decreasing the gap between wage earners and profit earners. Competition is what allows these tendencies toward equalization. Here we see how it is possible to have actual gaps within wage rates and profits rates: limits to competition are roadblocks on the way to equalization. They create injustices. The solution is thus to eliminate those roadblocks and to allow competition to do its job.

PART I: INEQUALITIES ARISING FROM THE NATURE OF THE EMPLOYMENT

Smith is not too worried about differences in monetary wages that the nature of the employment may cause. They do not generate real inequalities. In fact, they counterbalance other factors, creating equality. So he tells us he identifies five different reasons why monetary wages may not be the same across different jobs, while workers' compensation remains mostly equal – what today we call compensating differentials: the agreeableness and easiness of the job, the expense of learning it, its constancy, its trust requirements, and the probability of getting the job.

If a job is easy, clean, or honorable, it would have a lower wage than if it is hard, dirty, or dishonorable. The most detestable job – public executioner – is very well paid. Very few people want to be public executioners because others consider it despicable. So a high wage is needed to compensate for its detestability. The most agreeable one – fishing and hunting – is almost exclusively a recreational activity. No one can support himself with doing these things. The more pleasant a job is, the more people want to do it and the lower is the wage because the pleasantness of the occupation compensates for the work and competition drives down wages.

The same applies to the profits of stock. The harder the work, the higher the profits. An inn keeper is never fully the master of his home and needs to handle drunks quite often. Not easy, not pleasant. One needs very little stock (capital) to open and run an inn, but profits will be high, to compensate for the disagreeableness of its use.

Wages must compensate also for education and training costs. Educated men are like expensive machines; their wage must cover the expense of their education, so their wage will be higher than wages for jobs that require little or no education. In addition, education takes time. One starts working late, and given how uncertain life can be, one needs to make up for that cost relatively fast. Examples of jobs that have higher wages because of high educational/training costs are professions in the "ingenious and liberal arts" such as painters, sculptors, lawyers, and physicians. Their high wages are to cover the expense and the tediousness of their training. Professions requiring apprenticeship also tend to have higher wages because during the apprenticeship all the labor goes to the master and the apprentices need to be supported by their family. Their wage will eventually be higher than a common laborer, which makes them think that they are superior to the common laborer. But when one computes the lifetime earning of both, one sees basically no difference.

This difference in learning a trade does not apply to differences in profits.

The inconsistency of work makes a difference to wage rates, Smith continues. The work of a bricklayer is inconsistent, so his wage needs to be high enough to compensate for the times in which he cannot work, and for the anxiety he may have for not getting work. It will thus be higher than the wage for a more constant job. If one adds hardship to inconsistency, one would have even higher wages. The profits of stock are instead unaffected by the consistency of the employment. What matters is the trader, not the trade.

Professions like goldsmith, physician, and lawyer require trust. Because we tend not to trust poor people, jobs that require trust need to be more highly paid so that they are performed by richer individuals. Note that this is not a judgment that Smith makes, but a simple matter-of-fact description of what people believe. Also note that working with only a cost-based theory makes the analysis a bit chunkier than one based on willingness to pay. Today we would say that a higher price for the services of a physician may signal our willingness to pay for a higher quality service.

As far as profits, Smith observes that if one uses his own capital, the problem of trust does not arise. If one uses someone else's capital, then the profit rates will depend on the trust in the trader, not on the trade.

Finally, we may have some monetary wage inequality because, for Smith, getting some jobs is like winning a lottery. In a "fair lottery" (lotteries where our expected value is zero) the winner gains what others lose. Similarly, one would expect, because only 1 in 20 makes it as a lawyer, that one lawyer needs to be paid also for the other 19 who did not make it. But while the expenses of all who become shoemakers are the same as all the gains of all shoemakers, the expenses of all who study law is more than the gains of all lawyers. Law is indeed not a fair lottery. Why, Smith asks? And if we know that the probability of getting the job is so low and that the monetary returns do not compensate for the expenses, why do we still try to enter some professions? For two reasons, Smith tells us: our desire to gain a reputation of excellence, and our natural overconfidence.

Some jobs, like lawyers, are honorable, Smith tells us. Thus, many people are eager to enter the legal profession. The reason why people think being a lawyer is honorable is because, given that so few make it, one gains a reputation of "superior excellence". Our desire to gain a reputation of excellence is a strong characteristic of human nature for Smith. In his other book, the *Theory of Moral Sentiments*, he explains that we are always driven by our desire to distinguish ourselves from others. And here that driving desire reappears, explaining otherwise irrational behavior.

Sometimes, though, a reputation of superior excellence may not be enough to attract people into a profession. Public prejudice may kick in and consider a profession dishonorable. Despite their great talents, opera singers and dancers are considered prostitutes. They are, therefore, extremely well paid, not just for the rarity of their talents, but to compensate for the lack of reputation of their jobs, Smith observes.

But here Smith notes one thing: the nature of employment is not fixed. What is considered the nature of the job is a social construct and can vary in different times and places. If, in the future, opera singing becomes a reputable profession, then more people would go into singing and the wages will drop.

But there are other things being described as natural that are immutable parts of human nature. One of these, for Smith, is our absurd overconfidence in our good fortune, which any man in tolerably good health has. We systematically overestimate our probability of success, and systematically underestimate our probability of failure. Note this is a very different description of human nature than the assumption we tend to make in economics today. Today we tend to think of our mistakes as being normally distributed, so that, on average, we are unbiased in our errors: sometimes we err in one way, sometimes we err in the other way, so at the end, on average, we stay on path. Smith instead thinks we make the same mistakes over and over again. And it is not because we do not understand probability. Our systematic bias is caused by our self-love, not by probability ignorance, as we learn from the *Theory of Moral Sentiments*. We are born thinking we are the center of the universe and, though we understand that there is a high chance of failure, we do not think that it applies to us. The universe revolves around me. I am the lucky one.

This, Smith claims, is why we have lotteries, even lotteries that are not fair. A nonfair lottery is a lottery in which the expected winning (the amount won times the probability of winning) is less than the expected cost (the cost of playing), so that the expected value (expected gains minus expected cost) is negative. A fair lottery, instead, is a lottery in which the expected value is zero. Today we would say we have lotteries because we are risk loving over small amounts, but when dealing with large amounts we become risk averse, we purchase insurance instead. Smith does not buy into this, or at least he does not think in these terms. He thinks we are attracted by "vain hopes of great prizes". Lotteries are universally demand driven, even when they are not fair. As long as the prizes are high enough, our absurd presumption in our own good fortune will lead us to take part. Small prize lotteries, even if fair, are less popular. Big prizes are better vain hopes than small prizes. For Smith, this presumption in our own good fortune and contempt for risk is the same reason why lotteries are universally popular and, in his time, insurance is not a very profitable business. It is also the explanation for why so many volunteer to be soldiers or seamen.

Many ships are at sea without insurance, according to Smith. It is fine if they are part of a large company that has many ships, something in the rage of 20 or 30 ships, at sea. The saving from the multiple premiums compensates the loss of a ship. But Smith is willing to bet this is not the result of a rational calculation of the ship owner, but rather the result of this presumptuous contempt for risk.

Similarly, it is romantic hopes of honor and distinction that drive a young man from the lower ranks of society to enlist as a soldier. He will be paid less than a common worker and will have to work harder. But dreams of successfully surviving dangers are a positive incentive, attracting people into that dangerous profession and therefore lowering its wage. The lottery of the sea gives smaller and more frequent prizes and thus attracts less people. It is not by chance, for Smith, that a father usually lets a son join the navy but will always object to him becoming a soldier.

Differences in risk in the employment of stock (capital) will affect the profit rates too. When there is a high risk of failure, there is also a high profit. And indeed one of the most profitable professions is smuggling because it is one of the most hazardous. When a smuggler is successful, yes, his profits are going to be very high. But most of the time, given the dangers, he will fail and go bankrupt. But because of our presumptuous hope of success, we try anyway; the job becomes more and more competitive, increasing bankruptcy rates.

So, for Smith, of these five circumstances that affect wages, only two affect profits too: risk, as we just saw, and the agreeableness of the job, as we saw earlier. This explains why we see more variation in wages than in profits. If it looks like there is a great deal of variation among profits in different profession it is because we confuse wages for profits, Smith claims. Or, Smith also claims, it may also be because as the extension of the market increases, profits decrease, but transportation costs increase, therefore increasing the prices of commodities.

Smith observes that it is indeed rare to see sudden great fortunes arising from profits. If they exist, they come from trade speculations, but generally it is only lifelong industry and frugality that allows for great fortunes accumulation.

Now, all these differences are going, at the end, to equalize the compensation of labor and capital, but this will only happen under specific circumstances: if there is perfect liberty, if the employment is well known, if it is in its natural state, and if it is the sole employment of the worker. Indeed, Smith reminds us, if there are new kinds of jobs, they will have higher wages because they need to attract new workers. If there are many variations in supply and demand, like in the case of some commodities (wine, corn, hop, sugar, tobacco, for example), speculators will buy when they expect prices to rise and sell when they expect prices to fall. Finally, if a worker has more than one job, he would be willing to receive less from at least one of them.

There are other circumstances in which compensation for labor and capital do not equalize, according to Smith. Smith deals with them in the second part of the chapter.

PART II: INEQUALITIES OCCASIONED BY THE POLICY OF EUROPE

Smith identifies some inequalities of wages that persist and will not be compensated. They are due to policies. They are a source of injustice, and Smith condemns them.

The policies affect wages in three ways: by limiting entry in a profession, therefore limiting competition; by subsidizing entry, therefore increasing competition; and by limiting the free circulation of labor and stock (capital) both from employment to employment and from place to place.

The first cause of inequality of wages is the limit to competition that corporations impose, especially though apprenticeship. Corporations in Smith's time are not "Inc.", but are legal cartels, meaning groups of producers attempting create a monopoly, with several privileges guaranteed by law. Smith explains that incorporated trades were originally called universities, as in the university of smiths or the university of tailors, where members would become "masters of arts" after seven years. Mandatory apprenticeship is one of those attempts to reduce competition by regulating the number of apprentices (usually one or two) and the number of years they have to serve (usually seven).

Smith does not like apprenticeships. They are "a manifest encroachment of just liberty". Each man's "most sacred and inviolable" property is his labor. Property of labor is the foundation of all property, for Smith. Limiting one's employment is therefore a "plain violation of the most sacred property". Here again notice Smith's move: justice is the primary motivation. Apprenticeship is a violation of just liberty. And it happens to be inefficient too.

Smith tells us that apprenticeships do not help guarantee the quality of the work done. The employer is the best judge of it because his interest is at stake. Apprenticeships do not prevent fraud: a stamp does a better job at it. Apprenticeships do not teach how to do a good job, but being paid by the piece will, especially if the apprentice has to pay for the spoiled materials. Apprenticeships do not teach industriousness, but will teach how to be idle: because there is no reward in working, the apprentice will learn idleness.

Why do we have them, then, if they are "altogether unnecessary"? Because, for Smith, the master would lose out. The master would have to pay wages for seven years, while now he does not. The apprentice would also eventually lose out because it is easy to learn his trade, so without apprenticeship, he will have to face more competition and lower wages. The gainer would be the public, which could have cheaper goods. But the masters can easily get a corporation charter from the king so that competition is reduced, and price, profits, and wages are kept high. They just need to pay a fee for it and, because they control the governments of towns, the task is very easy.

Smith notes that the monopolistic privileges of corporations break down the natural equality we should expect to see between towns and country. Because of them, we see that the industry of towns is instead more advantageous than the one of the country: for each one hundred people of great fortune in a town, there is only one in the country. The town indeed gets its subsistence from the country paying it with domestic- and foreign-manufactured products. Corporations reduce domestic competition, creating high wages and profits. They also manage to impose high duties to reduce foreign competition, additionally raising wages and profits. Corporations and duties make it de facto cheaper for towns to get subsistence.

This is possible because in towns there is a higher density of population, Smith points out. Because of their proximity, people can easily combine into what today we call a cartel. Indeed we see even the most insignificant trades being incorporated. The monopolistic spirit prevails: there is jealousy of strangers, and aversion to competition, so that masters can reduce manufactures into a "sort of slavery to themselves". In the country this is not possible because of the low population density. People are dispersed in many places, so they cannot combine. This is a phenomenal Public Choice explanation, as we call it today.

It is not that farming lacks corporation because it is easier to learn farming than manufacturing. As a matter of fact, farming is much more complex than many mechanical arts. And it is not even that farmers are more stupid than traders. As a matter of fact, their understanding and judgment is superior because of the variety of activities they engage with (keep this point in mind because it will be used again later). The reason why wages are lower in the countryside is just because in towns there are corporations. Traders, joined in corporations and living in towns, can more easily concentrate and control each other to avoid cheating.

This leads Smith to believe that, in towns, people of the same trade can seldom meet without conspiring against the public on how to increase their prices. And merchants, with their "clamor and sophistry" are so well organized that they are able to persuade the people of the country that they need to pay higher prices for their products! They manage to persuade farmers that "the private interest of a part of society is the general interest of the whole".

Of course, the law should not prevent their meeting, but it should not facilitate it either, according to Smith. And laws that require members of the same corporations to register in public registry, or to have self-taxation to help their own poor, do exactly that: they facilitate if not make their meetings necessary.

To say that one needs corporations to make sure that trade is well governed is, for Smith, nonsense. If you want discipline in a profession, you need consumers, not corporations. The answer for this natural tendency to cartelize is competition. The policy of Europe causes inequality in employment of labor and capital instead.

This inequality is slowly decreasing in Great Britain, according to Smith. Given the increase in capital in towns, profits eventually decrease. So capital leaves the towns and gets to the country in search of higher returns. The demand for labor increases and so do wages. Yet, this opulence grows slowly, uncertainly, and with many accidents, being in every respect "contrary to the order of nature and reason" as we will see in Book III and Book IV.

Competition solves many problems, but too much of a good thing may not be good. It is possible to have too much competition, which will distort wages. How can there be too much competition, you may ask? Well, Smith tells us, you subsidize it. And scholarships are subsidies to incentivize the entrance into certain professions. The most popular one is the church, which subsidies young men to become priests. The fact that being a clergyman is considered honorable does not help. Wages are pushed down even further. Curates are the only professionals seeing laws attempting to increase their wage, to maintain a certain dignity for the church. It does not work.

Imagine, Smith says, if we subsided law and physics at public expense. So many people would try to enter these professions. Competition would be so great that wages would fall so low that people would not see the worth in educating their children at their own expense. This is what happens with men of letters.

Men of letters are people that the church educates at public expense, through scholarship, but who are not ordained. Because they are educated with scholarships, there is a high number of them. Their large supply pushes their wage down. So low, indeed, can their wage be that, before the invention of printing, scholars had the legal permission to beg! In antiquity, however, people would have to pay for their own education. Scholars were few and very well remunerated. Like lawyers and physicians today. Yet, in this case, not all that appears harmful comes to hurt us: cheap education is good. More in Book V.

The other factor that artificially creates difference in wages is, according to Smith, the inability of labor and capital to move freely either across professions or across places. This is, again, the fault of corporations and apprenticeships. With their absurd laws, they block the circulation of labor, and, as a consequence, the circulation of capital too (which is still called stock here), as the capital employed depends on the availability of labor.

For Smith, there are fewer laws limiting the circulation of capital. It is therefore easier for wealthy merchants to trade in different towns than for poor workers to move from town to town.

Indeed, Smith tells us, the laws are such to discourage or prevent the free circulation of the poor. In England before the sixteenth century, the charity of monasteries would support the poor. When monasteries were forced to close, the poor had no support. Now each parish had to provide for its poor. The incentives for each parish were to send their poor away and not to receive any. The result was a set of laws, called the Poor Laws, meant to regulate the parishes' relief of the poor, but that, in practice, made it impossible for a poor to move: "it is more difficult for a poor man to cross to the next parish than to change country", Smith declares. The scarcity of hands in one parish cannot be compensated by the movement of hands from parishes where they are abundant.

What is Smith's judgment of this? "It is an evident violation of natural liberty and justice". It is a "cruel oppression". Again justice is the judging criterion here. Efficiency is a consequence.

The conclusion of the chapter is similarly based on justice, with Smith's typical Public Choice bent. Smith repeats an issue he brought out earlier: the treatment of masters and workers in the law is not symmetrical. If masters combine to reduce wages, they succeed. If the workers try to do the same, the law punishes them severely. Whenever the legislature regulates the difference between workers and masters, the counselors of the legislature are always the masters. Thus, if there is ever a regulation that favors the workers, we can be sure that it will be just and fair.

FURTHER READINGS

Aspromourgos, Tony. 2013. "Adam Smith on Labour and Capital", in *The Oxford Handbook of Adam Smith*, ed. Christopher Berry, Maria Pia Paganelli, Craig Smith. Oxford: Oxford University Press. 267–289.

Martin, Christopher. 2015. "Equity, Besides: Adam Smith and the Utility of Poverty". *Journal of the History of Economic Thought* 37.4: 559–581.

Naldi, Nerio. 2013. "Adam Smith on Value and Prices", in *The Oxford Handbook of Adam Smith*, ed. Christopher Berry, Maria Pia Paganelli, Craig Smith. Oxford: Oxford University Press. 290–306.

Rosolino, Riccardo. 2018. "Resisting Economic Conspiracies: Adam Smith, the (Labor) Market and the Moral Basis of Antimonopolisitc Resistance". *History of Political Thought* 39.2: 297–324.

Samuelson, Paul. 1978. "The Canonical Classical Model of Political Economy". *Journal of Economic Literature* 16.4: 1415–1434.

Waterman, A. M. C. 2012. "Adam Smith and Malthus on High Wages". *European Journal of the History of Economic Thought* 19.3: 409–429.

———. 2009. "Adam Smith's Macrodynamic Conception of the Natural Wage". *History of Economics Review* 49: 45–60.

5

BOOK I, CHAPTER XI

BOOK I, CHAPTER XI: OF THE RENT OF LAND

The last chapter of Book I is on the last component of price for Adam Smith: rent (for his "classical" successors, rent does not enter into cost and is a price-determined surplus). But it is much more than just the explanation of the determinants of the natural rates of rent. It is an exceptional analysis of the problems with data analysis that can lead to gross misunderstandings and dangerous political manipulations. It is a great chapter, even if traditionally underappreciated.

For Smith, rent is the price of the use of land, and it is the highest the tenant can afford to pay, meaning that the landlord, when he can, will leave the farmer only with maintenance and will take the rest as rent. Of course, it is possible to have deviations from this: if the rent leaves the tenant a bit more than subsistence, it is just because the landlord is ignorant. If it leaves the tenant a bit less than subsistence, it is because the farmer is ignorant, though this is unlikely.

Immediately Smith warns us of the challenges of understanding rent correctly. Some people may, incorrectly, think that rent is the profit or the interest on the capital (what Smith calls here stock) used for improvement of the land. This cannot be right. The landlord charges rent also for the lands that have not been improved. As a matter of fact, when there is improvement, usually it comes from the stock of the tenant, not of the landlord. The landlord simply demands a higher rent after the improvement, with the renewal of the lease.

The landlord even asks for rent for lands that are not improved by human labor at all, such as rents for lands that give access to kelp (seaweed used to make soap) or fishing in the ocean.

But if rent is not based on the cost of improvement, what is it based on? One of the challenges of this chapter is that Smith gives us a second account of price determination. We have a cost-based account for competitive markets, as described in the previous chapters, and here we have a value-based account of price formation for noncompetitive markets. Monopolists can and do charge more than cost, and indeed the price of a monopoly seems to be independent of costs. The rent of the land is for Smith "naturally a monopoly price", so the rent of the land is not based on costs, but on willingness/ability to pay of the renter.

Rent is thus a residual for Smith. If the price at which the produce sells is more than the expenses of producing it, then there will be rent. If the price is less or equal to the expenses, then there will be no rent. And the price, the market price, depends on the demand for the good. It is different from wages and profits. Changes in wages and profits cause price to change, but variations in rents are caused by variations in price instead.

Let us see what patterns of demand and price we can find to determine rent.

PART I: OF THE PRODUCE OF LAND THAT ALWAYS AFFORDS RENT

Smith starts with a simple observation: as long as there are people, there will be demand for food. Indeed, as we know from the chapter on the wages of labor, Smith, like many eighteenth-century economists, and their predecessors too, believed that people multiply in proportion to the food they have.

Most of the time, the land produces more than what is needed to subsist. What is left, after paying all costs, including replacing the "stock" used, is rent. So rent will increase as there is more leftover after paying all costs.

For example, Smith explains, rent near towns is going to be higher than the rent in the countryside: the cost of cultivating the land is the same near or far from town, but the transport costs from the countryside are higher, so what is left near a town is going to be more than what is left in the countryside. Which is to say, rent, being a residual after all the expenses are covered, will be lower in the countryside because, given the same selling price of produce, the countryside produce faces the higher transport costs. Note that here Smith still uses a cost-based approach.

It is not by accident that, for Smith, good transportation counts among the greatest improvements in society. Good transportation introduces rival commodities. It also opens new markets, forcing the countryside to improve its own production. Monopoly, which is what the countryside would have over its neighborhood if transportation is bad, is the greatest enemy of good management: only free and universal competition forces management to be good "for the sake of self-defence", meaning that if you want to survive in a competitive environment, you have to manage your resources well.

Similarly, Smith continues, in the days of rude agriculture, meat is cheaper than bread. As civilization progresses, meat becomes more expensive than bread. The reason lies in their relative cost of production. A corn field produces more than a pasture, but it requires a great deal more work (remember that corn means edible grains in this context). When agriculture is not much developed, fields are left to cattle, which grow there on their own. There is more meat than bread. So much so that, in Buenos Aries, in Smith's time, an ox costs only the labor of catching it, but bread is quite expensive and rare.

On the contrary, with more sophisticated and extensive cultivation, cattle become less abundant and corn (read grains) less scarce. Cattle are no longer wild, and are fed with pasture cultivated on land, land that now can no longer be used to produce corn. The price of meat must now cover not only the cost of labor needed to care for it, but also the rent and profit forgone if corn were to be cultivated there. The price of meat will therefore be higher than the price of bread.

Now, the price of meat will be the same regardless of whether it comes from a moor or from a farm, Smith explains. Yet, the meat from a moor has a lower cost of production than the meat from a farm, so the landlord of the moor will receive a higher rent than the landlord of a farm.

This gives us Smith's pre-Ricardian view of the general principle of rent determination: the rent of improved lands regulates the rent of the unimproved lands, while the rent and profits of the improved lands is regulated by the rent of corn. On the same land, one can produce corn or meat. Meat takes longer to grow than corn – four years as opposed to one, give or take. So, one can produce less meat than corn, which implies that the price of meat has to be higher than the price of corn to compensate for the lower output. If the price of meat would be more than enough to compensate all its costs, more land would be turned into pasture. If instead the price of meat was not enough to compensate for the cost of not producing corn, more land would be turned into corn fields.

At the end of the day, according to Smith, the rent one receives from using land for pasture or for corn production has to be the same, and it will be regulated by the rent of corn production, because corn is what is most demanded as primary source of food.

But this equality of profits and of rent for grass and corn has its exceptions. Near a great town, for example, the value of grass may be more than value of grain because in a great town there is a relatively high demand for milk and for forage for horses. So in general, in area with great population, the combined quantity demanded of corn and grass may be larger than the quantity supplied.

The land will be used as pasture because meat, dairy, and forage are more difficult to store and transport than corn, Smith continues to explain. Corn is easy to store and transport so it can easily be imported.

Another exception comes from the cultivation of "artificial grass", which is turnips, carrots, and cabbage. These "artificial grasses" can feed more animals than regular grass, so in this case the price of meat will be lower than otherwise.

What about other primary food? Smith realizes that corn may not be the primary food for everybody. Indeed in some nations, the primary form of nutrition is rice, in others it may be potatoes. But it is not easy to turn rice fields into fields for the cultivation of other things, so rice cannot easily regulate the rents of the land. A field that produces potatoes, however, can easily produce other things too, so the rent of that land can regulate all other rents. Potatoes are more nutritious than wheat, so the same amount of land can maintain more people. And if there is a large surplus of potatoes, population will grow and rent will increase too. But potatoes do not last very long, so it is unlikely they can become the principal food of all people, Smith concludes.

So, for Smith, the general principle of rent determination can be: in all great countries, rent and profits of land producing food for men and food for cattle regulate rent and profits of all other lands. If other products give more, less land will be used for food for man or cattle. If other products give less, more land will be used for producing food for men or animals.

There are no exceptions to this, according to Smith. What look like exceptions, such as special produce with special prices, do not generate special rent. They just have special costs. A fruit garden, for example, requires greater expense: it is more labor intensive, it requires more care, it is riskier, and it is practiced by the rich as an amusement. Vineyards producing expensive wines may have high profits only because of laws restraining free cultivation. These examples for Smith mean that the rents and profits of things that require extraordinary expenses just compensate those great expenses and are regulated by the profit and rent of corn production.

Smith believes that the only real exception is for those special lands whose production is limited, so that its supply cannot equal its effectual demand. Some fancy wines, for example, can be produced only in limited parts of some countries. Fashion and scarcity induce some people to be willing to pay more for it, given that the quantity demanded is less than the one supplied. Price therefore goes up, as does rent. In these cases, it is the higher price that causes the more careful cultivation, not vice versa. If the farmer is not careful, the wine may spoil, and he would lose a great deal. Thus, given how much he can lose, he has all the incentives to take a great amount of care.

Another example Smith gives is sugar. Sugar is also one of those goods for which the effectual demand exceeds the supply, therefore increasing its price, profits, and rents.

Tobacco is another of these goods, but for different reasons. For Smith, tobacco could be produced in Europe, but its cultivation in Europe is prohibited. Why? Tobacco is heavily taxed, and it is easier to collect the taxes from a single custom office than from a large number of producers spread all over the country. Tobacco is thus monopolistically imported from the colonies, especially from Virginia and Maryland. Its supply thus is limited. But tobacco is not as profitable as sugar. The evidence? The limit of its cultivation seems artificial. There are rumors, Smith reports, that some plantation owners burn the excess tobacco to keep its supply low and its price high, which implies that the advantage over corn may not last long.

So, in this part of the chapter Smith shows that for the land that always generates rent, the rent of the lands that produce human food regulate the rent of other lands. It cannot generate less rent for long, or production will shift. It can generate more rent, but only if there are ways to limit supply of the produce of land to be less than its effective demand.

PART II: OF THE PRODUCE OF LAND THAT SOMETIMES DOES AND SOMETIMES DOES NOT AFFORD RENT

People do not live on bread alone. We also need clothing and shelter. Land not only gives us food, but it can also give us clothing and lodging. Yet, as important as clothing and lodging are for our existence, Smith reminds us that population increases only with abundant food, not with abundant clothing or lodging.

In Smith's account, in a "rude society", land can produce clothing more easily than food, but in an "improved society" the reverse is true. When hunting is the primary source of subsistence, game will provide for both food and clothing, and much waste. When commerce is introduced, what was previously wasted may now be sold. If things are so abundant to be wasted, there can be no rent. But where there is scarcity, then someone will be willing to give more for what they want, so rent will be possible. This is why in "rude societies", there are no rents. Rents are present in "improved societies", though, due to scarcity.

In a "rude society", the materials for producing lodging, being more difficult to transport, will not be an object of trade, Smith explains. As a consequence they cannot generate rent. As a matter of fact, landlords often grant the use of their land and their timber to whomever asks for it. This may not necessarily be the case in wealthier countries, though.

Smith goes on saying that once we have enough to eat, we want to satisfy our other wants: our wants for ornaments and distinction. A rich man consumes more or less the same quantity of food as a poor man, because the stomach of the rich is not significantly different from the stomach of the poor. Yes, the rich may eat better quality food and food with more elaborate presentation, but the desire of food remains limited by the size of our stomach, however rich or poor we are. By contrast, our desire for ornaments is infinite, or so Smith claims. Clothing, lodging, and furniture are where we can see significant differences between rich and poor, not just in quality but also in quantity.

For Smith, the rich have more food than they need, and use it to gratify their endless desires. The poor gratify the rich to get food. So, as the amount of food increases, so does the number of workers, in its turn increasing the demand for food, and therefore the rent on land producing food. The division of labor lets us produce more, as the demand for the materials for ornaments increases, which also increases rents as a consequence. What this means is that food is therefore the origin of all rent.

In a different context, Smith makes a similar argument to the one made here. The wealth of the rich does not stay in their hands. It trickles down to the poor. The desire for distinctions, that is typical of our nature, can find some satisfaction when the rich employ the poor to produce those means of distinctions. In this way, the rich share part of what they have with the poor. It is like there is an invisible hand that distributes wealth among people, so that the poor get some of what the rich have, through the work they provide to the rich. This account comes from Smith's other book, *The Theory of Moral Sentiments*, and it is the only other place in his published works where he mentions the invisible hand.

That said, let's go back Smith's analysis of rent. Smith just told us, again, that food is what matters to us. Food is what keeps us alive, what allows population to grow both in number and in wealth, and what regulates all rents. The comparison to what follows may, therefore, appear to be quite striking – it is a way of cutting the legs off the argument he is fighting against: precious metals are not wealth and do not create wealth. Believing so is incorrect and dangerous.

Here is what Smith says. Mines differ from the land producing corn. They may or may not afford rents, and their rents depend on both the fertility of the mines and the historical circumstances in which the mines operate. The value of coal mines depends both on their fertility and their circumstances. The value of metallic mines depends mostly on their fertility.

Coal mines have to be in a convenient place (circumstance) to generate rent. A fertile mine in a sparsely populated place with poor transportation may not be mined. Similarly, some mines in good location may not be fertile enough to justify their mining. Yet, in all cases, the most fertile mines will regulate the price of coal of all other mines. The owner of the most fertile mine can undersell his competitors. They will need to lower their prices too. Profits and rent will go down as well. For some, they will go down so much that they may have to close. So usually the price of coal will give no rent to the owner of the mine.

Smith estimates that the rent on land is about one-third of the gross produce, while the rent on mines is about one-tenth. And coal mining is not that bad because it is not in long-distance competition, as metallic mines are.

The market for precious metals is a worldwide market. Because precious metals are valuable, their price can cover transportation costs worldwide. So it is the most fertile mines in the world to determine the price of metals. In fact, the discovery of the fertile mines of Peru caused many European mines to close. Mining can eventually cover only its expenses. It is rare to have high rents. The price usually covers just wages and profits. Not surprisingly, now even in Peru profits are approaching bankruptcy levels.

For Smith, mining is like a lottery: many ruin themselves attracted by the fortune of few. It is rare to find someone who became rich by mining silver, and even rarer someone who got rich mining gold. It does not help that the sovereign gets revenue from mining. The sovereign creates laws that encourage mining: who discovers the mine gets it, without the owner of the land's consent. This is a "violation of the sacred right of private property", which is sacrificed supposedly for the interest of public revenue. Note that, again, for Smith, what is unjust happens to be also inefficient.

Smith continues with a surprising analysis that seems to effortlessly solve the water-diamond paradox he mentioned earlier in the book. The high price of precious metals comes from their demand and from their scarcity.

The demand for precious metals derives in part from their utility and in part from their beauty. We can clean a silver boiler more easily than a copper one. But we prefer it to a copper one mostly because we think it is more beautiful. And we think it is so beautiful because of its scarcity.

And so Smith goes on. The great joy of the rich is parading their riches. And their riches are those signs of opulence that nobody else has. The value of something is in its beauty, in its utility, and mostly in its scarcity, which makes that object so expensive that nobody else can afford it.

It is therefore the utility (usefulness), beauty, and scarcity that give precious metals their high prices. This means that the value of metals is present before they are coined, and exists independently from it. Coining precious metals may increase their scarcity for other uses, increasing their value. Precious stones work in the same manner. They may be used only as ornaments, and their beauty is enhanced by their scarcity, Smith explains. Diamonds too? One may ask. ...

Two things to note here. One is the reliance on beauty and of our desire to show off as major motivation factors. This is a theme dominant in *The Theory of Moral Sentiments*. What we want most is for others to notice us. And, for Smith, the most effective way to attract people's attention is to show off our wealth. Wealth glitters after all. This is not an endorsement of the behavior, but a simple matter-of-fact description of it.

The other thing to note is the deepening of Smith's theory of money. Gold and silver emerge spontaneously as money because everybody wants them as a mark of opulence that can distinguish one person from another.

Smith concludes this section with a discussion that provides more ammunition against the mercantile system that he wants to criticize. More mines cannot and do not increase the wealth of the world because precious metals derive their value from their scarcity. The more abundant they are the less value they have. The only advantage there is to have abundant mines is to have cheap services of plate, that is, that silverware price will decrease.

And Smith concludes. Value comes from what is produced above ground, not below it. Producing more food creates more demand for the produce of other lands, increasing value and wealth. As the value of fertile land increases, the value of the barren lands also increases because the more people a fertile land can maintain, the more they create a market for the produce of the less fertile land. As the fertility of land increases, its value increases, bringing up the value of all other lands. The abundance of food creates the demand for metals and other ornaments too. It is, therefore, the abundance of food, not of metals, that gives value to other things.

PART III: OF THE VARIATION IN THE PROPORTION BETWEEN THE RESPECTIVE VALUES OF THAT SORT OF PRODUCE THAT ALWAYS AFFORDS RENT, AND THAT WHICH SOMETIMES DOES AND SOMETIMES DOES NOT AFFORD RENT

We just saw that when there is more food, there may be more demand for other things, such as ornaments. For Smith, this implies that the demand for clothing, lodging, and precious stones will increase too, and with that, the price of those things will increase as well.

What if their supply changes too? For some things the supply may increase more than the demand. We need to be able to distinguish among all these different factors, as well as among nominal and real changes.

The value of silver, used to express monetary prices, can change for two different and unrelated reasons: because of improvements in society and because of the discovery of new mines. The improvement in society will increase the demand for silver and thus its value will increase. But the discovery of new mines will increase its supply, decreasing its value. If the supply does not increase by the same proportion, the value of silver will be higher than the value of corn, meaning that the average money price of corn will go down. But if the supply increases more than demand, silver will become cheaper and cheaper, meaning that the money price of corn will increase. And if supply and demand of silver increase by the same proportion, the average money price of corn would stay about the same, despite the improvement in society.

The digression on silver that follows is Smith's marvelous analysis of the distinction between nominal and real prices and of the importance of recognizing that what we see and commonly believe may not be correct.

DIGRESSION CONCERNING THE VARIATIONS IN THE VALUE OF SILVER DURING THE COURSE OF THE FOUR LAST CENTURIES

Smith opened Book I by noticing that what we commonly see is not necessarily correct. We are often misled by what we see. We see how the division of labor takes place in full in a small shop and we commonly think that is where it exists the most. But in reality, the division of labor is more extensive in large manufactures. We do not commonly think so because we do not see all the pieces in one place.

Book I also ends by noticing mistakes we commonly make because we are misled by what we see: we commonly believe that the value of silver decreases with the increase in wealth. But we are mistaken. We see the nominal price and stop there, being misled by what we see. We just look at the nominal price, not at the real price, which is where value is. To understand the relation between value of silver and wealth, Smith warns us, we need to look with care at changes in relative prices, not nominal prices. Then we will notice that correlation is not causation. It just happened that Europe grew richer over the last four centuries and that the nominal value of silver decreased. But if we look at historical events and relative price changes, we see the mistake. The two phenomena happened simultaneously, but independently. They are correlated, but one did not cause the other. They have separate and independent causes.

Smith is going to separate the last four centuries into three periods in which the changes in the value of silver and corn are compared, to show their disconnection, and therefore the error that is commonly believed. The following is his account of it.

FIRST PERIOD

Between the middle of the fourteenth and the middle of the fifteenth century the quantity of silver in silver coins tended to decrease. At the same time the value of silver increased. The two effects cancelled each other out.

But from the end of the fifteenth century the value of silver increases compared to the value of corn. This could be because the demand for silver increases while its supply stays the same, because the demand for silver stays the same while its supply declines, or both.

Indeed, between the end of the fifteenth and the beginning of the sixteenth century, Europe experiences an increased security, thanks to more stable governments, which allows industry and improvement to increase, fueling a demand for luxuries. More coins are, therefore, needed to circulate the larger quantity of produce. But European mines are old, so the supply of silver is not enough to keep up with the demand for it. The value of silver increases, that is, money prices decrease.

However, the popular, yet incorrect, notion that from the time of Julius Caesar to the discovery of America the value of silver diminishes, that is, prices increase – the idea that an increase in the quantity of silver is related to an increase in wealth so that the value of silver decreases as the wealth of a country increases – is groundless and is based on poor understanding of what one sees, according to Smith.

When one looks at the variations of the recorded prices of corn, one needs to understand what the records say, and not take for granted that they say what we want them to say. One needs to consider the three following factors. First, ancient records do not record market prices, but conversion prices of corn. Rent used to be paid in corn. The landlord could ask to covert the payment in money prices. That is the conversion price, which may not be the same as the market price. Second, we can't assume that there are no mistakes in the records, especially because they were copied by hand, and copiers can be lazy. Third, what is often recorded are the lowest (and the highest) prices, not the actual market price. Prices do indeed look lower in the past, but it may be because we may not be looking at the right prices.

Many people look also at the price of "unmanufactured commodities" such as cattle and poultry, which are more common in "rude ages". One sees lower prices. One sees lower nominal prices. One infers they are caused by the high value of silver, and their increase by the decreased value of silver. But ... Smith tells us one needs to look deeper than what one sees. Things are cheap; yes because of the high value of silver, but also, as is the case here, because those goods are able to buy less quantity of labor than in more "advanced societies". The low money price here indicates that the value of those commodities is low, not that the value of silver is high. In the early stages of development, cattle are produced by nature and are abundant. There are also few people. The value of cattle is low, due to their relative abundance. They represent very little labor. In more advanced societies, however, when there are no longer more cattle than what people can consume, the value of cattle is higher, and they command more labor than before.

Looking at nominal changes in the price of cattle may tell us nothing about the changes of the value of silver.

Corn, by contrast, Smith reminds us, is always produced by labor. With similar soil and climate, regardless of the level of improvement, producing corn always requires the same quantity of labor. Even when the improvement in the productive power of labor improves cultivation, the increased price of cattle (which is the principal instrument of improved cultivation) counterbalances it. Equal quantities of corn, therefore, will always more or less represent equal quantity of labor, regardless of the state of improvement of society. Corn is, therefore, a better measure of value and a better measure of value of silver. We knew this already. But it is worth being reminded of it, because to evaluate the value of silver, we need to compare it to the value of something of stable value: corn. It is the relative price that matters, not the nominal one.

If there is no reason to infer that the value of silver decreases by looking at the nominal price of corn, there is even less reason to infer that a decrease in the value of silver is connected to an increase in wealth and improvement. We need to be careful about where we look and what we see, Smith seems to imply.

Now, the quantity of precious metals increases for two different and independent reasons. One is the increased abundance of mines. In this case, the large quantity of silver will decrease the value of silver. The other case is the increase in production. But in this case the value of silver will not decrease. To the contrary, the value of silver will increase.

With an increase in wealth, we experience an increase in production, which means that we need more coins to circulate that larger produce. An increase in wealth also means that we increase the demand for things that satisfy our vanity and our desire for ostentation. Our demand for plate will increase, just like our demand for paintings and statues. The price of gold and silver will, therefore, increase in richer countries. More gold and silver will go there, like all other things for which there is a higher price, Smith explains.

Again, wealth increases the value of silver, not decreases it. Among "savages", who are very poor, precious metals have scarcely any value.

Corn is more expensive in towns than in the countryside, but we would not say that it is because real price of silver is lower in towns than in the countryside, but because the real price of corn is more in towns: it costs the same to bring silver to towns or to the countryside. But it costs more to bring corn to towns than to the countryside. Substitute towns with rich commercial states, say Genoa or Holland, and countryside with poor agricultural state, say Poland. Price of corn is higher in Holland than in Poland because Poland produces corn and transports it to Holland, which produces manufactures instead. Now, imagine Holland without its wealth, without the power of getting corn for Poland. What would happen to the price of corn? It would skyrocket. It would require a very, very large quantity of labor to get corn. Corn is a necessity and we are willing to give up many superfluities in time of scarcity to get necessities.

Smith reiterates that with poverty and/or dearth, superfluities are cheap and necessities are expensive. With wealth and/or abundance, necessities are cheap, and superfluities become expensive. The real price of corn rises in times of poverty and falls in time of abundance. The real price of silver will move in the opposite way: it falls with poverty and rises with wealth because silver is a superfluity, while corn is a necessity. The opposite of what is commonly believed! Smith's implied warning: Careful what you look at, you may very well be misled by what you see.

SECOND PERIOD

From 1570 to 1640, the value of silver sank and the value of corn rose nominally, Smith reports. This can be uncontroversially attributed to the discovery of the mines in America. The demand for silver also increased because of economic growth. But the supply of silver rose by much more. Easy enough.

THIRD PERIOD

Smith now explains the last period, when the supply of precious metals increases at about the same rate as its demand, leaving the price of corn about the same.

By 1636 the effect of the new mines ends. The profits of the mines used to be quite high, but now are just enough to cover the expense of operating them, a sign their peak production is past. We also have to keep in mind that not all the gold and silver of America comes to Europe, just a part of it.

The demand for silver experiences a gradual increase. This gradual increase in the demand for silver, which counterbalances its increase in supply, happens because there is a larger market: Europe is growing, with the possible exception of Spain; the Americas are now a new market; even Mexico and Peru are now larger markets than before; and the East Indies are also a larger market. Add to this that some metal is lost during its transport, and that some is buried in the ground and then forgotten there. Furthermore, there is always an increasing demand for silver due to the consumption of the coins by wearing and the consumption of plate by wearing and cleaning (the continuous rubbing of metals against other things in people's pocket or in their daily use causes the metals to wear out – the "wearing" of the coins and plate). This demand due to the wearing of silver is like the demand for brass and iron due to the wearing of the tools made with it. When we see an increase in iron and brass so that they can replace the worn tools, we do not think that the increase in this quantity was caused by a decrease in their price, but by the wear and tear of the tools made with them. The same works for silver: the increase in its quantity may not be caused by a decrease in its price but by an increase in its demand.

At the same time there are also events that caused the price of corn to increase. Here again Smith warns us that we need to be careful to decompose the changes to see which ones depend on changes in the value of silver and which ones do not. There was a civil war, which caused the price of corn to rise, by making it scarce; there is a bounty (a subsidy) on the exportation of corn in combination with pretty bad season; and there is also a great debasement of silver coins through clipping of the coins and wearing, which increases its nominal price. The value of silver, therefore, increased in proportion to the increase in the value of corn. And the nominal price of corn does not change much over this time.

But – yes, there is always a "but" in Smith – at the time of the discovery of American mines, the money price of corn increased. People thought that the real value of silver went down. They did not think that the real value of corn may have gone up. Similarly, we can think that around 1700–1764, the money price of corn goes down because the real value of silver goes up rather than the real value of corn down. Relying exclusively on nominal price changes is, not surprisingly, misleading for Smith. We need to understand if that change is caused by a change in money supply (the quantity of silver and, therefore, the value of silver) or by a change in the supply or demand of corn.

Think of the effect of the bounty. It is true that a bounty (subsidy) on the exportation of corn will increase the real price of corn by increasing its scarcity both in good seasons, because of the subsidized exports, and in bad seasons, because the extra grain of the abundant years has not been saved but sold abroad. But it is also true that during those same years, France prohibits the exportation of corn, and yet its price goes up there too. This means that the increase in the price of corn in this era can be attributed to a monetary phenomenon – that the value of silver decreased. Otherwise we cannot explain how two opposite policies (prohibition and subsidized exports) can generate the same price effect.

Similarly, Smith continues to explain, the money price of labor in Britain increases. But if at the same time it decreases in France, it is difficult to attribute these changes to a change in the value of silver. It is more likely they come from a change in the demand for labor and, therefore, a change in the prosperity of a country.

Also, it is true that a bad season increases the price of corn. But it is also true that a bad season is a temporary event and it will have a temporary and immediate effect. Changes in price due to changes in silver are instead very slow to observe. So whenever we have sudden changes in prices, we can be confident that those are due to accidental variation of seasons. Long trends are less likely due to seasons but more likely due to changes in silver. The prices of metals tend to be remarkably stable year after year, especially compared with the prices of the produce of the land. The corn consumed this year is the corn produced last year. But the iron used today may be produced three hundred years ago. Corn production is about proportional to its yearly consumption. The production of the mines can vary a great deal from year to year, but because metals are very durable, they can be stored, so the yearly variation in production has almost no effect on price, which remains stable.

VARIATION IN THE PROPORTION OF THE VALUE OF GOLD AND SILVER AND GROUNDS OF SUSPICIONS ON THE DECREASE IN THE VALUE OF SILVER GOOD

Now, Smith observes, the quantity of silver in the market is probably more than the quantity of gold, even if the value of gold is more than the value of silver. This is consistent with the fact that generally the whole quantity of a cheaper commodity is greater and of greater total value than an expensive one. Bread is cheaper than meat, but there is much more bread than meat, and the total value of bread may exceed the total value of meat. Yet, the profits of gold mines may be less than the profits of silver mines.

Here Smith hammers home once again that mining is not a profitable activity. We see that mining costs are increasing because taxes on metals are decreasing. But this decrease in taxes will just postpone, not avoid, the increase in the value of metals. Especially because as wealth increases, the demand for gold and silver increases too, like the demand for all luxury goods does. This rise in nominal price is not rooted in a decrease in the value of gold and silver, but in an increase in their value, in an increase in their real price.

Imports of metals more or less match their consumption. As we import more, the value decreases; and as the value decreases, we use more metals and we use less care in handling them, wearing and tearing them more. So consumption increases to match imports. Then, Smith claims, we start importing less because the consumption is more than the imports, which pushes the value up and consumption down to match imports again.

DIFFERENT EFFECTS OF PROGRESS OF IMPROVEMENT ON THE REAL PRICE OF THREE RUDE PRODUCE

Smith tells us that we can see that the price of things can change independently from the changes in their value by looking at three different kinds of things: things that we cannot increase, things that we can increase, and things for which there is limit and uncertainty on what we can do.

If we can't increase the quantity of a good, it may seem like the price may rise to no limit. For things that we can increase, price may increase but not by much, and for things that are uncertain there is uncertainty on the direction of change of the price.

FIRST SORT

Smith explains that nature produces only a limited amount of some things. And they may be perishable. Rare fish or rare birds, for example. As wealth increases, and their quantity cannot increase, their prices can reach extravagant levels. Those high prices are not an effect of the low value of silver but of the high value of their rarity.

SECOND SORT

Smith continues explaining that human industry can multiply something in proportion to its demand. For example, there are animals, say cattle, that are abundant in nature, but they can become scarce as civilization progresses because we give space to more profitable produce. So, as civilization advances, the quantity of cattle decreases. Yet its demand increases. The value of cattle, therefore, increases so that it is worth producing.

Poultry, hogs, and dairy products work in a similar way. They are "save-all" products. Pigs and chicken eat leftovers, so they cost little to maintain. They sell for little. Milk too is perishable and abundant; the extra quantity sells at very low prices. But with the increasing wealth and luxuries, the price of all these increases, and it becomes profitable to use land to explicitly produce them. The only rude produce that still has not gone through this process, and unlikely will, is venison. Even a high price will not compensate the expense of maintaining a deer park.

In all these situations, the increase in the money price of the produce is not due to a decrease in the value of silver but to an increase in the real price of the produce. So the increase in their price is not a public calamity but, on the contrary, a sign of greater prosperity.

Interesting enough, here is where Smith introduces the solution of a different problem: How do we get to increase the stock (i.e., capital) that we will need to improve the land, given that without the improvement in the land we cannot increase our capital? Smith throws in the seed of his answer: with a long course of frugality and industry. The idea will be developed in the next book. Here we just have a taste.

THIRD SORT

The third kind of goods whose price varies, but not necessarily because of changes in silver value, are, for Smith, those goods whose price would increase with improvement of society as well as accidents. The direction of change of these prices is, therefore, uncertain.

Wool and raw hides are good examples of these goods. In a sense they are like butcher's meat: their price increases with the increase in wealth. But they differ from butcher's meat because the meat market can be only domestic. In Smith's time, with no refrigeration and no steam engine means of transport, it was too difficult to move fresh meat long distance. But the market for wool and hides is an international one because they are easy to transport. At least they do not rot easily.

In poorly cultivated countries, as we saw already, the price of wool and of hides is more than the price of the whole animal. There are many animals and much meat, and they cannot be easily shipped abroad. Wool and hides can be sold abroad. But with progress and the increase in population that progress brings about, the price of the whole animal increases too.

Yet, in Smith's time, both the real and nominal prices of wool and raw hides are low. Why? Because of "violence and artifice", Smith claims. "Violence and artifice"? Yes, "violence and artifice". The price of wool is low because there is an absolute prohibition of exporting wool, there is permission to import wool from Spain duty free, and there are impositions on Ireland so that they can export wool only to England. Why on earth does England have those kinds of regulations? Smith explains it as he explains why the price of hides is low: the price of hides is low because British tanners are not as successful as clothiers in convincing the nation "that the safety of our commonwealth depends upon the prosperity of their particular manufacture". The merchants and manufacturers of clothes want to have cheap inputs for their productions. They are able to convince "the nation" that to benefit them is good for everybody. Of course this is not true, but they encounter little resistance. Smith will more fully elaborate this few pages later, in the conclusion. Here he simply notes that the lack of resistance comes from the indifference of the landlords. When regulations decrease the price of wool or hides, the price of meat has to increase to compensate for it. What is not paid by wool or hides has to be paid by the meat. The landlord gets his rent independently by which part of the animal is sold at high or low price. But this kind of regulation would not fly as easily in poorer countries where the price of meat is very low because of its abundance and where the value of an animal comes almost exclusively from its wool or hides. The interest of the landlords and farmers here would be greatly affected by an artificial decrease in the price of wool or hides: their profits and rents would decrease.

With this solid economic logic, which today we would call Public Choice analysis, Smith concludes that the attribution of a prohibition of the exportation of wool in the fourteenth century has to be false. It would have been "the most destructive regulation which could well have been thought of". What a jewel of analysis!

This is a long way – but Smith never loses a chance to attack what today we call special interest groups – to say that the price of wool and raw hides may change independently from changes in silver, and in ways that are not strictly dependent on domestic production.

So now we can go back to metals. The price of metals is also independent from the local situation, but rather dependent on the fertility of the mines worldwide. The quantity of metals in a country does not depend on its mines but on the state of its industry and the produce of its land, and on the barrenness and fertility of the mines in the world. But the fertility and discovery of new mines depend on luck, according to Smith. In addition, given that what matters is the real value, that is the real quantity of labor that something can command, which is independent from its nominal value, having more mines would bring only one advantage: cheap plate, that is, cheap silverware.

CONCLUSION OF THE DIGRESSION CONCERNING THE VARIATION IN THE VALUE OF SILVER

Here we have the explicit justification of this long digression and its fundamental importance in Smith's intellectual machine.

Past writers linked low money prices of corn, meaning high value of gold and silver, with barbarism and poverty. This way of thinking is grounded into the idea of gold being wealth. But as Smith just told us, the high value of metals is not a proof of poverty but only a proof of barrenness of the mines in the world.

Just because an increase in the quantity of gold and silver and an increase in manufacture and agriculture happened at the same time, it does not mean they came from the same cause and that are connected with one other.

Look, Smith tells us: China is richer than Europe, but the value of precious metals is higher than in Europe. Then think, since the discovery of the mines in America, the wealth of Europe has increased and the value of silver decreased. But the value of silver decreased not because of the increase in wealth but because of the increase in the number of mines.

The increase in gold and silver is a mere accident.

The improvement in agriculture is the result of the fall of feudal system and of the establishment of governments that offer tolerable security so that one can enjoy the fruits of his own labor, which is the only encouragement that industry needs, as will be elaborated in Book III.

You do not believe it? Look at Poland, Smith says. Poland is still a feudal system, it has no improvement in agriculture, yet the real value of metals has decreased there just like in rest of Europe. Similarly in Spain and Portugal, the quantity of metals increased but their industry did not.

Higher money prices, or a lower value of gold, are not a proof of wealth, just like low money prices, and low prices of corn in particular, are not a proof of barbarism. If money prices increase from a decrease in value of silver, then all prices would be equally affected. Again, Smith seems to imply: when you look at something, make sure you understand what you are seeing.

From low or high prices in general, or of corn in particular, we can only infer the fertility of mines.

We can infer if a country is rich or poor only from the relative price of some goods compared to others. As wealth increases, the price of some provision will increase too because of the increased value of land, due to the increase in its fertility. So the increase in wealth will not affect the price of all provision equally. Low money prices of cattle in proportion to the money price of corn is a better estimator of poverty.

Why does this matter? Because some "inferior servants" may be on a fixed monetary compensation. If the prices increase because of a decrease in the value of silver, their monetary compensation needs to be adjusted or their real compensation will go down. If instead prices increase because of improvement, then it is more difficult to evaluate if the fixed monetary compensation needs adjustments.

An increase in the price of venison affects the poor less than an increase in the price of potatoes, Smith continues. Similarly, in times of economic growth, a change in the price of corn will affect the poor as much as changes in taxes on salt, soap, candles, malt, and beer.

Why does this matter today, we can ask? Because it is a powerful lesson in the importance of looking at relative prices rather than nominal prices as well as on the importance of understanding that correlation is not causation.

EFFECTS OF THE PROGRESS OF IMPROVEMENT UPON THE REAL PRICE OF MANUFACTURE

Now let's look at the last piece of the puzzle. The division of labor causes improvement and causes prices of manufactures to decrease. Less labor is needed to make the same things. But the increase in wealth causes the real price of labor to increase. The increased quantity of manufactures compensates for the increase in the price of labor.

The price of some raw materials increases too, due to the higher demand, but the price of manufactures drops enough to compensate for it. The price decline is more present in the industries in which labor can be divided the most. So, for example, the decrease in price of coarse manufacture is less than the decrease in price of fine manufacture. Smith uses a nice anecdote to explain the idea: at the time of Edward IV (in the fifteenth century) socks were made with common cloth and knitting stocking were nowhere to be found. Allegedly, the first person to wear stocking was Elizabeth I. Now they are commonly used.

CONCLUSION

And so Smith concludes. Some improvements in society increase rent of the land. Add to this that the price of manufactures is dropping. This means that the real rent on land is even higher. The landlord can buy more manufactures with the produce of his land. He can buy more and more ornaments.

But because those who live by rent live without having to work or to care, they tend to be indolent, ignorant, and incapable of understanding the consequences of public regulation. This is too bad, because this is a group of people whose interest coincides with the interest of society.

The interest of society also coincides with the interest of the people who live by wages. But they are also incapable of understanding it because of their lack of time and education – a point elaborated on later. In public deliberation, they have no voice, unless they clamorously protest – a point previously elaborated.

The interest of society is instead opposite to the interest of those who live by profits. They want high profits, which means less competition, while society benefits from more competition and lower prices. Because of their wealth, they attract a great deal of attention and admiration, so they are listened to (a point further developed in the *Theory of Moral Sentiments*). They know their interest well, and they are able to persuade other groups that their own interest is somehow the same as the interest of society, despite being the opposite of it. These are Smith's last words in this chapter –the foundation of what today we call Public Choice and of the criticism of mercantilism that will see its full power in Book IV:

> The proposal of any new laws or regulation of commerce which comes from this order, ought always to be listened to with great precaution, and ought never to be adopted will after having been long and carefully examined, not only with the most scrupulous, but with the most suspicious attention. It comes from an order of men, whose interest is never exactly the same with that if the public, who have generally an interest to deceive and even to oppress the public, and who accordingly have, upon many occasions, both deceived it and oppressed it.

FURTHER READINGS

Brewer, Anthony. 1995. "Rent and Profit in the Wealth of Nations". *Scottish Journal of Political Economy* 42: 183–200.

Gee, J. M. A. 1981. "The Origin of Rent in Adam Smith's Wealth of Nations: An Anti-Neoclassical View". History of Political Economy 13.1: 1–18.

Rutherford, Donald. 2012. *In the Shadow of Adam Smith.* London: Palgrave Macmillan.

Schliesser, Eric. 2005. Some Principles of Adam Smith's Newtonian Methods in the Wealth of Nations. *Research in the History of Economic Thought and Methodology* 23A: 33–74.

6

BOOK II

After seeing the causes of the improvement in the productive power of labor – the division of labor – Smith tackles what is needed for that division of labor to take place. He again opens the book and the chapter by mentioning labor. Labor is always center stage: labor is the source of wealth.

So, what do we need to have division of labor? Smith tells us that when there is very little division of labor, little exchange, and little "stock" accumulation, we are still in a "rude" society. Under these circumstances, we would expect to have not much more than self-sufficiency.

Let's suppose we have some increase in the division of labor. Now we can no longer supply our own wants by ourselves: we need the labor of other people. If I specialize in the production of pins, I will not produce food, so I will not have much to eat. I need the baker, brewer, and butcher to have my dinner. If we do not allow for credit, we have a problem: we can buy the labor of others only after we sell our own labor. So in the time during which our labor is not yet sold, we need something on which to live: some "stock". This means that we cannot have division of labor before some accumulation of "stock". This also means that the more division of labor there is, the more accumulation of "stock" we need to have. Which, in its turn, means that it is only through this accumulation of "stock" that improvement is possible.

So let's look at how we can get and use this "stock".

BOOK II, CHAPTER I: OF THE DIVISION OF STOCK

If someone has something on the side, some stock, to support himself only for couple of days, he will not think to use that stock to generate revenue for himself. He will get his revenue only from his work, and this is the condition of most workers. If, however, someone has enough stock to support himself for a few years, he will use the stock that he does not consume to generate revenue for himself.

So, stock can be divided into two types: one that generates revenue, called capital, and one for immediate consumption.

Capital, the part of stock we do not use for immediate consumption, in its turn, yields profits in two ways. If we make a profit by separating from it, that is by buying and selling or by making and selling goods, we call it "circulating capital" because it is its circulation that generates profits. And, if we get profits by keeping it, rather than by circulating it, we call it "fixed capital". Land improvement and machineries, for example, are capital that does not change hands, thus fixed capital.

Merchants tend to have circulating capital, manufacturers both circulating and fixed capital, and the mining industry mostly fixed capital in the form of big equipment needed to mine. Agriculture also has fixed capital, but it is more of a mix. Wages of the workers are circulating capital. "Cattle for fattening" are circulating capital – the farmer makes a profit by selling them – while "cattle for labor" are fixed capital – the farmer makes a profit by keeping them. Similarly, sheep for wool are fixed capital because farmers make a profit by keeping the sheep.

Smith explains also that the stock of a country is divided in the same three parts: there is a stock for immediate consumption, such as housing (which gives no revenue and so no profit); fixed capital, such as machinery, shops, warehouses, stables, granaries, improved land, and useful skills of all the inhabitant of society (which generate profits without changing master); and circulating capital, such as the money used to circulate the other capital, provisions, the input materials for future production, and inventories of finished goods that are waiting to be sold (which generate profits by changing master).

Note that for Smith what we called today human capital (the skills of the members of society) is part of the fixed capital, while wages paid to workers are circulating capital.

Fixed capital needs circulating capital to yield revenue. A machine cannot function without inputs and workers. Circulating capital is what brings them to it. Furthermore, parts of circulating capital go into fixed capital and stock for immediate consumption, which means that circulating capital needs to be continuously replenished or it will end. This replenishment comes from the produce of land, fishery, and mines.

This argument, as appropriate as it may have been in the eighteenth century is a bit unsettling today. Natural resources replenish the circulating capital, which in its turn supports both fixed capital and stocks for immediate consumption. It is a unidirectional flow that requires constant extractions from nature. With the exception of mining, Smith does not yet see the possible difficulties of sustainability of the finite resources of the planet.

Smith concludes the chapter with a remark on the fixity of human nature and the importance of good institutions. If there is tolerable security, people use their stock for either present enjoyment – current consumption – or for future profit – fixed or circulating capital: not doing this is "perfectly crazy". But if there is violence, and only if there is violence, it makes sense to bury stock in the ground or hide it.

This is an implicit argument against those thinkers who suggested that hoarding stock may be a good way to encourage low domestic prices and therefore a mild stimulation of industry. For Smith, instead, unless there is violence, hoarding is "perfectly crazy".

A final consideration is spelled out in this chapter. Smith seems to be setting up his attack: the purpose of both fixed and circulating capital is to maintain and increase the stock for immediate consumption. This means that the goal of production is consumption. In fact, we judge wealth or poverty by the abundance or scarcity of stock available for immediate consumption. Labor is the only source of wealth and wealth is our ability to consume. Gold and silver? They have nothing to do with either.

BOOK II, CHAPTER II: OF MONEY CONSIDERED A PARTICULAR BRANCH OF THE GENERAL STOCK OF SOCIETY

With this second chapter Smith seems to continue his criticism of who does not seem to appreciate the advantages of money and banking, and his much-stronger criticism of those who believe, incorrectly, that gold and silver are wealth. Smith's argument is based on the idea that only one's ability to consume is wealth.

Here Smith starts by tiptoeing around aggregation fallacies. A private estate has a gross rent, which is the value of all the rent collected, and a neat rent, which is what is left after covering all the expenses, including the maintenance of fixed and circulating capital. The stock for immediate consumption comes from the neat rent. Similarly, a country as a whole has also a gross revenue and a neat revenue; and the stock for immediate consumption is what comes out of the neat revenue. How do we know a landlord's real wealth? We look at his neat rent. How do we know a country's real wealth? In the same way: we look at its neat revenue.

The costs of maintaining fixed capital cannot be part of the neat revenue of society, just like the costs of repair in a private estate are not part of its neat rent. They are, though, both necessary and beneficial.

The expenses needed to maintain circulating capital are more complicated. The circulating capital in the form of provisions, raw materials, and finished goods regularly become either fixed capital or stock for immediate consumption. The stock for immediate consumption is neat revenue, as we just saw. Here Smith realizes we need to differentiate between individual and society: the content of a merchant's shop is not for his immediate consumption, so it is not part of his neat revenue. But it is part of society's neat revenue because it is for society's consumption. So the maintenance of these three parts of the circulating capital in the form of immediate consumption will not decrease the neat revenue of society. When, however, circulating capital is transformed into fixed capital, it will.

Money, which is a part of circulating capital, is even more complicated. The maintenance of money may decrease neat revenue. Money, despite being part of the circulating capital, behaves as if it was fixed capital.

For Smith, money is like a machine. They are both expensive to make and to maintain. Some valuable materials (gold and silver in case of money) and labor have to be taken away from consumption to support this "great but expensive instrument of commerce". Now, machines, being fixed capital, are *not* part of the gross or neat *revenue*. Similarly, money is not part of any revenue, neither neat nor gross. Money just circulates revenue. It is not by chance that Smith claims that money is "the great wheel of circulation [which] is altogether different from the goods which are circulated by means of it". Goods are the revenue of society; wheels are not revenue.

Smith believes that a possible reason why we may get confused about this is an ambiguity in the language. If a person has a pension of a guinea (a coin originally containing a quarter of an ounce of gold) per week and spends it all each week, his weekly revenue is not equal to both the one guinea and what he bought with it. His weekly revenue is a guinea's worth of stuff, not the guinea. Similarly, the metal pieces in society are not the revenue of the members of society. Don't believe it? Then think: most metal pieces pay several people, so there are fewer metal pieces around than the value of the whole money pensions annually paid through them. In today's language: the value of all dollar bills in circulation is less than the value of all the things that those dollar bills buy, because the same bill changes hands multiple times, buying more than one thing.

Smith thus concludes that the revenue of society is the purchasing power it has, not the number of metal pieces used as money. Again, Smith tells us money is just a great wheel of circulation, a great instrument of commerce, a part of capital, but not a part of the revenue. The people who think that money is wealth are mistaking the wheel for the produce it carries.

The final reason Smith offers to explain why money is like fixed capital, like a machine, is that the less one spends to maintain it, the more neat revenue one gets. The capital saved can be used in productive ways. Substituting paper money for gold and silver money is like replacing a very expensive high-maintenance machine with a cheaper but equally convenient one. Paper money is a wheel of commerce too, and a cheaper one.

To better understand the rest of Smith's argument, we need to consider that the monetary system he lived with is different from ours. The first big difference is that today we have a fiat system, while Smith did not. Fiat money is a form of paper money. It is not convertible into precious metals. The paper is declared money by government decree, by fiat. And it is usually monopolistically produced by a central bank. This form of money did not exist in Smith's time. When Smith talks about money, he usually talks about commodity money: a commodity, like gold and silver, which emerged as a commonly accepted medium of exchange. Paper money, in his day, was not fiat money, but a sort of certificate that could be converted into gold and silver more or less upon demand. The other difference is that rather than a monopolistic production, the issuing of paper money was competitive. Anybody could, in theory, issue paper money. Smith indeed describes a monetary system in which there are several banks of issue. The final main difference to keep in mind is that the kinds of banks Smith talks about are not like our commercial banks. They did not generally accept deposits. They lent money on credit, or better, rather than actual gold and silver, they lent a piece of paper that was redeemable for gold and silver upon request. While there were no legal restrictions for who may become banker, there were some practical ones. A banker needed to be wealthy enough to guarantee that all the paper he issued could be converted into gold and silver. Unlimited liability was typical of the time: the entire personal assets of a banker were on the line and could be used to fulfill his obligations. The other fundamental characteristic that a banker needed to have was trustworthiness. A banker needed to be renowned, not just as having a large fortune, but also as being prudent and honest. After all, one businessman accepts a piece of paper as payment for his goods or services because he trusts that that piece of paper will be accepted by others and that it will be convertible into gold and silver upon demand. This is why paper money is also called fiduciary money, because it is a form of money based on trust.

Now, Smith tells us that the most common form of paper money is circulating notes of banks. If there is confidence in the fortune, probity, and prudence of a banker, and that he will pay his promissory notes on demand, those notes will be as good as gold and silver. When a banker lends by issuing his own promissory notes, he gains interest on them as if he was lending gold or silver. And because not all notes come back for payment at the same time, he can keep only about 20 percent of the value of the notes in circulation in gold and silver to answer occasional demands. This means that 20,000 pounds of silver can perform the same operations of 100,000 pounds, which means we can save 80,000 pounds of silver. This precious metal is now freed from having to circulate as money. Ergo, paper money is cheaper than and just as effective as a wheel of circulation.

How is that possible? Smith works with an implicit assumption: the demand for money is constant, at least in the sense that it depends on the level of economic growth. If so, he can say that money circulates in fixed "channels". When these channels are full, their content "overflows". So if paper is introduced, it will substitute for gold and silver. Gold and silver will go abroad to seek profitable employment. Paper money, however, cannot go abroad because it is difficult for people to accept it, as they do not know or trust the issuers. Gold and silver do not go abroad as gifts, though. They go to buy foreign goods to bring either to other countries, through the so-called carrying trade, or to the domestic market; or they go as foreign investment.

So, Smith continues, while banking cannot directly increase the annual produce of a country, it can free gold and silver from being used as currency at home, so that they can be used to promote industry instead. But careful: it is the extra material to work with, the extra tools, the extra wages that put industry into motion, not money. Here, again, Smith differs from some of his contemporaries who would say that the introduction of paper money would increase domestic prices and discourage domestic industry, the high prices making it less competitive internationally and encouraging consumption of foreign goods. For Smith, banking does not affect prices. Smith agrees that gold and silver will go abroad, but for Smith they will not encourage idleness, instead they will bring back more industry.

For Smith, the banks in Scotland did just that. Almost all business in Scotland was now done with paper. Silver and gold were rarely seen. Yet, trade and industry increased significantly. At the time of the Union of Parliaments between Scotland and England (1707), there was in Scotland about one million worth of gold and silver. At the time when Smith was writing, there was only half that amount. But real riches had increased significantly. And that is what matters.

So let's go back to the circulating notes of banks. What exactly are they? A bank discounts bills of exchange, which are promises that a specific amount will be paid on a specific date, with interest. Discounting bills of exchange means advancing the money of the bill before the bill is due, but deducting from the advance the legal interest. When the payment of the bill is due, it replaces the advance, and the interest remains as a clear profit for the bank.

Smith does not give us an example, but it may help. I buy flour from you to make bread for my bakery. I pay you with a note that promises to pay you $x + %$ interest in one year. You go to a bank, give them my note in exchange for $x in cash. A year from now, the bank comes to me, with my note. I pay them $x + %$ interest. The bank gave $x to you earlier, so the $x I gave them covers that. But I also gave them % interest, which is the clear profit for the bank.

Let's continue with Smith. Usually, rather than advancing actual commodity money, the bank would issue its own promissory notes. In this way, the bank could discount more bills.

Now, for Smith, the greatest innovation in paper money and banking comes from the so-called cash accounts. A cash account is a way for a bank to give credit to people who can provide two guarantors. The advance should be paid on demand and with interest. But the innovation with the cash account is that the advance can be paid back a little at a time and there will be no interest charged on the portion that is repaid. The bank advances the money with its own promissory notes; the merchant uses the notes to pay the manufacturer; the manufacturer uses them to pay the farmer; the farmer uses the notes to pay the landlord; the landlord uses them to pay the merchant; and the merchant returns them to the bank to balance his cash account. Without cash accounts, merchants need to keep money unemployed to answer demands for payments, which means that they have less money with which to do business. With a cash account, when bills come in, they can pay with the cash account, which they can then pay back when they sell their goods.

You may ask, as many did in Smith's time, wouldn't having many independent banks of issue create inflation or instability? The answer Smith gives is no. Smith already took care of the problem of inflation, and he will return to it again later in the chapter: banking does not create inflation because the demand for money is fixed. When too much is poured into a canal, it overflows. Gold and silver will go abroad in search of productive and profitable activity. Banking will also not create instability, for the same reason. Here is why.

The total amount of paper money cannot exceed the value of gold and silver it replaces. If there is more paper than needed, today we would say if the quantity supplied of money is larger than the quantity demanded (remember that for Smith the demand and the quantity demanded of money are not affected by the quantity of money in circulation, but by the level of development), the excess paper money would return to the bank. Paper money cannot go abroad. If it is not needed for domestic circulation, it returns to the bank to be exchanged for gold and silver, which can go abroad, and are indeed sent abroad. If the bank is not ready to pay, it may very well start a bank run. A bank run takes place when many customers run to the bank to make sure they get their gold and silver, before the bank runs out of them through excess demand. If the bank runs out of money, it is a problem. The problem can be so severe that it can cause bankruptcy. It is, therefore, in the interest of the bank not to overissue paper.

Here is a more detailed explanation of what came to be known as the law of reflux. A bank faces two kinds of expenses: the expense of keeping the money in coffers to answer occasional demand, and the expense of refilling the coffers as they are emptied. If a bank overissues, it needs to increase the quantity of gold and silver it has for its payments, and it needs to do it in a proportion larger than the amount overissued because the notes come back for conversion at a much-faster rate than in normal circumstance. Remember that people pay interest on the notes they hold. This is why they will hold only what they need. Now, the additional coins received as payment for the unwanted paper will go abroad as investment, which makes it even more difficult, and thus more expensive, for the bank to find gold and silver to replenish its coffers.

The Bank of England, which has to supply coins to support the English and Scottish overissuing, due to the high price of bullion, is forced to coin gold and silver at a 2.5 percent to 3 percent loss.

Many Scottish banks keep an agent in London to get the gold and silver needed. Add shipping and insurance cost, Smith tells us, and the replenishing of metals in their coffers becomes quite expensive. Sometimes, if they cannot find enough gold and silver, they have to use bills of exchange with other banks, and the interest they have to pay on those bills is another significant expense. At 8 percent cost and 6 percent interest received, overissuing is a receipt for bankruptcy.

But if overissuing increases both kinds of expenses of a bank and can lead to bank failure, why do banks overissue, as some have done? Banking is still something relatively new, Smith claims. Overissuing is something that banks have not always understood. And some "bold projectors" want to overtrade. Note here who gets the blame: bankers are ignorant; they make mistakes because they do not know any better. Projectors know the consequences of their actions, but they do it anyway because it is in their short-term (deluded?) interest.

So what is it that banks have not always understood for Smith? First, if banks advance only real bills from real creditors to real debtors, if debtors really repay the bills, and if the advances are really only for that part of ready money needed for occasional demand, then the coffers of a bank are like a pond: what goes out will come back in. The pond will stay at the same level at little cost. No problems here.

In addition, it is difficult for a bank to evaluate the prudence of all its debtors, if it has 500 of them. What today we call asymmetry of information would be overwhelming. But a solution may be possible, even if not always well understood. If, like Scottish banks do, banks require frequent and regular payments, so that a merchant can pay back his advance within few months, the bank will experience few problems. It will be in a better position to judge whether its debtors are doing well. If a merchant does pay regularly and repays within few months, this merchant is a good customer. He is a keeper. If, by contrast, he does not, it is not safe to deal with him anymore. Solution for asymmetry of information problem? Check.

Finally, the successful bank is a bank that does not lend circulating capital. Long-term loans are not good for a bank: the repayment time is too distant in the future. Lending to finance fixed capital? Even worse. The returns on fixed capital are even further out in the future, often several years in the future. They are too slow to come in. If someone wants to borrow to finance his fixed capital, he should borrow from private people upon bond or mortgage, not from a bank. There are enough people who want to live on interest without taking the trouble to employ their capital themselves. Debtors would prefer borrowing from a bank because there is less paperwork and expense than issuing a mortgage, but these debtors are "the most inconvenient" for a bank.

There is more to understand. "Bold projectors" overtrade, thus creating losses for a bank. Traders want more and more credit. Banks, if they understand the risk associated with it, will not extend credit. But these bold traders will start using a trick: a "shift of drawing and redrawing", a technique usually used as an act of desperation before bankruptcy. It consists in paying a loan with another loan, which makes it very expensive because of the commission and the interest. Profits barely make it to 6 percent, and drawing and redrawing costs no less than 8 percent: an "enormous expense". This practice is also called raising money by circulation. With this technique, all bills are paid, but with another bill of a larger amount. So, even if bills are paid, they are not paid: they are fictitiously paid. This kind of overtrading is often done without the banks' knowledge, or consent, or even suspicion. If one draws and redraws from the same bank, the banker will know and will prevent it. But if this is done with different banks, it is difficult to know where the money comes from. By the time the banker eventually discovers it, it will generally be too late. Refusing to discount further has the very concrete risk of making all parties involved bankrupt. So the vicious circle will continue until something breaks.

Without ever naming it, Smith tells us that a "new bank" is created to relieve the distress of some of the Scottish banks. Unfortunately, its execution was "imprudent". "This bank" discounts all bills indiscriminately, real and fictitious ones: a problem. Of course, it overissues, and its bills return immediately to be redeemed for gold and silver. But the coffers are not well filled: another problem. The proprietors of the bank open their own cash accounts, which the directors think they cannot refuse: yet another problem. They lend to improve land, which means that the returns are too slow for the bank to be profitable. "This bank" loses 3 percent on more than three-quarters of its dealing: a big problem. So big that the bank does not last two years. It lasts so long because of its unlimited liability: the immense estates of the proprietors of the bank are the pledge used to continue doing business. But, for Smith, rather than solving the problem, it made it worse because it extended the activities for an additional two years. Smith brings back the pond metaphor: water goes out but not in. The attempt to keep the level constant is to get water from a distant well by carrying it in buckets. What Smith does not tell us is that the failure of "this bank" is the most catastrophic one in Scottish history. And yet, all the creditors will be paid with the sale of the estates of the bank's backers: the largest land redistribution in Scotland. This nameless bank does have a name: it is the so-called Ayr Bank. One of the proprietors is the Duke of Buccleuch, the pupil for whom Smith quits his job at Glasgow to become his private tutor and eventually lifetime friend, who pays Smith a hefty pension for the rest of his life.

Smith describes two additional kinds of bank: a land bank and the Bank of England.

A country can issue paper in proportion to the value of the land, creating a so-called land bank. A Scot, of all people, came up with this idea. His name was John Law. Scotland did not consider his model. So Law went to France, which adopted the idea. The result was the Mississippi Scheme: "the most extravagant project ... the world ever saw" and also the biggest financial bubble at the time. For Smith, a bank that lends to "chimerical projectors" and "extravagant undertakings" cannot benefit a country. It will transfer capital from prudent and profitable to imprudent and unprofitable activities. Something to keep in mind when Smith talks about usury laws.

The Bank of England was incorporated in 1694 to lend to the government, which at the time must not have had good credit given that it was borrowing at a higher rate than usual, Smith claims. The capital stock of the Bank was less than its loan until it bought the South Sea Company, a trading company that was the cause of another big financial bubble. Now, for Smith, the stability of the Bank of England is basically the same as the stability of the British government. The Bank is not an ordinary bank but acts as an engine of the state: it pays annuities to the public, circulates exchequers bills, and advances land and malt taxes to the government. And, of course, it overissues.

So there are risks and costs associated with banking, mostly associated with ignorance, which can be overcome. There are benefits too. If banking learns to be judicious, which Smith believes it does, benefits are significantly larger than expected costs. The judicious operations of banking increase the industry of a country. Banking, if judicious, does not increase the capital of a country though. It renders a greater part of it active, which otherwise wouldn't be. It converts dead stock into an active and productive stock.

Smith exemplifies money as a highway: the land used as highway is used to bring produce to market but does not produce anything. Paper money is like a "wagon-way in the air", a suspended highway: it lets us convert old highways into pastures. But like Daedalus who flies in the sky with his wings, but ends up dead by flying too close to the sun, the "Daedalian wings of paper money" are never as safe as the solid ground of gold and silver. Indeed, if there is an unsuccessful war, if the enemy gets the treasury or the capital that supports banking and paper money, there is much more confusion than otherwise. But what are the chances that a capital, say London, is conquered by a foreign army, one may ask.

According to Smith the judicious operation of banking alone may not be enough to assure security. He proposes two banking regulations – a ban on small denomination notes and the abolition of the optional clause – to ensure safety and justice.

In Smith's account, the circulation of paper money takes place between dealers and dealers, and between dealers and consumers. A dealer-to-dealer exchange usually implies exchanges of large sums, which require large denomination bills. A dealer to consumer exchange usually implies exchanges of small sums, requiring small denomination notes. If issuing of small notes is allowed, there will be many bankers of dubious stability because small change is easily accepted without checking it. But this implies that bankruptcy among these bankers will be frequent. This can be a calamity for the poor who received these notes as payment. It is therefore better not to have notes under five pounds.

An added benefit of restricting notes only between dealers is that there will be more silver in circulation, like in London, as opposed to very little silver in circulation if there are notes also between dealers and consumers, like in Scotland or in the North American colonies.

The ban on small denomination notes can be seen as a "manifest violation of natural liberty". It is, Smith admits. But if the liberty of a few endangers the whole society, it makes sense to violate that liberty. Party walls, after all, are built to prevent fire to spread from house to house in cities, and can be similarly considered violation of natural liberty. Yet they are accepted because of the greater good they produce. The same is true with small denomination notes: innocent poor may face catastrophic consequences. If this can be avoided, then it should be. It is too bad that Smith does not consider that the prohibition of small denomination note issuing may cause de facto a reduction in competition, raising barriers to entry in banking. The small notes are promissory notes used by suppliers and employers. They fill a vacuum in the market. Their elimination not only creates a shortage of means of payment but also, and most importantly, imposes in practice higher capital requirements for banks. This means that only fewer and larger banks could now enter the market. And, in combination with the abolition of the option clause, the other banking regulation Smith favors as we will see in a moment, it increases what today we call balance-sheet risk and therefore the likelihood of bank failure.

The second regulation Smith favors is the ban on the optional or option clause. His logic is as follows. Paper money does not increase prices, as long as it is fully convertible on demand. When David Hume published his *Discourses*, in 1751–1752, prices of provisions were high because of bad weather, not because of an increase in paper money. Hume was fooled and mistaken. Smith's criticism of Hume's understanding of money and banking is explicit, as he calls him out by name. Back to the option clause. For Smith, if paper is not immediately convertible, the value of paper money would fall below the price of gold and silver because of the uncertainty of its conversion. The optional clause, the option to convert paper into metal at a later time, and paying interest for the time in which it is not converted, as opposed to pay on demand, should therefore not be allowed.

Recent studies indicate that Smith here again may not note the unintended consequences of this policy. The optional clause, which allows banks to temporarily suspend convertibility of their notes, is in practice not used, but it does serve as a deterrent against raids by rival banks. Domestically, it functions as a deterrence against overissuing, as opposed as a means to overissue. It is instead used, very selectively, as a private form of capital control. In addition, without the option clause, solvent but illiquid banks are now forced to temporarily close their doors when faced with overwhelming demand for specie. But closing their doors implies indiscriminate suspension of all payments and uncertainty regarding their reopening. The increased uncertainty prevents notes from being acceptable as payment and increases redemption demands, encouraging bank runs and instability. The opposite of what Smith hopes to see.

The final form of paper money Smith considers is the paper currency of North America, which is government paper and not bank notes. It is something to avoid. It is made legal tender and it carries no interest. So a 15-year note at zero interest when the interest is at 6 percent forces a creditor to accept only 40 pounds of ready money for a debt of 100 pounds. This is a "violent injustice" "never attempted by governments of any other country which pretend to be free". It is a fraudulent scheme for debtors to cheat their creditors.

The chapter ends with the juice of its content. If small denomination notes are banned, and if there is immediate and unconditional payment of the notes, if there is genuine competition, that is, then the multiplication of banking will increase security rather than decrease it. Competition will force banks not to overissue to avoid bank runs. And by dividing circulation in greater number of parts, by having several banks of issue, the failure of one will have only local consequences not global ones. As for any branch of trade, the freer and more general the competition, the more benefits for the public. Competition remains the answer.

BOOK II, CHAPTER III: OF THE ACCUMULATION OF CAPITAL OR OF PRODUCTIVE AND UNPRODUCTIVE LABOR

As we saw, "stock" is fixed capital, circulating capital, or stock for immediate consumption. Capital is the productive part of it. How do we increase it so we can be more productive? Smith's answer is as easy as it is alien to a modern reader: put capital in productive hands rather than unproductive hands. This turns out to be an odd distinction and it makes this chapter one of the most problematic of the *Wealth of Nations*. Smith uses a distinction made by the French economists, the physiocrats, (and he was unjustly accused of some form of plagiarism for it), but he changed the meaning of "productive" and "unproductive" so that he could *criticize* the French physiocrats. Some earlier editors of the *Wealth of Nations*, such as William Playfair, editor of the 1805 edition, saw this, but many other commentators took this an endorsement of the physiocrats and fueled confusion.

Yet again, Smith starts from labor. Here he claims that all labor is valuable and needs compensation. But some labor produces something that adds value, something that stores up labor for future use: that is, some labor produces something that reproduces itself. Some labor, instead, despite being valuable, does not increase value, it does not reproduce itself. It produces something that perishes the moment it comes into existence. Smith calls the labor that reproduces itself "productive labor", and the one that perishes the moment of performance "unproductive labor". One grows rich by hiring productive labor; one grows poor hiring unproductive labor.

We need to be careful in understanding Smith's words. He does not use "unproductive" as a derogatory term; it is not a moral description of something useless or wasteful. Unproductive here simply means that it does not reproduce its own value.

Unproductive labor can thus be honorable, necessary, as well as frivolous. But it is always valuable. The sovereign, the officers of justice and of war, churchmen, lawyers, physicians, men of letters, buffoons, musicians, opera singers, and dancers are all unproductive laborers. They are servants of the public; they are maintained by the industry of other people. The product of their labor this year will not give more product next year.

Smith may have borrowed the terminology from the French economist Quesnay, whom he met in France during the grand tour of Europe Smith did with the Duke of Buccleuch. But while Quesnay claims that only agriculture is productive and manufacture is unproductive, Smith twists the roles and shows that manufacture is not only productive, but even more productive than agriculture because of the different behaviors of landlords and manufacturers. Here is how.

The produce of the land supports all labor. That produce is not infinite, thus the more unproductive labor there is, the less productive labor we can maintain. And if we maintain less productive labor, produce will have to decrease. The proportion of productive and unproductive hands depends on how much the produce of land and productive labor is destined to replace capital, and that proportion varies from rich to poor countries, as Smith told us in his own introduction to his work.

Now, the produce of land creates enough revenue to replace used capital and also to create profits of stock or rent of land. The great landlord spends his profits and rent to feed more unproductive than productive hands. Also the produce of the great manufacturers replaces the used capital and creates a profit, which is the revenue of the owner of capital. The part of it that replaces capital goes to maintain productive hands, while the part of it that goes into profits or rent can maintain either productive or unproductive hands. If that stock is used on productive labor, it is considered capital. If it is used on unproductive labor is considered stock for immediate consumption. Also rich merchants maintain both productive and unproductive hands with their activities and their expenses. Finally, even common workers maintain unproductive hands. They may go to a puppet show and surely pay taxes. Not just landlords, but all landlords, manufacturers, merchants, and workers are productive and support unproductive labor.

Today, Smith tells us, a large part of revenue goes to replace capital. In the past, that part was small because the amount of capital then was small. You can also think of it in these terms: rent increased in absolute terms, but it decreased as a share of the produce of the land. In rich countries, there is great capital in trade and manufacturing, while in ancient times, there was little trade, so there was little capital and thus large profits. How do we know? We can look at the interest rates.

In the past the interest rate was more than 10 percent while today it is less than 6 percent, closer to 4 percent. As we saw in Book I, the interest rate is a good indicator of profit rates because one needs to generate enough profits to pay interest. This also means that the part of the revenue derived from profits is always larger in rich than poor countries. Why? Think of a cake. A large slice of a small cake may be smaller than a small slice of a large cake. Here it is the same. The stock is larger, even if in proportion to the stock, profits are smaller. So, the part of the annual produce coming from the ground and from productive labor destined to replace capital is larger in rich countries and it is a larger proportion to profits and rent, just like the fund for the maintenance of productive labor is not just greater, but it has a greater proportion to that used to maintain unproductive labor.

An implication of this larger pie? We are more industrious than in the past, because the funds for industry are proportionally more today than in the past. Our ancestors were idle not because they were lazy, but because they had too little capital to work with: "it is better play for nothing than work for nothing", Smith cites the proverb. We can see this also in Smith's time if we compare manufacturing towns with court cities. People in manufacturing towns are more industrious, sober, and thriving. In court cities, people are more idle, dissolute, and poor. The only exceptions, according to Smith, may be London, Lisbon, and Copenhagen, but that maybe because they are both trading and court cities. Edinburgh was idler before the union than now, even if it is still less industrious than Glasgow because it still has the court of justice of Scotland and the boards of customs and excise (where Smith eventually would work). Thus, the proportion between capital and revenue regulates the proportion between industry and idleness. The more capital, the more industry. The more revenue, the more idleness.

So, how does capital increase?

Smith answers categorically: capital increases thanks to parsimony and it decreases because of prodigality and misconduct. When someone saves, he can use the capital himself or lend it at interest letting someone else use it. It is, therefore, parsimony, and not industry, that increases capital. Industry gives us something to save. But we can have industry and no parsimony, and therefore no capital accumulation. Note, again, that saving and investment are for Smith equivalent.

For Smith it is also true that saving and consumption are quite similar, in the sense that they are both spending, even if on different things. What is consumed is spent on idle guests or menial servants and once it is spent, it is gone. What is saved is employed as capital and is spent on laborers and manufacturers who reproduce with a profit the value of their consumption.

Now, are prodigals public enemies and frugal men public benefactors? The frugal man's saving maintains additional productive men. We do not need laws to guarantee this productive use of resources, Smith claims: it is in the interest of their owner to invest his savings productively. However, the prodigal encroaches upon his capital. He is like someone who uses the revenue of a pious foundation to profane purposes, an example that Smith will use again to describe how the "High Church" (the Roman Catholic Church) loses power. The frugal needs to, and usually does, compensate for the prodigals, or the country will get poorer. Smith's choice of words is careful. The prodigal "appears" to be a public enemy. Is he? Maybe. But we are not sure.

For Smith, for sure we know that the people who think that as long as the prodigal spends on domestic goods, gold and silver will remain in the country, and so all will be fine, are wrong. Money cannot stay at home when the value of the annual produce decreases, which will decrease because of the decrease in productive labor. If there are fewer ways to use money at home, money will go abroad. So the exportation of silver is the effect, not the cause, of the decrease in industry. Similarly, the quantity of money increases as the value of the annual produce increases, as it requires more money to circulate. So part of the increased produce goes to get gold and silver, which are needed to circulate the rest. Again, the increased quantity of money is the effect not the cause of public prosperity. Here again, Smith seems very cautious of the problem understanding what we see: reverse causation is more common than not.

Smith explains that also misconduct, like prodigality, diminishes the funds for the maintenance of productive labor, even if the project was undertaken by productive hands. This is because the project, in failing, cannot reproduce its value. This will become even more relevant in the next chapter, when Smith talks about usury laws. As for now, Smith is not too worried. The frugality of many generally compensates for the imprudence of few, he claims.

The explanation is grounded in a psychological description of human behavior that Smith seems to take (implicitly) from his *Theory of Moral Sentiments*. Profusion is a passion of present enjoyment, but it is a short-lived passion. By contrast, saving comes from our desire to better our condition, which is, yes, a calm desire, but a desire that is always with us. We always want to better our condition, and the means to do it is to increase our fortune, which is most likely done with saving. Frugality dominates, on average at least.

Similarly, successful undertakings are usually more frequent than unsuccessful ones. And the threat of bankruptcy, for Smith the greatest and most humiliating calamity an innocent man can experience is a strong deterrence. True, though, deterrence does not work for everybody: some do get bankrupted, just like some get to the gallows.

Let's go back to the prodigal. The prodigal may only appear to be a public enemy because, in reality, private prodigality never impoverishes a nation. But sometimes public prodigality does. The majority of public revenue is used to support unproductive hands. Worse, great courts can multiply the unproductive hands they support to an unnecessary number. Even wars cannot compensate for the expense of the military, which, remember, is unproductive just like the king, the courts of justice, and the buffoons. Courts can consume so much that productive labor decreases and frugality cannot compensate for all caused "by this violent and forced encroachment".

And yet, most of the time, individual frugality can compensate both individual and public prodigality. The desire to better our conditions is such a powerful force that it can maintain the natural progress toward improvement "in spite both of the extravagances of governments and of the greatest errors of administrations", just like we are able to restore the health "in spite not only of the disease, but of the absurd prescriptions of the doctor".

Not all prodigals are the same, though. There are two different kinds of prodigality. One is the expenditure on immediate consumption, such as banquets; the other is the expenditure on durables, such as clothes, ornaments, or furniture. The magnificence of who spends on durables increases over time because all add up and it becomes a stock of goods with value. The one of who spends on immediate consumption, such as banquets, disappears and leaves no trace of it in the future.

Another advantage of consumption on durable, Smith continues, is that the durable goods can be resold. When a rich man stops using his house, his furniture, and his clothes, people from inferior ranks will buy them and use them. In addition, consumption on durables is somehow favorable to frugality. If one needs or wants to cut down expenses, nobody will notice. But if one spends on nondurables, such as on servants and banquets, one cannot cut his expenses without it being noticed, and it is more likely that he will go bankrupt trying to keep up appearances. Durable goods maintain more people and are more productive in this sense. Hospitality, the pinnacle of nondurable consumption, generates much waste with its banquets, and is in this sense more unproductive. Hospitality, however, is an expenditure on other people, while durable consumption is an expenditure directly to the self, which unleashes our "selfish disposition". Yet, the consumption of durables is more favorable to growth and public opulence. Here Smith is setting up Book III, where the transition from consumption on hospitality to consumption on durable goods is at the base of the transition from an agricultural society to a commercial society.

Now let's go back to capital accumulation. Smith tells us that the annual produce increases only with the increase in the number of productive hands or with an increase in the productive power of labor. The increase in productive labor increases with an increase in capital; the increase in the productive power of labor increases with better machines or better division of labor. In either case, more capital is needed. That is to say, if the annual produce has increased, it must be that capital had increased.

And in most nations, despite imprudent governments, we do see that improvement, especially if we look over a long span of time. Smith realizes that there are always people complaining that wealth decreases over time. That may be true in times of expensive and unnecessary wars, where there is much waste and destruction. But when there is no war and destruction, the annual produce does increase. The profusions of governments may retard it, but cannot stop it. Capital does increase over time, gradually and silently, because of individual's frugality and our universal and uninterrupted efforts to better our conditions, especially if those efforts are protected by laws and allowed by liberty. For the third time in eight paragraphs, Smith tells us that our universal and constant desire to better our condition is the driving engine of prosperity, despite wars, fires, plagues, and prodigality.

Governments can protect our efforts to better our condition by law, but can at the same time be prodigal, impertinent, and presumptuous enough to want to restrain the expense of private people with sumptuary laws or with limits on the importation of luxury goods. For Smith, this is hypocritical. For Smith, governments are always, and without exception, the greatest spendthrifts in society. If their extravagance does not ruin the state, that of their subjects never will. Prodigal individuals seem, but after all are not, public enemies. Governments may be.

BOOK II, CHAPTER IV: OF STOCK LENT AT INTEREST

So we accumulated some stock. What if I do not want to use it myself? I can let someone else use it, by lending it at interest. For the lender, the stock lent at interest is therefore always capital. For the borrower, it can be either capital if it is used to reproduce its value, or stock for immediate consumption if it cannot restore itself or pay back the interest, Smith explains.

If one borrows to spend, he will soon be ruined. Lenders will soon regret their decision. Borrowing to spend is contrary to both parties' interest. It does not happen frequently. It is, therefore, more common to lend for productive uses than for immediate consumption. Only the country gentleman borrows without expectation of repayment, but his situation is different because he borrows upon mortgage, meaning he borrows using his asset as collateral: he will be forced to sell it, should he not be able to pay. He bought so much on credit already that needs to borrow to repay. In a sense he is not borrowing to spend on immediate consumption, but to replace capital already spent.

Smith continues explaining that because capital is lent out and paid back in money, lenders are called monied interest. Monied interest is different from landed interest and trading interest because these use their own capital. The lender instead gives their capital to others to use, giving others power to purchase.

But this does not imply that lending is a monetary phenomenon for Smith. What is borrowed and lent is capital. Indeed, the same money can be lent several times. This implies that the stock lent is the value of all the goods that can be bought with it, which is more than the money used to buy it.

Furthermore, Smith claims, we can see that even if loans are always made in money, be it paper or metal, the stock lent at interest is not regulated by money, but by the value of capital, through the interest rate. A borrower does not want money per se, but the money's worth. And the amount of capital demanded and available will depend on how much extra capital there is after replacing the existing one and how much extra capital the owner of it does not want to employ himself. The more capital, the more stock will be lent at interest. And as the quantity of stock lent increases, the interest decreases, that is, the price to use that stock decreases. Interest rate decreases also because as capital increases, profits decrease because it is more difficult to find profitable ways to use capital.

In this, Smith is closer to Hume than Locke and Montesquieu. For Smith, interest rates decrease not because of an increase of gold and silver, as Locke and Montesquieu believe. Hume got this right: the increase in gold and silver increase, not the real value but the nominal value only.

Two more things about interest rates:

First, for Smith, interest rates regulate the market price of land. If you have extra capital, you can either buy land or lend at interest. Land is safer, so you would prefer land to lending at interest. But if rent is much less than interest, land will attract few buyers and the price of land will decrease. And, vice versa, if rent is significantly more than interest rate, then there are incentives to buy land and its price will increase.

Second, and quite controversially, in some countries interest is prohibited by law. But this does not prevent usury, which is the charging of high interest. It makes it worse. For Smith, the debtor will pay for the use of money and for the risk that the creditor incurs: he will now have to pay also for the insurance against penalties the creditor may face.

For Smith, there should be usury laws, laws dictating the maximum rate one can change, but they should fix the interest rate a bit above the safest interest rate. If the law fixed the interest rate lower than the safest one, it is as if it was fixed at zero or close to it. If it is fixed much above it, prodigals and projectors will end up being the only ones willing to pay such high interest rates, as sober people would not borrow. In either case, capital would flee from those who could use it productively toward those who would waste it. If, by contrast, the interest is fixed a bit above the minimum, the sober investors would get the capital, because a sober investor is more attractive than a prodigal projector: the lender would get the same back, but one is a safer bet. And lenders prefer safer bets, all else equal.

Smith's call for legal control of interest rate is a controversial aspect of his thought. From the beginning, he was harshly criticized for this proposal. Jeremy Bentham, with his "In Defense of Usury" is probably his most famous critic, suggesting that Smith would strangle entrepreneurs and innovators. New ideas are risky. They would not be able to be legally financed with a low legal interest rate.

BOOK 2, CHAPTER V: OF DIFFERENT EMPLOYMENT OF CAPITAL

Recall that in Book II, Chapter III, Smith distinguished between productive and unproductive labor, and that distinction was also used to differentiate between different types of stock. Capital is productive stock. Now Smith goes back to look at capital and its different productive uses. As he will more explicitly explain at the end of Book IV, agriculture is not the only productive sector of the economy. Contra the physiocrats, he will argue that trade and manufacturing are productive too. The use of capital in these activities is his evidence for this.

Here Smith tells us that capital can be used in four different ways: to support rude produce for consumption, which means for the cultivation of land; to support manufacturing; to support transport of rude produce or transport of manufactures, which means wholesale business; and to support dividing goods for occasional demand, which means retailing business.

Each of these uses of capital is necessary for the other uses. If there is no rude produce, there cannot be manufacture and trade. If there is no manufacture, there cannot be produce because there is no demand for produce, if there is no trade. If there is no transport, there cannot be production, and if there is no division, things will be too big to be bought.

Breaking and dividing goods, such as a butcher does, is therefore a valuable activity that benefits all, especially the poor. Restricting the number of retailers hurts the public; increasing it benefits the public because it increases competition and thus lowers prices. And the more retailers, the lower is the chance they can collude successfully. Occasionally, a consumer may be deceived into buying something he does not need (allegedly a reason to want fewer retailers), but that is not going to go away with the decrease in number of retailers, just like the number of ale houses is not what causes drunkenness, but it is drunkenness that causes the presence of ale houses. The prejudices against shopkeepers and tradesmen are therefore without foundation.

Retailers have little capital. Wholesalers have more. Manufacturers even more. Farmers have the most, claims Smith.

The farmer's capital is the one that puts in motion the largest quantity of productive labor. In agriculture, in fact, man and nature work together. The rent charged by the landlord can be seen as the landlord lending nature's work to the farmers. Agriculture is the most advantageous use of capital in society, states Smith.

What is interesting about the capital used in agriculture and in retail trade is that it is linked to a country and does not move from it. The capital of wholesale merchants, instead, does not have a fixed residence. It goes where it can buy cheap and sell high. The capital of manufacturers is rooted to where the manufacture is, but where that is may be far from home.

Smith goes on, setting up parts of Book IV. When domestic capital is not sufficient to support agriculture, manufacture, transport, and retail trade, it means that a society is not wealthy enough to support all these activities, and trying to do all of them prematurely will lead to failure. One should concentrate first on agriculture, then on manufacturing, and finally on trade. But historically it is difficult to find examples in which a country did agriculture, manufacturing, and trade all with its own capital. America sees fast growth because all its capital is in agriculture, it has no manufactures, and exports are done with British capital. If they try to do manufactures or exports with their own capital, their growth would be slower. China, Egypt, and Indostan were big in agriculture, but had no foreign trade, Smith continues. That was done by foreigners.

Wholesale trade is of three kinds: domestic, international, and carrying trade, where the domestic capital transports goods from a different country to yet another country: for example, the Dutch carry the corn of Poland to Portugal. Usually all these are done by exchanging goods for gold and silver. It is easier to buy imports with gold and silver than with exports because of the lower costs (transport and insurance) of gold and silver compared to goods of equal value that would be bulkier and more difficult to carry.

Now, when the produce at home is more than the domestic demand, the surplus will find its way abroad. Without exports, productive labor would decrease as well as the value of the produce. Only with exports does the surplus get enough value to be worth producing. When foreign goods at home are more than the demand for them, their surplus will also go abroad. The carrying trade is, therefore, the natural effect of the great wealth of a nation, not the cause of it. In addition, the returns of foreign trade come more slowly than home trade. The returns on carrying trade are even slower because they depend on two separate foreigner trades.

We should not, therefore, encourage one branch of trade over others, Smith suggests. It will inevitably happen on its own accord, without constrains or violence. The consideration of his own profits is the sole motive that the owner of capital has when he uses it in agriculture, manufacture, or trade. How much productive labor he puts in motion never enters his thoughts. This idea will come back with much more power later on in the volume, in Book IV's account of the invisible hand in particular. For now, we are just told that in the next book (Book III) there is an explanation for the circumstances that give trade in towns an advantage over the trade in the country.

FURTHER READINGS

Checkland, S. G. 1975. *Scottish Banking: A History 1695–1973*. Glasgow: Collins

Goodspeed, Tyler Beck. 2016. *Legislating Instability: Adam Smith, Free Banking, and the Financial Crises of 1772*. Cambridge, MA, and London: Harvard University Press.

Hollander, Samuel. 1999. "Jeremy Bentham and Adam Smith on the Usury Laws: A 'Smithian' Reply to Bentham and a New Problem". *The European Journal of the History of Economic Thought* 6.4: 523–551.

Paganelli, Maria Pia. 2016. "Adam Smith and the History of Economic Thought: The Case of Banking", in *Adam Smith: A Princeton Guide*, ed., Ryan Patrick Hanley. Princeton, NJ: Princeton University Press. 247–261.

Rockoff, Hugh. 2013. "Adam Smith on Money, Banking, and the Price Level", in *The Oxford Handbook of Adam Smith*, ed. Christopher Berry, Maria Pia Paganelli, Craig Smith. Oxford: Oxford University Press. 307–332.

Selgin, George and White, Lawrence. 1997. "The Option Clause in Scottish Banking". *Journal of Money, Credit, and Banking* 29.2: 270–273.

7

BOOK III

BOOK III, CHAPTER I: OF THE NATURAL PROGRESS OF OPULENCE

After the previous two books of what is often considered Smith's economic theory, this book is often considered an historical book: an account of how Europe developed. But it is also possible to read Book III as a continuation of the economic theories exposed before. We know that division of labor and capital accumulation are the foundation of prosperity. We know that it is our desire to better our condition that drives us to seek improvement, and that the desire to better our condition can take different forms, depending on our habits. Here more explicitly than previously, we may interpret Smith as telling us how economic growth and development depend on human passions, some of them rational, some of them not rational. However one wants to look at these passions that drive the economy, the process of development is not planned, it is not intentional, and it is not mechanical. Price signaling plays a smaller role than vanity in the efficient allocation of resources over time, and human institutions mediate our vanity and passions.

So, Smith asks, given that division of labor and capital accumulation bring about prosperity, why are some countries richer than others? Why do some countries grow faster than others? Two factors play a role: "the natural inclination of man" and "human institutions". The "natural inclination of man" generally leads development through some sort of more or less linear "order of things", but "human institutions" make things unpredictable and nonlinear. Economic growth is, therefore, an unpredictable mix of economic forces, human passions, and human institutions.

Smith explains that the basic process of economic growth is based on the growth of commerce between towns and country. The towns receive their wealth and subsistence from the country, and the country finds in the towns both a market for its products and a supplier for its manufactures. The larger the number of inhabitants in towns and the larger their revenue, the larger is the market. So the more division of labor is possible.

We need to have something to live on first, Smith reiterates. Then we look for conveniences and luxury, so the improvement of the country "must necessarily be prior" to the increase of the town. In this sense it is true that towns cannot survive without the country, but this does not make one better off and the other worse off, as some may wrongly think, Smith says. Both gain from trade because of the increased division of labor. In another sense, the inhabitants of the country and of a town are "*mutual* servants" to each other (my emphasis). The employment of the town depends on the country demand, and the country demand depends on the improvement in cultivation.

If towns are in geographical locations where transportation is easy and cheap, like next to water, trade thrives. Recall Book I, Chapter III, where Smith tells us that the division of labor is limited by the extent of the market? The towns that historically flourished the most are the ones that can take advantage of water carriage. Here Smith picks up that idea again. Towns do depend on the country for their subsistence. But that country does not have to be next door. If towns are easily reachable (by water), they can easily receive subsistence from the country far away rather than depend on geographical proximity.

What about the natural inclination of man? Given a choice, and given similar profits, people would prefer investing in land than in manufacture because they prefer to keep things under their "view and control". What we call monitoring costs today will affect the allocation of capital. Furthermore, people think the chance of misfortune is lower in agriculture than in manufacture or trade. A trader depends more on "winds and waves" and on "human folly and injustice" than a farmer. All else equal, what is our first choice for investing, given our natural inclination? Agriculture.

But here Smith kicks in his other, often more powerful explanation based on other natural inclinations, which are not necessarily economic inclinations: we are naturally attracted by the beauty of the countryside, by the pleasure and tranquility of country living, so we do prefer agriculture to manufacture also because we believe that cultivating the land "was the original destination of man". A reference to physiocracy? To stoicism? Sarcasm? Genuine love of nature and agriculture? It is up to our interpretation.

Look at the North American colonies, Smith says: all capital is used to improve uncultivated lands. They have no manufacture for distant sale. And the colonials cultivating their land very much enjoy the feeling of being "master, and independent of all the world"!

Then Smith resumes. It is only when there is no more uncultivated land that capital goes to manufacture. Indeed, given the choice of manufacture and foreign trade, all else equal, people prefer manufacture for the same reasons why, all else equal, people prefer agriculture to manufacture: in manufacture, capital is more under "the view and control" of its owner and it is more secure, than in foreign trade.

Foreign trade can be carried equally by foreign or domestic capital. It does not normally matter, unless there is not enough domestic capital. In that case, foreign capital would be better to carry trade. Indeed, in many places trade is carried by foreigners: China, Egypt, Indostan, and even the North American colonies.

So, Smith recaps, the natural course of things is that agriculture develops, then manufactures, and then international trade. This must happen in one form or another in all countries, if "human institutions [had] never disturbed the natural course of things". But human institutions do disturb the natural course of things. All the time. So much so that in Europe this natural course of things did not happen. In Europe the order is "entirely inverted", not a little bit inverted, but "entirely inverted". Europe developed foreign trade first, then manufactures, and then agriculture. The manners and customs that the nature of government introduced forced Europe into this "unnatural and retrograde order". So much for the natural order of things.

BOOK III, CHAPTER II: OF THE DISCOURAGEMENT OF AGRICULTURE IN THE ANCIENT STATES OF EUROPE AFTER THE FALL OF THE ROMAN EMPIRE

The order of development of Europe is so "inverted" that not only the order of development is backward but also agriculture rather than developed first, was first discouraged. How did it happen? By accident. The German and Scythians invaded the Roman Empire and the institutional setting changed.

The barbaric invasions caused the interruption of commerce between towns and country, Smith tells us. The towns became deserted and the country uncultivated. Poverty prevailed. The new leaders acquired all available land so that no piece of land remained without owner.

Primogeniture and entails prevent the division of landed estates. Primogeniture is the law that gives the entire estate to the eldest heir and nothing to the other members of the family. Entails is the law that prevents an estate from being divided as gifts or other means. Under the circumstances, it makes sense to put aside the natural law of succession, which is to divide an estate equally between all the children, given that land is the primary source of subsistence. Now land becomes a means of power and protection, given the continuous wars and the uncertainty. Tenants become subjects of landlords, and landlords become their judges, their legislators in peace, and their leaders in wars. It makes sense to keep the land undivided to better defend it and its inhabitants by preventing the weakening of power through its division.

But to whom should the land go? Merit is questionable and can start disagreement. Gender and age are less questionable. And so primogeniture is introduced. Smith tells us that, in his time, primogeniture persists even if all the land is perfectly secure and there is safety for all. This makes the law not just useless, but also unjust as it benefits one child at the expense of all others. Why is it still there? Not for economic reasons because it is now inefficient, but because it supports the pride of family distinctions. Similarly, we still have entails, which were meant to preserve a lineal succession to protect the security of thousands from the caprice of one man, even if today the law provides security. Today it is absurd to continue following the will of someone who died 500 years ago, especially because these regulations are based on the "absurd supposition" that "not all generations of men have a right to the earth". Yet, we still have it because it preserves exclusive privileges for the nobility – some military and civil honors require noble birth.

What makes primogeniture (and entails) inefficient in times of secure laws is that big proprietors are generally not great improvers. They are useful in times of disorder because they provide defense. As they provide defense, they do not have time to think about improvement. In times of order, they do have time, but they are unwilling and unable to do it. If they have some capital, they use it to buy more land, not to improve the existing one. An improvement that generates profits requires attention to small savings and to small gains. But someone born to great fortune can rarely do it. He cares more about his ornaments than his profits because ever since he was a child, he was taught to care for elegance more than anything else. To improve, for him, means to embellish, even if it comes at an expense ten times more than what it is worth. Evidence? Compare old big estates with small proprieties: you will immediately see how unfavorable to improvement large estates are, claims Smith.

Note that, despite the criticisms of the landlords, Smith maintains that there is no natural difference between landlords and nonlandlords. What makes a difference is just habit.

If we expect little improvement from landlords, we expect even less improvement from tenants, Smith continues. Tenants are basically slaves, according to Smith. They have no incentives to improve. Even if they belong to the land, not to the master, and can be sold with it, not separately from it, they cannot acquire property.

For Smith, slave labor is the most expensive kind of labor because, if you cannot acquire property, you will eat as much as you can and work as little as you can. If they work a bit more than mere subsistence it is because that labor is "squeezed out of him by violence only".

So why do we have slave labor if it is so expensive and ineffective? Smith believes it is because we "love to domineer": we think it is humiliating to have to persuade those whom we consider our inferiors. So, whenever the laws allow it, we prefer slave to free labor. The North American Quakers freed their slaves only because they were few and the cultivation of corn did not generate enough revenue to support that expense. Only sugar and tobacco can afford slaves because the profits are so high.

Again, note how Smith mixes economic incentives with human passions, not necessarily rational ones. Note also how the argument about slave labor in sugar and tobacco production is also normative: for Smith slavery is both wrong and inefficient. Having slaves (unjust) is possible only because the high profits allow that expense (inefficient), as opposed to having those high profits in sugar and tobacco because of slave labor and the zero expense on wage.

Smith suggests that the Church of Rome claims the merits of the abolition of this form of slavery, but in reality no one listened to it. The engine for abolition of slavery is the landlords and the king who are jealous of the great lords. Probably these freed slaves take the form of the metayers. Metayers can own property. Yet, they do not have any capital of their own, so they need to use that of their landlord. They then divide their produce between them and the landlord, keeping half of the crops (*medium* from which *meta* is derived means half in Latin). By being able to keep half of the produce they have incentive to produce more. But having to give half of the produce to the lord is a 50 percent tax, which gives farmers little incentive to use their own capital to improve.

Eventually, Smith continues, tenants start to pay rent, even if they still have to perform many services to the landlord and to the public. They need to provide for the king's troops, giving them horses, carriages, and provisions in case of wars.

Public taxes are also still oppressive and irregular. The *taille* is an example of this. It is a tax on the profit of the farmer, which gives the farmer incentive to lie and to appear to have as little as possible, discouraging improvement.

So now there are longer-term leases, but they are still too short for real improvement, according to Smith. Landlords offer these leases to protect tenants against heirs and purchasers, but these are meant to favor the landlords. The length of the lease is still not enough to incentivize improvement. Smith lapidary states: avarice and injustice are always shortsighted.

It is only when farmers pay rent to the landlord, and their leases are long-term leases, that they have incentive to use their own capital to cultivate the land and, thus, to improve it. Add the security of possession of the land that a change in law brings, so that the tenant is guaranteed possession. Add also that the leasee is able to own enough now to get to vote for a member of parliament, gaining the respect of the landlords. And now you have all the elements that allow England to grow to its grandeurs.

So, who are the best improvers? The farmers who improve the most are the owners of land. The tenant farmers will improve their land more slowly than the owner farmers because the tenant farmers need to pay rent. Part of the capital farming generated cannot be reinvested because it needs to go toward rent payment. Generally, all the great capital used in farming comes from farming, which, ironically, is the slowest way to accumulate capital. But that makes small owners the greatest improvers.

And why didn't ancient Europe grow much? For Smith, it is because the ancient policies of Europe were unfavorable to improvement: they prohibited the exportation of corn, restrained inland commerce, and gave privileges to fairs and markets.

Smith is telling the story of the order of events that brought wealth to Europe. The first step was agricultural decline. The second "retrograde" step is the rise of cities and towns.

BOOK III, CHAPTER III: OF THE RISE AND PROGRESS OF CITIES AND TOWNS AFTER THE FALL OF THE ROMAN EMPIRE

The barbaric invasions not only cause the country to become abandoned and its improvement to halt and be discouraged but it also causes changes in the nature of cities.

Before the fall of Rome, Smith tells us, landlords live in cities surrounded by walls for defense. With the fall of Rome, the land-lords move into fortified castles on their estates. The towns are left to merchants and artisans, who are in servile conditions and poor. They have to travel around from fair to fair with their goods to make a living. They have to pay taxes as they travel over bridges, roads, and to fairs.

But, sometimes, the king gives them some special exemptions in exchange for an annual pool-tax to compensate for their pro-tection. These traders are known as free traders because of their exemption from some other taxes. These exemptions are personal. But eventually they became impersonal, meaning that all burghers receive these exemptions. For Smith, burghers also benefit from being able to collect their taxes themselves and pay them directly to the king, freeing themselves from the "insolence" of the king's officers. They are jointly and severally answerable for the whole rent of the land of the town. This rent eventually becomes perpet-ual and fixed, and with it also the exemptions become permanent, and therefore impersonal. This is when the burghs become known as free-burghs.

Smith here candidly admits he is speculating: "I cannot produce evidence", he tells us, on whether the freedom to marry, to succes-sion, and to dispose of possession at will come with the freedom of trade or later. Regardless, Smith believes, free-burghers are now free "in our current sense of freedom".

Because burghers pay taxes directly to the king, they need some compulsory jurisdiction. Towns are thus elected into corpora-tions, with their own magistrates, their own town councils, and their own militia. This is for Smith extraordinary: it is unprec-edented that sovereigns exchange the right to collect taxes for a certain rent. It creates independent republics in the heart of the sovereign's dominions.

How is it possible? This is the key explanation for the freedom and therefore growth of some parts of Europe to levels never seen before, according to Smith. This can also be interpreted as an example of the power of Smith's analysis: combining economic incentives with human passions, recognizing the tensions between different interests, and analyzing their balancing or unbalancing.

So, Smith tells us that sovereigns need to protect their subjects from the oppression of great lords or will lose their authority. The burghers are unable to defend themselves individually, but if combined in large leagues of mutual defense they can. These are regular incentives. Then there are our passions. The lords hate the burghers because they are envious of their wealth. They looked down at the burghers, as no more than emancipated slaves. And yet, they are getting rich (more on how in a bit). How horrible! The burghers hate and fear, for good reasons, the lords. The king hates and fears the lords too, but has nothing against the burghers. So the king and the burghers have the lords as common enemies. And because the enemy of my enemy is my friend, the king grants the burghers their own magistrates and their own ability to defend themselves, which means security and independence. And to signal he means it, he grants the burghers the right to collect his rent. The princes on worse terms with the barons are the ones who give the most to the burghers. Not a surprise, given Smith's analysis.

The problem is that sometimes, in Smith's account, that security and independence is so great that cities *do* become independent, as it happened in Italy between the twelfth and the sixteenth century. In France and England, instead, the king maintains some power over the cities, but can't arbitrarily ask for more taxes. To so do, he needs the consent of the cities. So cities now send representatives to parliament, just like the clergy and the barons. They generally side with the king, creating a counterbalancing power to the great lords.

These conflicts among different interests are thus resolved in such a way to create order, good government, liberty, and security for the cities. In the country there is still violence and, therefore, poverty. But whenever one has the security of enjoying the fruits of one's own labor, one will exert himself to better his conditions, Smith consistently claims. And after having provided for basic needs, one strives for elegance.

With their order and good government, freedom, and security, industry grows in cities first. Farmers, still oppressed with servitude, if they have a little capital, they hide it and then run away from the lords into towns. Towns would give them protection. In this way, both people and capital run into cities: "the only sanctuary in which it could be secured to the person who acquired it".

So you see how Smith builds on his theory? What are the causes of the wealth of nations? Division of labor; accumulation of capital; order and good government; and security and freedom. We humans desire to better our conditions and our passions somehow do the rest. But our passions have to be channeled into the right institutional settings (order and good government, and security and freedom), or it will not work.

Back to Smith's description of the history of Europe. The natural order of things implies the development of agriculture (country), manufacture (town), and international trade, in this order. In reality this does not happen. Not in Europe at least. In Europe the country does not develop, but is abandoned instead. By contrast, the towns develop first. How is that possible? Well, Smith says, through the development of international trade first, and of manufacture later. A complete reverse of the natural order.

Cities must derive subsistence from the country. But it may not be from the country closest to it. If a city is near the sea, or navigable rivers, it can get subsistence from far away, from anywhere in the accessible world. So cities start to carry trade for others to get subsistence, growing in wealth and splendor by trading with many countries, even when there is poverty near them. The Italian cities are the first to grow to opulence though commerce. They do it thanks to their location and thanks to the crusades (again, an exogenous random shock, that is, an uncontrollable unplanned event). The great armies going through the country need transport and supply their provisions. Venice, Genoa, and Pisa are there to help. In exchange, they import expensive luxuries from richer countries to feed the vanity of their landlords.

Foreign commerce introduced a taste for finer and improved manufactures. With an argument implicitly similar to David Hume's, Smith tells us that when we discover these finer products and we establish a taste for them, people start to produce these products at home to save on transport cost. And so manufactures develop, again in reverse order. First foreign commerce, then manufacture.

Smith tells us also that there are two kinds of manufactures. A rude one and a refined one. The rude one is always present because it is what gives small tools and common things to common people. This is produced domestically and is meant for the domestic market of the common people. It is not that interesting for this story. The manufacture that is relevant here, for Smith, is the refined manufacture, the manufacture of luxury goods. These are the only goods worth exporting or importing, given transportation costs. These are generally referred to as manufacture for distance sale.

Manufacture for distance sale is introduced in two ways. One we just saw. It is what Smith calls the introduction by "violent operation of the stock of a particular merchant". It is the off-spring of foreign commerce. It is introduced as imitation of foreign manufacture, most commonly in places near water carriage.

The other way is a more "natural" way that grows out of the gradual improvement of some existing coarse manufacture inland. If there is abundance of provisions, provisions are cheap. They attract workers there as they can more easily feed their families. The cheap provisions and the higher demand, in their turn, facilitate the growth of manufacture on the spot, therefore saving transportation costs. Manufacture keeps improving, eventually reaching the same refinement as the manufacturers destined for more distant markets, Smith claims.

Rude produce and course manufacture cannot support transport costs, especially by land. But, for Smith, the more improved manufacture can. Even if small in bulk, refined manufacture is high in value and can stomach transportation costs. This kind of manufacture is the offspring of agriculture, as it should be, but it does not often happen.

BOOK III, CHAPTER IV: HOW THE COMMERCE OF THE TOWNS CONTRIBUTED TO THE IMPROVEMENT OF THE COUNTRY

The last step in Smith's account of the "inverted" order that Europe experiences is the development of the country, which in theory was to be developed first, but in reality develops last.

Rather than the country improving the towns, the towns improve the country. Towns improve the country in three ways, according to Smith.

One: as cities grow bigger, they became larger markets for the country, therefore encouraging the improvement of the country, even faraway country.

Two: merchants, lured by the idyllic appeals of country living, want to become country gentlemen, so when they retire, they buy land and move to the countryside. They prove to be the best improvers. They end up improving the land, and do a good job with it, because they are accustomed to using money profitably. They are not like the actual country gentlemen who instead are accustomed just to spend the money on immediate consumption. They are bold undertakers (the word Smith uses for entrepreneurs), while old landlords tend to be timid instead.

Three: calling out Hume by name as the first and only to recognize this, Smith tells us that commerce brings "order and good government" and "liberty and security" to all individuals. Before the introduction of commerce, there was "servile dependency" and continual violence.

Here is the story of this transformation that Smith tells us.

When foreign commerce is little known, where refined manufacture is little known, there is only rustic hospitality because there is not much on which to spend one's revenue. So a landlord has a multitude of retainers and dependents. They must obey him because they have nothing to give back for the food they received. Indeed ancient hospitality exceeds today's notion of it. Just think that Westminster Hall was meant as a dining hall and was not even big enough to accommodate all the guests! The lord's tenants are fed in their own homes too, provided for from the "landlord's bounty and good pleasure".

The ancient barons have thus power over their tenants and retainers as they are their judges in times of peace and their leaders in times of war. The king is too weak to do either. He is not strong enough to be a buffer between the landlords and the people they keep in servitude.

It is a mistake, Smith says, to think that territorial jurisdictions originate from feudal law. The lords had those rights centuries before the law. The feudal law may be seen as an attempt to moderate, not to extend, the authority of the lords. But it does not work. The king remains incapable of restraining the "violence, rapine, and disorder" that the lords create in the country.

But, "all the violence of feudal institutions" could never do what "the silent and insensible operation of foreign commerce" do. And what does commerce do? For Smith, foreign commerce gives to the great lords something in exchange for their whole surplus of their land. So "for a pair of diamond buckles, or something as frivolous and useless, they exchanged the maintenance of thousands of men and the authority it would give them". "To gratify the most childish, the meanest, and most sordid of all vanities, they bartered away their power and authority".

In the past, great lords would directly maintain 1,000 families who were necessarily at their command. Today, Smith says, they directly maintain 20 at best, but indirectly they maintain many more by contributing to 1/10, or 1/100, 1/1,000, or even 1/10,000 part of their annual maintenance. They contribute to the maintenance of them all, but they are all more or less independent of him because they can live without him. Each tradesman has a thousand customers. He is obliged to all, but not dependent upon any of them.

This passage implicitly echoes the section in Smith's other work, *The Theory of Moral Sentiments*, which is the only other place where he mentions the invisible hand. There, even if in a different context, Smith tells us that the luxury consumption of the rich feed many, distributing wealth from the hand of a few people to the mouths of many. Here too, the luxury consumption of the rich distributes not just wealth, but also power, from the hand of the very few, generating freedom for all.

The reason why the landlords lose power and authority generating freedom for their dependents and tenants is the following, for Smith. The landlord's expenditures are too high to sustain. He can't afford both diamond buckles and immense banquets. He can have either one or the other. So he dismisses his retainers and asks his tenants for higher rent. The tenants agree, conditioning to longer leases. Longer leases mean independence for them. So now, without dependents, because the tenants are independent and the retainers dismissed, the great proprietor is no longer able to interfere with the regular administration of justice and to disrupt the peace. He sells his birthrights "for trinkets and baubles".

For Smith, now we have regular government, and nobody has too much power to disturb it!

Smith remarks also that, in commercial societies, it is rare to have very old families with large estates, despite laws trying to maintain them. They are common in noncommercial societies instead, despite having no law to support them. If one can only spend on others, one will not go bankrupt. Benevolence is seldom so intense to try to maintain more than one can afford. But if one can spend on his own person, one can and does go bankrupt, because our vanity is boundless. Laws going against human passions are not effective, as Smith will explain later.

Smith concludes with his moral of the story. Commerce brings about "a revolution in public happiness". Yes, it is the word *happiness* that he uses. Remember after all when he described a growing economy? A society with positive economic growth is a happy society, a stationary economy is dull, and a declining one is miserable? Economic growth brings prosperity, freedom, security, order, good government, and happiness too, but unintentionally. The people who cause this silent revolution do not care about the public and do not intend to bring about public happiness. It is because of the "childish vanity" of the great proprietors and the "peddler principle of turning a penny where there is a penny to be made" of the merchants and artificers that the feudal system crumbles. Neither group had "knowledge or foresight of that great revolution which the folly of one and the industry of the other brought about".

And so in Europe the order of development, contrary to the natural course of things, sees the development of commerce and manufacture of the cities as the cause of the improvement of the country, not the effect. It may be slow and uncertain, but it is there.

Smith tells us that North America seems to be the closest place to see a possible natural course. And, there, it is fast. The North American colonies are based on agriculture alone and their population seems to double every 25 years. In Europe, population doubles every 500 years. In Europe, the law of primogeniture slows growth down. Estates are too large. It is difficult to know how to improve them. Not enough land can go on the market, leading to monopoly prices. Buying land thus is the most unprofitable use of small capital. Yet it is done because of the security that the land gives once one retires. Buying land is good for old people, not for young and ambitious ones. If there was no primogeniture law, the growth of Great Britain would be closer to the colonies' growth because so much more land would be available on the market.

Would the North American colonies grow so fast without "the protection of the genius of the British constitution" as Smith claims in Book I? He does not mention it here. What he does mention is that the laws of England favor agriculture, both in a way that is "altogether illusory" and in a way that is really effective. The illusory way, as he will explain in the next book, is the one based on bounties (subsidies) on corn, duties on foreign corn, and no importation of live cattle from Ireland. These laws establish a monopoly against their countrymen for the two most important products of land: bread and butcher's meat. The effective way, as explained in this book, is that the farmers of England are as secure, as independent, and as respectable as the law can make.

The very end of Book III is additional fuel for who claims that Smith has a preference for agriculture. The capital acquired by commerce, he claims, is not secured until it is used to improve the land. The wealth coming from agriculture is solid and durable and can be destroyed only by events such as the barbaric invasions. Revolutions, wars, and governments can easily dry up the sources of wealth coming from commerce only. And a merchant, not being a citizen of any country, can easily move his capital to different places.

The history that Smith presents here can be read as a strange economic history. Economic growth and development cannot be separated. They depend on some economic incentives, but not necessarily on the signaling of prices. Human passions, rational or not, are what drive that silent revolution of commerce, which is more powerful than any laws or armies. It is our childish vanity as well as our charm for the countryside. It is clashing interests and their reciprocal jealousy. It can be read as a strange history also because it is an impersonal unheroic history. It is a history told in almost the opposite way form David Hume. Hume, in his *History of England*, goes through king after king, war after war, name after name. We can read Smith as telling a nameless history. It is an anonymous history. Changes do not come from kings and do not come from specific acts of parliaments. Changes come from the actions of several anonymous individuals who have no intention or knowledge of the changes they are bringing about. The real revolutions are the slow, impersonal, and silent revolutions of commerce. This is why this book is read as an historical account of Europe but also as a continuation of Smith's economic theory.

FURTHER READINGS

Brewer, Anthony. 1998. "Luxury and Economic Development: David Hume and Adam Smith". *Scottish Journal of Political Economy* 45.1: 79–98.

Forbes. D. 1975. "Sceptical Whiggism, Commerce, and Liberty", in *Essays on Adam Smith,* ed. A. Skinner, T. Wilson. Oxford: Clarendon.

Haakonssen, Knud. 1981. *The Science of a Legislator: The Natural Jurisprudence of David Hume and Adam Smith*. Cambridge: Cambridge University Press.

Skinner, Andrew. 1975. "Adam Smith: An Economic Interpretation of History", in *Essays on Adam Smith,* ed. A. Skinner, T. Wilson. Oxford: Clarendon.

Smith, Craig. 2006. *Adam Smith's Political Philosophy: The Invisible Hand and Spontaneous Order*. London: Routledge.

Winch, Donald. 1978. *Adam Smith's Politics: An Essay in Historiographic Revision*. Cambridge and London: Cambridge University Press.

8

BOOK IV, CHAPTERS I–VI

INTRODUCTION

Book IV is a bit of a shift in gears because it is where Smith describes different systems of political economy. It is about two different theoretical systems that attempt to offer not just understanding to men of learning, but also to influence princes and states: the system of commerce, or mercantile system, and the agricultural system. He will start with the commercial one because it is by far the most popular.

But what is political economy? Smith defines it as the "science of the legislator". It is meant to help us understand how to enrich both the people and the sovereign by providing plenty of revenue to the people, or, better, how to enable them to provide for themselves thereby supplying the state with the revenue for public services.

BOOK IV, CHAPTER I: OF THE PRINCIPLE OF COMMERCIAL OR MERCANTILE SYSTEM

Smith opens the first chapter of this Book by addressing his major enemy: the popular notion that money is wealth. Smith believes this mistake is so popular because of the double functions of money as an intermediary in exchange and unit of account. We always want money because we want the things we can buy with it. We measure the value of everything in money. So we think that to grow rich is to get money. Indeed, in common language, wealth and money are used synonymously. Similarly, allegedly, a rich country is a country that has lots of money, and getting rich should mean accumulating gold and silver.

The notion that money is wealth is a mistake, though, according to Smith. The Tartars, the Turco-Mongol nomadic population of Central Asia, understand it better than the Spaniard conquistadores or some modern philosophers, Smith claims. To evaluate if a new territory is worth conquering, the Tartars ask: Are there sheep here? Instead, the Spaniards in America asked: Is there gold here? The Tartars demonstrate a better understanding of wealth than the Spaniards. This could be interpreted as a stab to his intellectual enemies: Tartars are considered "barbarians", but even barbarians have better economic understanding than mercantilists.

Even the British philosopher John Locke, like the Spaniards, but unlike the Tartars, thought that money is the movable wealth of a nation, Smith claims. The mistake is so luring that some unnamed "other" thinkers who say that in a closed economy money is irrelevant, end up saying that in an open economy we need to accumulate money. Money is needed to finance foreign wars; therefore, we need to accumulate money in times of peace. So every country, following the example of Spain and Portugal, tries to keep its gold and silver at home with export prohibitions, under the assumption that it is keeping its wealth at home. Not only are they making a mistake, but also their attempts are in vain.

The prohibitions of exporting gold and silver eventually become inconvenient for merchants as commerce expands. Smith suggests that advocates such as the merchant and eventually director of the

East India Company Thomas Mun (1571–1641) push for a change in policy. Mun claims, according to Smith, that trying to keep gold and silver at home with prohibitions does not work. Smuggling is quite easy, given the small volume and high value of precious metals. This means that prohibitions do not prevent exports of metals but make them more expensive, which means they lead to more metals leaving the country. If one wants to grow rich, one should focus on the balance of trade rather than on prohibitions.

If the value of exports is more than the value of imports, it means that gold and silver will have to come into the country to pay for those excess exports. This is a much better way to grow rich, according to Mun. Smith, of course, disagrees. For Smith, Mun is correct in saying that the prohibition does not prevent smuggling gold and silver out of the country. But Mun is incorrect when claiming that the government needs to regulate trade to get the desired quantity of money.

According to Smith, everybody knows that trade enriches the country, but nobody knows how. Merchants claim to know trade. Parliament members, councils of princes, nobles, and country gentlemen are aware of their own ignorance of trade. It is, therefore, easy for merchants to convince parliament that their views are correct and that they would benefit the country. But what merchants know is how to enrich themselves, not the country. They say that foreign trade brings money to the country, but the current laws limit it. More money would come in if the laws were changed: rather than focusing on the prohibition to export gold and silver focus instead on the balance of trade: a "much more embarrassing, and just equally fruitless" idea. After all, Smith notes, if a country does not have mines, it gets gold and silver from abroad, just like if a country does not have vineyards, it gets wine from abroad. Freedom of trade provides us with wine, why shouldn't it provide us with gold and silver too?

Here are some of the "embarrassing" reasons used to justify policies favoring a positive balance of trade.

The government should take measure to preserve gold and silver in a country. But this is unnecessary because, if the quantity of gold and silver is more than the effective demand, no government can prevent its exportation. A sign of it, which is not an accident, is that the price of gold and silver is very stable, much more stable than the price of any other commodity. Gold and silver are easy to transport because of their small weight and a high value, so it is easy to keep supply and demand in balance and their prices somewhat stable. Other commodities are bulkier, harder to transport, and indeed their prices are more volatile.

But what if there is not enough gold and silver? Well, Smith answers, if there are not enough provisions, people will starve, as there are few substitutes for basic food. But if there was really not enough money, we can have plenty of substitutes: barter, credit, and paper can all do the job of gold and silver. Yet, the most common complaint is that there is not enough money. Why? Because many people want money but have nothing to exchange it for and cannot easily borrow. For example, if one overtrades, one buys on credit too many goods to send to a distant market in hope that the returns will arrive before the payments are due. But the hope is ungrounded: the payments come in before the returns. Ergo the complaint.

Another "embarrassing and fruitless" reason to want regulation to increase the quantity of gold and silver in a country is that we want gold and silver because they are more durable than any other commodities. This is absurd, Smith claims. We want money because it is easier to exchange it for other things than any other commodity. We do not want money for its own sake, but for what it can buy. Pots are also very durable. But it makes no sense to force people to accumulate more pots than what they need. The quantity of money is similarly limited by its use. It makes no sense to accumulate more than what is needed. It just takes up space, meaning we are just wasting otherwise useful resources.

Another common and wrong reason why people want to accumulate gold and silver, for Smith, is the incorrect belief that wars are financed with gold and silver. But fleets and armies are maintained by consumable goods, not gold and silver. In theory, a country could maintain troops in foreign countries by sending abroad gold and silver, by sending abroad some part of the annual produce of its manufactures, or by sending abroad part of its annual rude produce. Let's examine each one.

The gold and silver accumulated in a country usually consists of circulating money, the plate of private families, and the treasury of the prince. There is seldom little to spare from the gold and silver used as circulating money. True, with foreign wars there are more people abroad and less people at home, so fewer goods circulate at home, which means less money is needed at home and more goes abroad. But using circulating money to finance wars is not very effective, especially long wars. Melting private plate is insignificant. France did it, and its loss in fashion was not compensated by the gains of extra money. Also, the treasury of the prince may have worked in the past, but today the prince does not accumulate much of a treasury and the expense of the wars are enormous. The last war that Britain fought cost three times the amount of gold and silver present in Britain! Even if we think in terms of bullion, the gold and silver that circulates among commercial countries, that is the "money of the great commercial republic", would not be nearly enough to support a modern war.

Exporting raw materials cannot finance foreign wars. The transport costs are too high and there is too little to spare from home consumption.

So, for Smith, wars are paid with refined manufactures. Merchants sell goods in foreign countries and are paid with foreign bills. The government buys the foreign bills from merchants and uses them to pay for provisions for troops abroad. That is how wars are financed, not with gold or silver. As a matter of fact, during wars manufacturers have a double demand: they produce goods to be sent abroad to pay for the foreign provisions of the troops and they produce for the domestic market. During the most destructive foreign wars, some manufacturers may flourish and decline when peace returns.

Another way to think about how incorrect it is to want to accumulate gold and silver to pay for wars is to think that in ancient times it was difficult to have long uninterrupted wars. Not so today, Smith says. The past inability of long wars was not caused by lack of money but by lack of manufactures. Without commerce, one needs to rely on the treasure because a sovereign cannot tax much more than usual even during emergencies. It works there because noncommercial societies are parsimonious: there is little to buy, so little on which to spend. With commerce, we can indulge our vanity in extravagant expenditures. The treasure disappears. But manufactures pay for the (now longer) wars.

Smith concludes this chapter with a reminder that foreign trade has two benefits: it carries out the surplus part of the produce from which there is no demand at home (what later will be called vent for surplus), and it brings back something for which there is a demand at home. So division of labor is not limited by the domestic market, but it can expand and improve the productive powers of labor and increase the wealth of society.

And so Smith reminds us that the discovery of American gold did not make Europe richer, but made service of plate (silverware) cheaper. It was a good thing, though, even if not necessarily because of the cheap plate. The new and inexhaustible markets for European commodities helped create a new division of labor and new improvements. Unfortunately, it came at a high price: "The savage injustice of Europe rendered an event which ought to have been beneficial to all, ruinous and destructive to several of those unfortunate countries". Smith will soon tell us more about the European atrocities in America. Here he just gives us a first taste.

For now, just think that trade brings benefits, and the richer is a trading partner the more benefits one receives, Smith tells us. But Europe benefits more from its trade with America than with East Indies, even if in America there were "savages" (remember that for Smith savage means hunter-gatherer and poor). The only "advanced" societies (Mexico and Peru) were destroyed as soon as discovered. China, Indostan, and Japan were more advanced and cultivated, even if they did not have mines. But the East India trade is monopolized by the East India Companies. Worst, the exclusive privileges of the East India Companies caused much envy, and envy makes people believe that "trade is pernicious". Something went wrong.

Indeed, the policy prescriptions of the mercantile system are based on its two wrong ideas, according to Smith: that gold is wealth and that metals come into the country only with a positive balance of trade. Policies should therefore, incorrectly, focus on increasing exports and decreasing imports. There are two kinds of import restrictions: a restriction of foreign goods for home consumption that can be produced at home and a restriction of imports of any kind of foreign goods. High duties or absolute prohibitions are the ways to implement these restrictions. There are four kinds of export encouragements: drawbacks, which are tax refunds for goods that are exported; bounties, which are export subsidies; treaties of commerce, which give privileges to some specific countries; and colonies, which create privileges and monopolies for the goods of those countries.

These are the six, wrong, principal means to increase gold and silver in a country by bringing the balance of trade in its favor, according to Smith. The following six chapters will analyze each of them.

BOOK IV, CHAPTER II: OF RESTRAINTS UPON THE IMPORTATION FROM FOREIGN COUNTRIES OF SUCH GOODS THAT CAN BE PRODUCED AT HOME

The first means to create a favorable balance of trade that Smith analyzes and criticizes are the import restrictions of goods that can also be produced at home.

High duties or absolute prohibitions of goods that can be produced at home create monopolies in the home market for the domestic industry "against their countrymen". Smith spells out loud and clear who benefits and who loses from monopolies: monopolies benefit the monopolized industry, never society.

Indeed, for Smith, the general industry of society cannot be more than the capital that society has, and no regulation can increase the industry beyond what its capital can maintain. It can only divert part of the capital in directions different from where it would otherwise go and not necessarily for the best. An individual looks for the most advantageous use of his capital. And even if he has in view only his own advantage, not the one of society, yet, his advantage is what is most advantageous for society.

As the first choice, according to Smith, one would use his capital at home, supporting the domestic industry, all else the same. Given similar profits, one prefers home trade over foreign trade and foreign trade over carrying trade. Why? Because we like to keep our things close to us. We want to keep an eye on what we own. What we can see matters. With domestic trade, one can keep his capital within his sight and control. Additionally, one knows more about the home market and the domestic laws than about those of different countries. With carrying trade, all capital is out of sight all the time. Some are willing to pay extra to have their shipment stop at home just to have it within their sight. This is why, for Smith, the home ports of the country engaged in carrying trade are the emporium for all the goods of all the countries whose trade it carries.

Merchants are trying to convert carrying trade into foreign trade, and foreign trade into domestic trade just to have their capital close to their sight. Today we would say that monitoring costs and local knowledge is what makes a difference.

The home market is, therefore, the center around which all capital circulates, even if sometimes external forces push it off. Note that this image is not that different from the image Smith uses to explain that the natural prices are the prices around which market prices gravitate, unless some exogenous forces interfere.

When capital stays at home, one directs it toward the industry that has the greatest value. After all, one uses his capital only to get profits. This is why capital will go in the industry that produces the highest value, which implies that the annual revenue of society will be as great as possible. The owner of capital, seeking his profits, does not intend to promote public interest. As a matter of fact, according to Smith, he does not even know he is promoting public interest. He cares only about his own security and his own gains. He "is led by an invisible hand to promote an end which is no part of his intention".

This is the one and only mention of the invisible hand in *The Wealth of Nations*. There is an invisible hand in *The Theory of Moral Sentiments* and one in the *History of Astronomy*, a "juvenile" essay that Smith spared from the flames at his death and was published posthumously. In *The Theory of Moral Sentiments* the invisible hand redistributes goods from the rich to the poor: the conspicuous consumption of the rich unintentionally feeds many poor. In the *History of Astronomy*, the invisible hand of Jupiter is believed to move the planets in an orderly way. This belief helps us explain otherwise mysterious events that would cause us anxiety. The invisible hand of *The Wealth of Nations* has received an impressively large amount of attention, given its only mention. Its meaning is still an open question, ranging from being the hand of God to being an "as if" statement. What I think is clear so far is that the invisible hand is not an endorsement of unethical or even amoral greediness as some occasional caricatures of Smith may portray it. It is also difficult to see it as an unconditional endorsement of laissez-faire. As we already saw on more than one occasion, Smith does support a wide range of government interventions. One may agree or disagree about whether they are many or few, but not on the fact that they exist.

Smith explains why it is better to let capital find its way to the domestic market. He continues with the recurrent theme waved in all chapters since Book I: not all interests in society are always harmonious. The interest of some groups, those of merchants and manufacturers, clash with the interest of the great body of the people. If they are able to capture political power, they will enrich themselves at the expense of society. As he just explained in the previous chapter, they are very persuasive and often trusted, which is dangerous.

> I have never known much good done by those who affected to trade for the public good.... [E]very individual ... can, in his local situation, judge much better than any statemen or lawgiver can do for him. The statesman, who should attempt to direct private people in what manner they ought to employ their capitals, would not only load himself with a most unnecessary attention, but assumes an authority which could not safely be trusted, not only to a single person, but to no council or senate whatever, and which would nowhere be so dangerous as in the hands of a man who had the folly and presumption enough to fancy himself fit to exercise it.
>
> (WN IV.ii.10)

In *The Theory of Moral Sentiments*, Smith describes a man of system who is enamored of his system and tries to implement it, forgetting that he is dealing with real people and not with inanimate pieces on a chessboard. It can, therefore, be dangerous if he tries to move the "pieces" against their will. Here the argument is similar, but also more complex. The problem is not just that the love of system is blinding. The problem is that someone sees extremely well what his interest is and uses the power of the state to get it, at the expense of society. The same interest, without political power, unintentionally promotes the interest of society. But if able to capture the legislature, it will hurt the interest of society, intentionally or not. And unfortunately, merchants and manufacturers know their interests well, and are willing and able to get political power to implement the policies that favors them, as the mercantile system does.

Smith then explains that domestic producers' monopolies of the home market are either useless, if the goods are done more cheaply at home, or hurtful, if it costs more to make them at home than to buy them from abroad. If a foreign country can produce more cheaply than us, buy from them with the produce of our industry; if not, the industry of our country will decrease because capital is diverted from more productive uses toward less productive uses.

Smith says that some may claim that protections are useful because they may help some industries to develop faster than otherwise. Not true. Such protections cannot increase the industry of society. The industry of society can increase only as capital increases; and capital increases only as saving increases. The immediate effect is a decrease in revenue.

Scotland is not famous for its wines, given its weather, Smith explains. The wine industry does not grow that fast. It does not grow at all, actually. Why not protect it so it could grow faster? Smith asks: Would it be reasonable to make wine in Scotland at 30 times the costs at which it can be imported?

Who benefits the most from monopoly of the home market then? Smith tells us the answer: merchants and manufacturers of finer manufactures. Because of lower transport costs, it is easier to export finer manufactures than cattle and corn, so they are the primary beneficiaries and the primary promoters and supporters of these monopolies.

Indeed, if there were free imports of manufactures, home producers would suffer a great deal. Some may even go to ruin, which simply means that their capital will find different employment. But if trade in cattle was free, Smith says, so few would be imported anyway because the transport of live cattle is so expensive, especially by sea, that it would make little difference. Even the freest importation of salted meats would make little difference because it is also bulky and expensive to transport, and the quality of the salted meat is much less than fresh meat that it is not a real competitor. So we would not see much change in the price of butcher's meat. Also free importation of corn would affect British farmers very little, according to Smith, because corn is too bulky to sustain the transport costs needed to be sold at a competitive price.

Furthermore, repeating again what mentioned in the previous books, country gentlemen and farmers are the least subjected to the spirit of monopoly because they are many and dispersed, thus they cannot easily combine. They demand privileges just because they want to mimic manufacturers.

That said, for Smith there are two cases for which it is okay to tax foreigners to develop domestic industry. One is defense. British defense depends on its number of sailors and ships. The Act of Navigation is thus justifiable even if it is not favorable to trade. Foreign ships cannot come to Britain to take exports, but they can come to bring imports. But if someone cannot sell, they cannot buy. Coming with an empty cargo is too expensive. The act gives de facto a monopoly of the British trade to British ships. But for Smith, the act is good because defense is more important than opulence.

The other justified tax on foreign goods is when there are taxes on the same goods domestically made. In this way, the competition between domestic and foreign-made goods remains the same before and after tax.

What is not justifiable is to extend these taxes on the necessaries of life and on all sort of foreign goods. A tax on import of necessities such as soap, salt, leather, or candles would increase domestic labor costs and, therefore, the price of all commodities. Taxing incoming necessities is like having a poor soil or bad climate. And if the tax is too high it becomes equivalent to the "curse" of "barrenness of the earth and inclemency of the heavens". Only rich countries can afford those absurdities. Here again we have a problem of understanding that correlation is not causation: rich countries are rich not because of these import taxes, but in spite of them.

There are two additional cases in which taxing foreigners could be justifiable for Smith. These are not general principles but are situations that need to be evaluated case by case. One situation is to evaluate if we should continue to import freely when another country is taxing our goods. Retaliation may be appropriate if it induces foreigners to repeal their tax.

The other situation that requires evaluation on a case-by-case ground is whether to restore free import when domestic industry grows enough with protection. This is a difficult decision. It needs to be done very slowly and with a good deal of advanced notice, according to Smith. If done too fast, many may lose their jobs and subsistence, causing disorder. Yet, Smith suggests optimistically, disorder may be less common than expected.

After all, at the end of each war, thousands of sailors come home and need to find a job. They do it without problems. Similarly, displaced workmen should be able to find different employment. After all, the capital of the country remains the same, so the demand for labor remains the same too, just in different occupations. It only needs to have freedom of employment and of movement, which means to abolish apprenticeship and the Poor Laws, which, as explained in Book I are the main source of labor impediments.

Smith is more realistic than optimistic about the future of free trade, though. His Public Choice analysis, as we would call it today, is impeccable. He believes that to expect freedom of trade restored in Great Britain is to expect to find Utopia. The prejudices of the public are too strong, and the private interests behind them are "unconquerable". They are as dangerous as an "overgrown standing army"; they are "formidable" and can "intimidate the legislature".

If someone is promonopoly, they gain a reputation of understanding trade and they feel important because they become popular among the wealthy, Smith says. If someone is against monopoly, nothing can protect them from "infamous abuses, insults, even real danger from the insolent outrage of the furious monopolists". Policy prescription? Do not establish new monopolies or extend existing ones.

BOOK IV, CHAPTER III: OF THE EXTRAORDINARY RESTRAINTS UPON IMPORTATION OF GOODS OF ALMOST ALL KINDS FROM COUNTRIES WITH WHICH THE BALANCE OF TRADE IS SUPPOSED TO BE DISADVANTAGEOUS

PART I: OF THE UNREASONABLENESS OF THOSE RESTRAINTS EVEN UPON THE PRINCIPLES OF THE COMMERCIAL SYSTEM

The second expedient to increase the quantity of gold and silver has its origins in national prejudice and animosity. This expedient is even more unreasonable than the ones originating from private interests and spirit of monopoly, according to Smith. The expedient is to restrain imports of foreign goods. The high duties used to restrict imports make smugglers the main importers.

Where do these pernicious national prejudices and animosity come from? For Smith they always come from the private interest of some traders. It would be otherwise difficult to justify the popular support for a favorable balance of trade, given the difficulties in measuring it.

Let's see why measuring a balance of trade is tricky for Smith.

First, if we import wines from France, true, the balance is worsened against France. But we would be buying less wine from Portugal. And French wine being cheaper than Portuguese wine, the value of all imports may be less. Second, some imported goods are reexported. Third, customhouse books are famous for their inaccuracy, especially in terms of reported value, and Smith working in one knows it well. Fourth, debts and credits do not cancel each other out, as countries deal with many different places. And, fifth, all the previous problems do not count that (a) mint standards are unreliable because the coins are clipped and worn so that the same ounce of pure gold and silver seldom buys the same amount of money, and (b) bank money has often *agio*, that is that bank money is more valuable than currency.

DIGRESSION CONCERNING BANKS OF DEPOSIT, PARTICULARLY CONCERNING THAT OF AMSTERDAM

A large state uses its own coins. A small state uses its own coins and the coins of all other states too, Smith tells us. Thus, differently from a large state, if a small state wishes to reform its own coins, it would not reform the currency used in the state because in circulation there are coins also from several other places. This implies that when one wants to exchange a foreign bill, there is potentially lots of uncertainty regarding what kind of coins one would receive. So the bill is exchanged below what it is worth.

A solution, for Smith, is to have foreign bills of exchange paid with transfer in the books, established on credit with the protection of the state, rather than in currency. By law, the bank will always pay in money of the standard of the state. Small states such as Venice, Genoa, Amsterdam, Hamburg, and Nuremberg use this bank money. And because the money of these banks is better than the local currency, it calls for *agio*, a premium.

Amsterdam is one of the cities that adopt this form of money. The Bank of Amsterdam is possibly the most famous bank issuing bank money.

The Bank of Amsterdam was established in 1609. It receives deposits and gives credit in its books to the true value of money. Its bank money is always to the standard of the mint. And by law, every merchant has to pay large foreign bills of exchange with this bank money. Because bank money is superior to currency and safer, so it exchanges at an *agio*. This means that if someone demands payment, the *agio* is lost. The Bank can, therefore, claim that all the money deposited is still and always is in the Bank.

Note that this bank is very different from the merchants banks of Scotland that Smith describes in Book II. The Scottish banks would not accept deposits. They just give loans based on their capital. The Bank of Amsterdam is instead a bank of deposit and with 100 percent reserves, as we would say today. Meaning that it keeps 100 percent of its deposits and does not give loans.

So how does it stay in business?

The Bank receives deposits in coins, which become its capital, Smith explains. The value of bank money is supposed to be the same as the value of the coins deposits.

The Bank also receives deposits in bullion (uncoined metals). It issues credit at 5 percent less than mint price, which is the government set price of the coined metal. The price difference is a sort of warehouse rent for bullion. The depositor gets a receipt and needs to take out the bullion within a specified time, usually six months, and paid in bank money. If not, the deposit goes to the bank. It is, therefore, rare that receipts expire.

The owner of bank money (given for deposited coins) is generally different from the owner of receipts (given for deposited bullions). Thus, receipts are tradable, and they trade between the mint price (price of coins) and the market price (price of bullion). The receipts cannot draw out bullion without giving the bank the equivalent in bank money. If the owner of the receipt has no bank money, he must buy some. Similarly, bank money cannot draw bullion without giving bank receipts for the same amount. If the owner of bank money does not have a receipt, he must buy it.

In times of peace, all is good. But in times of public calamities, there can be some sort of runs on receipts, so that their price may increase significantly.

The city gains from the presence of the Bank thanks to the warehouse rent, the different fees, the sale of foreign coins, the expired receipts of bullions, and the *agio* of bank money. But the gains are not intentional, in a sense, Smith tells us. The Bank was meant to relieve merchants from some of the inconveniences of exchange, and accidentally it turned out to be profitable for the city.

PART II: OF THE UNREASONABLENESS OF THOSE EXTRAORDINARY RESTRAINTS UPON OTHER PRINCIPLES

Let's go back to the nonsensical mercantile ideas on trade.

If we really want to look at a balance, we should look at the balance of production and consumption, not at the nonsensical balance of trade, Smith states. If a country consumes more than it produces, it may grow into decay. But if a country produces more than it consumes, then that country will have savings. And because savings are at the base of economic growth, that country will flourish. The balance of trade can be negative, but if the balance of produce is positive, the economy is in good shape.

And yet, we have the popular notion that the balance of trade is the most important indicator of economic growth. It makes no sense. The idea of the balance of trade is based on the idea of zero-sum game, as we say it today; that what a country gains is what another country loses. And for Smith, there is nothing more absurd than the idea of the balance of trade and that trade is a zero-sum game. Free trade is always advantageous for both countries, even if not equally. It is monopoly trade that is hurtful instead. And it is hurtful for the country that imposes it.

Of course the advantages of trade are not in terms of gold and silver, but in terms of exchangeable value of the annual produce: the annual revenue of a country increases with trade.

And yet again, some people claim that some trades are losing trades. Nonsense: all trades lead to gains. An alleged example of a losing trade is the one of an ale house, what today we call a bar. An ale house is just the result of division of labor and not the source of drunkenness. Cheap wine does not cause drunkenness; indeed, it seems to cause sobriety. Look at France, Smith tells us. In the north of France wine is more expensive than in the south of France. When troupes from the north go south and find its cheap wine, they drink a great deal at first. But then, the novelty wears out and they become sober like the locals. The restraints on wine that England has do nothing to promote sobriety. They just favor Portuguese wine over French wines with the excuse that Portuguese are better customers of British goods than the French.

But merchants do their business by buying where it is cheap, independently of who produces the merchandise, Smith reminds us. Why should all British people not be allowed to do the same? The spirit of monopoly is directly opposite to the interest of the great body of the people. People, like merchants, want to buy from the cheapest seller. But the merchants want monopoly of the home market. So they ask and obtain high duties and prohibitions. Smith does not seem to lose an opportunity to condemn the hypocrisy of merchants.

Merchants are perversely and dangerously clever in fooling who believe in them, Smith tells us. They perverse what commerce is and ought to be. Commerce is and ought to be "a bond of union and friendship" among nations. The wealth of one's neighbor may be dangerous in war, but it is beneficial in trade. A rich man, after all, is a better customer than a poor one. Open ports enrich cities and towns, and do not ruin them. Look at Amsterdam. But, for Smith, the "passionate confidence of interested falsehood" of merchants is such that they make every nation look with envy at the prosperity of other countries. The manufactures of rich nations are dangerous rivals, even if this competition is beneficial to the great body of the people. They make the neighbors become necessarily enemies, and their wealth and power inflame violence and "discord and animosity".

Smith believes there are things that have remedies and things that do not. The universal violence and injustice of rulers has no remedy. The "mean rapacity" and the monopolizing spirit of merchants also have no remedy. But it can be, and it ought to be prevented from disturbing the tranquility of society. For Smith, merchants are not and ought not to be the rulers of mankind.

BOOK IV, CHAPTER IV: OF DRAWBACKS

When merchants affect politicians, they ask and generally obtain monopolies, Smith reiterates. Merchants want monopoly of the home market, and they want monopoly abroad too. But they can't get a monopoly abroad. So they ask for encouragement of their exports instead.

Drawbacks seem to be the most reasonable of these encouragements, in Smith's mind. They draw back, give back, inland duties or excise taxes if a good is exported or if an imported foreign good is reexported.

Drawbacks originate from the jealousy of domestic manufacturers. How do we know? There are import duties on imports prohibited in the domestic market. These are goods that cannot be sold at home. They are simply stored in domestic ports waiting to be exported. Yet, manufacturers are afraid that someone will steal them from the warehouses and sell them at home, making them become competition. The jealousy is such to even prohibit carrying goods, such as French ones. They are willing to give up a profit rather than let "our enemies" make a profit by our means.

Yet, drawbacks may have originated as an encouragement of carrying trade. Cargos are paid for in foreign money, so they bring gold and silver into the country. The motivation is foolish, but the institution turns out reasonable enough. It does not force more capital than it otherwise would into those activities. A drawback is not giving any special preferences to the carrying trade; it just removes some obstacles from it.

It is also good for customs as the customs revenue will increase because only part of the duties is given back. If all duties were kept, there would be very little gain from customs: those goods would be too expensive, so they would not come to the ports.

But drawbacks are justifiable only for goods exported from countries in which the home country does not have monopoly. They are not meant for European goods going into the American colonies. There, drawbacks would be just a loss of revenue. Also, drawbacks are useful only for goods that are really exported, and not smuggled back.

So far so good.

BOOK IV, CHAPTER V: OF BOUNTIES

But merchants want more. They want monopoly on foreign markets, Smith repeats. But we can't give domestic producers a monopoly in foreign markets. We cannot force foreigners to buy our goods either, as we do in domestic markets. What we can do is pay them to buy our goods. So we give bounties (subsidies) to domestic producers to help them export. If exports increase, the balance of trade would increase too. Win. Not.

A bounty is a subsidy given when trade would not happen without it. But be careful, Smith tells us, of the perversity of the logic: a subsidized trade is an unprofitable trade. It would not take place without subsidies. If it is a profitable trade, it does not need subsidies. So, for Smith, the reasons used to justify subsidies are the very reasons for which they should not be given.

Here Smith engages in a sort of dialogue with the supporters of bounties. He lists their objections to their critics, and then answers them to show how nonsensical they are.

The supporters of bounties claim that the value of the exports covers the expenses of the bounty. But they do not count the lost opportunity to use capital in a more profitable way. Without bounties, one would use capital in different ways. Bounties force trade in channels that are less beneficial than it would naturally be.

This means, that the national capital decreases as a consequence of bounties.

The supporters of bounties also claim that the price of corn decreased since the establishment of the bounty. This, for Smith, is a problem of mistaking correlation with causation. The price decrease happened despite the bounty, not as a consequence of it. Look at France. The price of corn in France dropped too, but there was no bounty. They fully banned exports. The reason why the price of corn dropped is because the real value of silver increased. It has nothing to do with the bounties. As a matter of fact, the bounty increased the price of corn at home. In times of plenty, the bounty encourages exports. With less corn at home, the domestic price increases. In times of scarcity, the bounty is suspended. But it is because there was an increase in exports in time of plenty that there is now less corn at home to make up for the bad times, so the price of corn increases also during bad times.

Ah, but high prices at home mean incentives for producers to produce more so the price will eventually decrease. No, not quite, Smith answers again. Every bushel of corn exported means less corn at home. It is the foreign market that expands, at the expense of domestic consumption.

In addition, domestic consumers have to pay two taxes to subsidize cheap consumption abroad: the actual tax to finance the bounty and the higher price of corn at home. But because the higher price of corn, all other commodities will increase in price too. And this is the highest tax of the two. Worst, everybody uses corn, so everybody pays for it. The poor are hurt the most because corn is part of their subsistence. The implication is that either population decreases or monetary wage increases, which means less people will be hired and industry will have to decrease. The home market shrinks. In the long run, the whole market and consumption of corn will decrease. Not good.

Fine, but a higher corn price means higher profits for farmers. Wrong again, Smith tells. The bounty does not affect the real price of corn, just the nominal one. What the bounty does is to decrease the real value of silver because corn regulates the price of all domestic commodities, the nominal price of labor, the nominal price of all the rude produce of land, and all materials used in manufacture. But if the value of silver decreases because of the discovery of new mines, the only thing that happens is that service of plate (silverware) will become cheaper. Everything else will stay the same.

But if the value of silver decreases only in a country, due to some peculiar situation of that country, that country will become poorer, not richer. It will face an increase in money prices and a decrease in industry. Spain and Portugal are examples of this. They want to prevent gold and silver from leaving the counties. They use taxes and prohibitions. Smugglers export them anyway. When a dam is full, the extra water must overflow. Smith explains that the water may be deeper behind the dam head than in front of it: Spain and Portugal have lots of plate in their homes. Silver is very cheap there, while everything else is expensive, which discourages agriculture and industry. If they removed the taxes and prohibitions to export gold and silver, the quantity of gold and silver at home would decrease, it would increase abroad, and the value of the metals would level.

The bounty on corn is as absurd as this policy in Spain and Portugal. It makes corn, and everything else, expensive at home and cheaper abroad. The bounty increases the nominal, but not the real, price of corn; it augments only the quantity of silver it exchanges for and discourages manufacture without any considerable service to the farmers or landlords. It gives only a little bit more money to farmers and landlords, but the value of that money is lower, so it makes little difference.

So who benefits from it, if the domestic population does not, and not even the farmers do? For Smith, the bounty does benefit one set of men: the corn merchants and the exporters and importers of corn. In years of plenty, they export more than otherwise. And in years of scarcity they import more than otherwise. In addition, the price is now higher because of the induced scarcity. It is not by accident that these men are the most zealous to maintain and renew bounties.

But also the country gentlemen support bounties. Why, if they do not benefit from them? According to Smith, they want to imitate the merchants: merchants want high import duties on foreign corn and bounties, a monopoly of the home market, and the market not to be overstocked. So the country gentlemen want to support an increase in the real value of corn, as if it was wool. But they do not understand that it is the nominal value of corn that increases, not the real one. The real value stays the same because corn is corn. The real value of corn is the quantity of labor that it can support. Money price cannot alter it.

If one really wants to increase production, Smith claims, then the bounties should be placed on production, not on exports. Bounties on production create only one tax, the one to pay for the bounty. The price in the home market will then drop (rather than increase, as in the case of bounties on exports), so in this case it is true that the lower price in part repays the tax. But, interestingly enough, we do not see bounties on production. Why? For Smith it is because it is not in the interests of the merchants and manufacturers to oversupply their market and have a lower price for the goods they sell. Bounties on exports instead undersupply the home market so that the price of the goods increases.

One could claim that there are some types of bounties on production, but this is not quite so, according to Smith.

There is a production bounty for fishing herrings and whales. But "our vessels are fit out for the sole purpose of catching not the fish but the bounty". The bounties encourage adventurers to go into businesses they do not understand. Their negligence causes losses greater than the gains from the bounties.

There are also premiums to artists or manufacturers that excel in what they do. But these premiums are different from bounties. They encourage extraordinary dexterity and emulation and they cost very little money.

Smith concludes that it is seldom reasonable to tax the great body of industry to support some particular manufacture. But it happens in prosperous times. In today's words, great folly is a luxury good.

A bounty may be justified only if the manufacture is needed for national defense, say, to support the export of British sail-cloth and British gun powder. Here, again, Smith is willing to give defense priority over trade.

DIGRESSION CONCERNING THE CORN TRADE AND CORN LAWS

The digression on Corn Laws is a sort of case study that exemplifies the analysis of the chapter and of the Book: some interests align with the interest of society, others do not. Avoiding putting obstacles on the path of the interests that align with society's interests promotes growth. Supporting interests that are opposite to society's does not.

Smith starts by stating that there are four kinds of corn merchants: the inland dealer, the importer for home consumption, the exporter of home produce, and the carrying trade dealer. With the exception of the merchant exporters, whose interest is the opposite of the interest of the majority of people, the interest of the other merchants is in line with the interest of society.

The interest of the domestic trader aligns with the interest of the majority of the people. He raises the price of corn as high as the scarcity of the season warrants it. This discourages consumption, so that it is possible to save for times of scarcity. Without intending to meet the interest of the people, but only his own, Smith says, he behaves like a prudent master of ship, preventing a famine. Should he be too avaricious, the merchant would lose out. He would have corn left over at the start of the new season when the price drops so he would have to undersell it. But if he keeps the price too low, there will not be enough later. He not only loses profits, but the chance of famine increases.

Why do we have famine, then? Not because of the corn producers. In Smith's time, it is difficult to create an extensive monopoly for corn. Corn producers are many and dispersed. They cannot easily collude. Not even the inland dealers can. As we just saw, inland dealers are never the cause of high prices of corn. Real scarcity, deriving from wars or bad weather, is the cause of high corn prices. And if the government orders to sell corn at a "reasonable price" either too little corn comes to market, causing famine, or too much corn comes to market, selling out soon, also causing famine. Thus, Smith says that the only source of famine is the violence of government, not inland dealers.

Yet, people believe that it is the avarice of corn merchants that causes famine. So corn merchants become the object of hate and indignation. They can even be in danger of ruin, having their warehouses plundered or destroyed by violence. But the years of scarcity are the only times in which they can make a profit. In regular years, they face losses from the perishability of corn and from the frequent fluctuations in its price. Add the popular odium against them, and very few people want to do this job. Remember from Book I, Chapter X that a job with bad reputation requires higher wages to compensate for it? Here we have a problem because there is bad reputation and the higher compensation is threatened away.

The ancient policies of Europe encouraged this hate against corn merchants, believing it would be cheaper to buy corn from farmers directly than through corn dealers, and called for the elimination of the middle men. For Smith, this was a bad idea because now farmers are forced to be corn merchants too. First, as a corn merchant, he cannot sell any cheaper than any other corn merchants. Second, he now needs to use his capital in different ways. Forcing farmers to be corn merchants is a violation of natural liberty, and thus unjust. Not surprisingly, it is also inefficient. For Smith, the law ought always to trust people with the care of their interest because with their local knowledge they generally are better judges of it than the legislator. This focus on local knowledge, also present among other places in the invisible hand passage, will find a place a couple of centuries later in particular in the works of F. A. Hayek.

Smith explains that when scarcity is real, it is better to spread the inconvenience over time. It is in the interest of the merchant to do so, and to do so as smoothly as possible. Nobody has the same interest, the same knowledge, and the same ability than the corn merchant. This is why corn trade ought to be left free.

For Smith, the popular fear that merchants are doing harm to society is the same as the popular fear of witchcraft: the law ending the prosecution of witchcraft put an end to the power of gratifying one's malice by accusing a neighbor of an imaginary crime. The same would be true for laws freeing the trade of corn.

The second branch of corn trade is the one of the importers of foreign corn for home consumption. These importers contribute to the domestic supply and thus benefit the great body of the people. They lower the average money price of corn, but not the real value of corn that, as we are reminded, is the quantity of labor that corn is capable of maintaining.

The third branch of corn trade is the one of the exporters of corn for foreign consumption. They contribute only indirectly to an abundant domestic supply. If a farmer cannot export his surplus, he will make sure not to have a surplus, so he will not produce much. Prohibitions to export therefore limit improvement.

But, for Smith, the problem with the merchant exporters is that their interest is the opposite of the interest of society. If there is scarcity of corn at home and famine abroad, the price of corn abroad will be higher than the one at home. So exporters have incentives to sell abroad, increasing the chance of famine at home. The problem would not necessarily arise if all countries would have free trade of corn. They would be like provinces of a great empire. The freedom of inland trade would be the best palliative against high prices of corn and the most effective prevention against famine. But freedom of corn trade is everywhere restricted, aggravating the misfortunes of high prices and the dreadful calamity of famine.

Interestingly enough, like the Neapolitan thinker Ferdinando Galiani (1728–1787) before him, Smith does not offer absolute principles to follow regardless of local circumstances. Smith sees that in small countries, such as Switzerland or in Italy, having a unilateral freedom of trade can be quite dangerous. If there are high prices at home and a famine abroad, corn may leave the home market making things worse at home. There, it may therefore be inevitable to limit corn exports. But this does not hold in a large country, such as France or Britain. Only in case of "the most urgent necessity" it may be justifiable to prevent farmers from sending goods to the best market, and to sacrifice the laws of justice.

But in a sense, for Smith, Corn Laws are like laws on religion. The government "must yield to prejudices to preserve public tranquility".

The fourth branch of corn trade is the one of carrying trade merchants, who import corn to export it again. They contribute to an abundant domestic supply, even if unintentionally. If a merchant can save the expense of loading and unloading his ships, he takes that opportunity. So if the opportunity comes, he sells at home, rather than exports his goods. The home country of a carrying trade is indeed a storehouse for the supply of other countries, and there are always many merchandises as explained earlier in Book IV. There, the money price of corn, but not its value, will be low.

Carrying trade of corn is de facto prohibited in Britain. Some claim that this prohibition is the cause of Britain's great growth. But, Smith corrects, the improvements of Great Britain are not caused by the Corn Laws. Again, we need to pay attention at what we see as correlation is not causation. The reason for the great improvement of Britain lays exclusively in "the security of laws, that each man can enjoy the fruits of his labor". Smith, who is usually very cautious and qualifies his statements, here drops all hesitations:

> that alone [the security of laws] makes any country flourish, notwith-standing other absurd regulations of commerce. The natural effort of each individual to better his condition, and the freedom and security to do so, are so powerful a principle that alone, without assistance, carry society to wealth and prosperity, and surmount the hundreds of impediments of the folly of human laws which encroach freedom and diminish security.
>
> (paragraph 42)

Correlation is not causation, Smith again seems to warn his readers. Prosperity came at the same time as the Corn Laws, but it came at the same time as national debt too. Nobody, though, says that national debt is the cause of prosperity of Britain. Nobody should dare say that the Corn Laws are the cause of its prosperity either.

Can we test this? Do we have a counterexample? Yes. Spain and Portugal have bounties too. But only Britain is rich. Spain and Portugal are the most beggarly countries in Europe. Why? Because they do not have good laws to counterbalance the bad effects of bad policies. Their civil and ecclesiastical governments do not offer general liberty and security of the people.

BOOK IV, CHAPTER VI: OF TREATIES OF COMMERCE

This short chapter is titled of treaties of commerce, but it is more about seigniorage, the tax on coining precious metals, than treaties. Smith admits it is oddly placed. It could have been inserted into the discussion on money. But because he claims the policy on seigniorage is part of the mercantilist scheme, he thinks better to put it in Book IV, which directly deals with mercantilism about mercantilism.

The connection between treaties and seigniorage is part of the rhetoric supporting the treaties. Allegedly, treaties give a country the needed gold and silver. Instead, seigniorage would do a better job in keeping gold and silver in the country, Smith claims.

A treaty permits trade of, or exempts from duties, goods of a specific country, causing a more extensive market, but only for the goods of that specific country, or a more advantageous market, but through a monopoly and higher prices. It grants a monopoly against itself in the hope that the balance of trade would become more favorable, so that more gold would come into a country.

Not surprisingly by now, we hear that merchants are better off, but the country worse off. The more gold comes in from one country, the less it comes in from other countries. We look at what we see, and do not think about what we do not see. But, as we know, the quantity supplied of precious metals cannot exceed the quantity demanded. If it does, gold goes abroad, purchasing things that are in demand. So for example, the treaty Britain has with Portugal makes Britain worse off because it forces her to produce for Portugal, get money from it, and then buy from other countries the products Britain wants. A direct foreign trade is for Smith always more advantageous. So again, merchants are able to capture the government to their favor, through treaties, using the rhetoric that what is good for them is good for the country, even if it is not.

To the ones who worry that if Britain does not trade with Portugal, which has a great deal of gold from its Brazilian colonial trade, Britain would not have enough gold, Smith answers: false. Importing gold is not useful to increase the amount of plate or coins in Britain. Plate and coins come mostly from melting down old plate and old coins. This is why seigniorage is relevant here.

If there is no tax or fee on melting down coins, people will melt their old coins for new coins. But if there is seigniorage, coined gold will be more valuable than uncoined gold because one needs to pay a fee every time it melts gold into coin and vice versa. Seigniorage, therefore, diminishes profit from melting down coins. So when money is received by tale (at face value), not by weight, seigniorage is the most effective way to prevent melting of coins into bullion, that is, seigniorage is the most effective way to decrease the exports of gold. One does not need a treaty of commerce.

Why does England not have seigniorage then? According to Smith, the Bank of England is in constant need to melt bullion into coins to replenish its coffers. It is for its interest that coinage is done at the expense of the government. The mint cost is irrelevant to the government but significant for the Bank. If there is no seigniorage, the government faces the expense of the mint and receives no revenue. For Smith, what the Bank of England does not understand is that nobody benefits from it.

FURTHER READINGS

Anderson, Gary M., William F. Shughart II, and Robert D. Tollison. 1985. Adam Smith in the Customhouse. *Journal of Political Economy* 93.4: 740–759.

Coats, A. W. 1975. "Adam Smith and the Mercantile System", in *Essays on Adam Smith*, ed. Andrew Skinner, T. Wilson Oxford: Clarendon.

Coleman, David C. 1988. "Adam Smith, Businessmen, and the Mercantile System in England". *History of European Ideas* 9.2: 161–170.

Samuels, Warren. 2011. *Erasing the Invisible Hand: Essays on an Elusive and Missed Concept in Economics*. New York: Cambridge University Press.

Skinner, Andrew. 2009. "The Mercantile System", in *Elgar Companion to Adam Smith*, ed. Jeffrey Young. Cheltenham and Northampton: Edward Elgar. 261–276.

West, Edwin. 1990. *Adam Smith and Modern Economics: From Market Behavior to Public Choice*. Brookfield, VT: Edward Elgar.

9

BOOK IV, CHAPTERS VII–IX

BOOK IV, CHAPTER VII: OF COLONIES

PART FIRST: OF THE MOTIVES FOR ESTABLISHING NEW COLONIES

Here Smith describes the last and possibly most dangerous tool merchants and manufacturers use to increase their own profits: building an empire through colonization.

The eighteenth century is not unique in having countries with colonial ambition, Smith tells us. Ancient societies had colonies too. But they were different and created for different purposes.

In ancient Greece, when the population of a city state expanded too much, the city state would look for new territories to relocate the extra people, forming a colony. The colonies were the children of their motherland, but they were more like emancipated children, according to Smith. The motherland did not have any claim of direct jurisdiction over the new colonies.

Ancient Rome also had colonies. There, colonization policies started as a way to reduce potential tensions that wealth inequality caused. In Rome, only the wealthy had land. Slaves would do most jobs. So the poor freemen had nothing to live on and would often protest, demanding some land. The rich and powerful thought that sending the poor away to form new colonies in new dominions would be a good way to satisfy them, with an additional side benefit: the colonies would form garrisons in the newly conquered land. The Roman colonies were different from Greek colonies. Even the origins of the names differed: for the Romans, colony derives from *plantation*, while for the Greek from *separate dwelling*. Yet, in both cases, colonies originated from necessity and utility.

Necessity and utility do not explain the European colonies in America and the West Indies. For Smith, avidity is the explanation. Here is how.

Venice in the fourteenth to fifteenth century had almost a monopoly trade with the East Indies. That monopoly, like all monopolies, gave Venice great profits. Those great profits, like all great profits, attracted the avid interest of others. Rather than going east by land, why not try to go by sea? The Portuguese thought they could circumnavigate Africa. And indeed in 1497 Vasco de Gama arrived in Indostan via the Cape of Good Hope.

But in the meantime, Christopher Columbus convinced Spain to get to the East via the West. And in 1492 he arrived in some uncultivated lands, covered in woods, and inhabited by some "naked and miserable savages". The place looked nothing like Marco Polo's descriptions. But Columbus refused to believe that he was not in Indostan.

In Smith's account, Columbus did not care what these lands were; Columbus wanted to show them off as important. The problem was that there were no animals or vegetation to show off, just iguanas and cotton. Because he could not find any impressive animals or vegetables, Columbus started to look for minerals. He did not find much of them either, just some bits of gold on some indigenous clothing.

Yet, he returned to Spain in triumphant honors, claiming he found inexhaustible sources of wealth. In what seems a sarcastic tone, Smith describes how Columbus showed off in solemn processions some small gold bracelets stolen from the native people, a few bales of cotton, some colorful birds, some curiosities, and some "natives of singular color". His inflated descriptions made Spain want to conquer these lands. As an added bonus, the indigenous people were obviously unable to defend themselves. So, with the excuse to convert them to Christianity, the Spaniards hid the real motive of this "unjust project": looking for gold.

To convince the crown of the greatness of his discovery, Columbus offered the crown half of the gold he found. Plundering defenseless people makes it easy to pay for this high tax. But after the natives were stripped from all they had (in 6–8 years), the Spaniards had to dig for gold, so they were no longer able to pay for the tax. And so for Smith, this is how the tax on gold had to be reduced to 1/20, and the one on silver to 1/10.

Smith's description of the Spaniards is not flattering. They found little gold. They exaggerated their reports. Their avidity became so inflamed that they went off in search for gold, even if there is nothing more ruinous than searching for new mines. They expected to find El Dorado even if mining is the most disadvantageous gamble. Mining does not replace capital; it absorbs both it and the profit. It is just the absurd confidence that almost all men have in their own good fortune that drives them to think that they can find veins of gold and silver as abundant as the veins of iron or lead. This is not something that sober reasoning would conclude, according to Smith. But it is an absurd idea dictated by human avidity. Sober reasoning would also have made them realize that gold and silver are valuable because they are scarce. Finding El Dorado would mean a decrease in the value of gold and silver. Avidity of immense riches of gold and silver is neither sober nor rational, Smith concludes.

Note how here again Smith seems to differentiate between the sober and prudent desire to make a living and earn well-deserved profits or wages, with this avid ambition of immense riches caused by dreams of gold. We all desire to better our conditions, but we ought to be wary of what shines too much and feeds our delusions. It is ruinous.

Note also how negatively we can read the description of Columbus. He is not described as a hero, but as a villain, greedy and overly ambitious, willing to lie and to commit the vilest injustices to bring glory to himself.

Eventually, Smith continues, abundant gold was found in Mexico and Peru. But that was 30 to 40 years *after* Columbus. It took more than a hundred years to find gold and diamonds in Brazil. In the English, French, Dutch, and Danish colonies no gold was found during Smith's life.

Smith concludes this part in what seems a lapidary way: this part of history is an accident. By accident, the discovery of the West happened unforeseeably trying to go East. Against all odds and all reasonable expectations, a project of gold and silver, with a course of accidents, which no human wisdom could foresee, was more successful than expected. Like in Book III, history is not made by human designs or by kings. A series of accidents and of deluded people in search for vain distinctions is what brings about historical changes.

PART SECOND: CAUSES OF THE PROSPERITY OF THE NEW COLONIES

So, European countries now have colonies in America, Africa, and in both the East and West Indies. Are these colonized places better off or worse off? This is not an easy question to answer. Smith is a British subject after all, a subject of one of the countries whose colonies he describes. Smith's perspective needs to be kept in mind. Yet, he is well aware of the irreparable damage done to the colonized population. Being either an accusation against the vicious injustices per se, or against the mercantile policies that caused those injustices, or against the British Empire, Smith's analysis reflects the mixed blessing of markets extended in brutally unjust ways.

If a land is empty, or if it is scarcely inhabited, Smith claims, it is easy to colonize it because there are no opposing forces. The colony will grow faster than any other land because the colonists carry with them their agricultural and institutional knowledge (which Smith correctly or not deems superior to the one of the indigenous "savages") and also their habits of subordination, regular government, the system of laws, and regular administration of justice. This speeds up the otherwise slow process of development.

Because of the low original population, there is more land than one can use. The farmer needs to pay no rent and little taxes. Superiors have to treat inferiors with more humanity and generosity, if there is no slavery, because of the disproportion between the abundance of land and the scarcity of people. They need to hire and pay labor well. The laborer will earn enough to leave and become a landowner. And the liberal reward of labor will encourage marriage, and children, so population grows fast. This was the case for Greece.

Rome was different. Its provinces were fully inhabited before colonization. There was little land for the colonists, and, differently from Greece, there was dependency on the motherland.

The European colonies are in between, Smith claims. They had scarcely populated land, like Greece, and dependency, like Rome, but were way far away, which made them more independent from their motherland, again like Greece. This combination of abundant land and independence explains their progress.

Spain kept closed ties to its colonies because of their gold and silver. For Smith, Mexico and Peru, in spite of the cruel destruction of the natives, are now more populous than they have ever been before. Portugal did not pay too much attention to Brazil because it seemed it had no gold. Brazil prospered. It is the colony with the most Europeans in it. The Danish St. Thomas and Santa Cruz were under the government of an exclusive company with the sole right to buy and sell there. The company could and did oppress. The government of an exclusive company of merchants is the worst of all governments. Yet, it was not able to stop progress; it just significantly slowed it down.

Of all colonies, the North American British colonies experienced the most rapid progress. There was plenty of good land and there was liberty for colonists to manage their own affairs. Both are important factors. But Smith tells us that free institutions are the most important. The land is not necessarily better than the land of the colonies of France and Spain, but the political institutions of the English colonies are more favorable to improvement and cultivation of land.

First of all, according to Smith, colonists can own only as much land as they can improve, there is no primogeniture, and taxes are moderate, so that people can save and invest in improvements. Their taxes are moderate because they have few expenses. Their government is modest and, a key factor, they do not have to pay for their own defense: Britain does. This is quite different from Spain and Portugal, which derive their power from taxing their colonies and have vain and expensive habits.

The British North American colonies also enjoy a larger market than other countries because, in Smith's account, even if monopolized, it is less monopolized than other countries.

So, Smith says there are three different ways to deal with colonial trade.

One is to give the whole commerce of the colonies to an exclusive company. Its interest is to sell at a high price and to buy at a low price. It will buy no more than what it can sell at a high price. Holland, Denmark, France, and Portugal adopted this kind of monopoly.

Another is to give the whole colonial trade to an exclusive port of the mother country. The port is open to all domestic merchants who pay a very costly license to operate there. The profits remain "exorbitant and oppressive", as in Spain and Portugal.

The final way is to let trade be free to all. Competition prevents exorbitant profits. So in France and Britain there are still high profits, but they are not exorbitant. In the case of Britain, Smith tells us, only a list of some commodities is confined to the home market: the so-called enumerated commodities. The non-enumerated commodities can be exported anywhere, even if only on British ships or in ships with a majority of British sailors. But this is limited to raw materials, not to manufactures.

For Smith, the colonies are lucky, in a sense, because their land is so cheap and their labor is so expensive that they can still be better off importing manufactures rather than trying to produce them themselves. But ... the advisors for regulations of colonial trade are the merchants. Not surprising, for Smith, their interest is considered more important than that of the colonists and of the mother country. British merchants and manufacturers convinced the legislature to impose high duties to prevent refined manufactures in the colonies.

Here again Smith does not seem to hold punches against the mercantile interests: to prohibit from making all they can from their own produce or from using their capital the way they think most advantageous is a manifest violation of the most sacred right of mankind. The interest of the colonies is sacrificed to the interest of the merchants. We can note the common pattern in Smith's analysis: it is unjust and it is inefficient.

Despite this monopoly, for Smith, Great Britain is the least illiberal with colonies compared to other countries. With the exception of foreign trade, the colonies manage their own affairs, secured like at home by an assembly of representatives, which also keeps in check the executive power. So, according to Smith, the meanest and most obnoxious colonist, as long as he obeys the law, has nothing to fear from the resentment of the government or of the civil and military officer. In addition, the colonies do not have hereditary nobility. There are old colonial families that are more respected, of course, but they do not have more privileges than others. In a sense, there is more equality among colonists than among the inhabitants of the mother country. They are more republican.

Thus, Smith claims, Britain is the only country to give perfect security to its distant provinces. Spain, Portugal, and France have a more absolute government. There may be more freedom in the capital city because the sovereign keeps the inferior officers in check. But in the distant provinces, away from the sovereign's sight, the inferior officers can become tyrant – with a possible exception: slavery.

Here Smith launches a counterintuitive argument: an arbitrary government is better for slaves than the government in a free country. With an arbitrary government, a magistrate can interfere with the private property of a master, defending the slaves. In a free country, the master is often a member of the colony assembly, so the magistrate does not dare go against him to protect the slave. This is another acute Public Choice analysis and criticism of British slavery. Furthermore, when the magistrate protects a slave, the slave gains some respect in the eyes of his master. The master will treat the slave more gently. In his turn, the slave will be more faithful and useful. This is why among the sugar colonies, where the sugar production is entirely in the hands of slaves, the French ones are the most prosperous. It is because of their good management of slaves. The British sugar colonies prosper too, but that is because of the great riches of Britain, not because of the good conduct of its colonists toward their slaves.

Here again, Smith ends the section with what sound like lapidary accusations: it was folly and injustice that motivated the establishment of the European colonies. The hunt for gold caused injustices for the harmless natives of the colonized lands, who, rather than injuring Europeans, welcomed them with kindness and hospitality. "It was not the wisdom and policy but the disorder and injustice of the European government which peopled and cultivated America".

Europe contributed with one thing – and one thing only – to the current prosperity of the colonies: "it bread and formed the men capable of achieving such great actions. The education and great views of their founders owe their greatness to scarce anything else".

PART THIRD: OF THE ADVANTAGES WHICH EUROPE HAS DERIVED FROM THE DISCOVERY OF AMERICA AND FROM THE PASSAGE TO THE EAST INDIES BY THE CAPE OF GOOD HOPE

Having established that the only benefits the colonies get from Europe is the education of their leaders, what are the benefits that Europe receives from the colonies, if any?

There are benefits of two kinds, according to Smith: general benefits and benefits specific to each country.

The general benefits, those that all countries share, are the increased enjoyment from having a larger variety of goods to consume, and the increase in industry due to a larger market for their products.

One country does not need to directly trade with the colonies to enjoy these benefits. Poland and Hungary do not send anything to America. Yet, they consume sugar, chocolate, and tobacco. They send their products to countries that will then send colonial products to them. Actually, a country does not need to even ever consume a colonial product to benefit from colony trade, Smith claims. As other countries do trade, directly or indirectly with the colonies, they become wealthier and consume more of everything, including the products of countries that do not consume colonial products.

Yet, monopoly trade, with its higher prices, will reduce both industry and enjoyment. Monopoly is a dead weight.

For Smith, it is, therefore, important to distinguish between colony trade and monopoly trade. Colony trade is always beneficial. Monopoly trade is always hurtful. In the case of the American colonies, it just happened that the benefits are much larger than the damages done by its monopolization. Again Smith, implicitly, seems to tell us to analyze with care what we see and to be careful between correlation and causation. Explicitly, he tells us that colony trade is beneficial not because of its monopoly, but despite its monopoly.

As a matter of fact, Smith tells us, we cannot take for granted that the benefits of colonial trade will always overcome the damages its monopoly causes. This is true for Britain. But that is because Britain has comparatively more liberty of trade, and most importantly, it has an equal and impartial administration of justice, where "the rights of the meanest subject" are as respected as the rights of the greatest. And where every man can safely have the fruits of his labor, which is the greatest and most effective way to increase industry. Things are different in Spain and Portugal. Their irregular and partial administration of justice protects the rich and powerful debtors from the injured creditors, decreasing, if not eliminating, the incentives to produce: Why produce if I am forced to sell to people who cannot pay? There, the damages of monopoly are more than the benefits of trade.

Smith continues with his taxonomy. The benefits specific to each country are divided into benefits that every empire receives, such as military force and revenue, and into benefits specific to the American empires, such as exclusive trade.

For Smith, an empire should benefit from its colonies because the colonies should increase its military force and its revenue. But it does not work this way. Not for the American colonies, at least. Only the colonies of Spain and Portugal contribute to the revenue of the mother countries. No colony contributes to the military force of the mother country. None of the colonies contribute even to cover the expenses of their own defense! It is always the mother country that has to face the defense bill. The American colonies therefore turned out to be a weakness, not a strength, for the countries in Europe. So much so that Smith claims that the unjust oppression of other countries falls back on the head of the oppressor crushing them.

The exclusive trade mother countries have with their colonies could be seen as the only benefit European countries may receive. But for Smith, it is a peculiar benefit because it is achieved by depressing others, rather than rising above others. It is not a benefit at all. For example, tobacco is received exclusively in Britain, so it has a high monopoly price. Britain then sells it to France at an even higher price. Free trade would allow lower prices for everybody. Not surprisingly, the higher monopoly prices of domestic products induce foreign merchants to undersell domestic merchants in all other markets. Not surprisingly, merchants complain. But they complain about high labor costs, not about their higher profits! They complain about the gains of others, not their own gains.

Another problem that Smith identifies is that the monopoly of the colony trade, with the great profits it generates, attracts capital in the colony trade away from other activities. At first sight, this seems great, to the undiscerning eye blinded with ambition. But every time Smith tells us "at first sight", we know to expect a problem. Indeed, this means that eventually profits in the colony trade will decrease (more capital poured in), but that profits elsewhere will increase (less capital available). Eventually they will equalize, but at a level higher than otherwise.

It is not an accident that since the establishment of the Navigation Act, trade with the colonies increased while trade with Europe decreased. One could object that after the introduction of the Navigation Act, profits decreased. True, Smith says, but they would have decreased even more without this monopoly.

We know from earlier, and Smith reminds us, that the mercantile capital naturally prefers to stay close to home, rather than going far, everything else equal. But if distant employments have high enough profits, capital will go there. Without laws, private interests and passions will naturally distribute capital in line with the interest of society. Regulation will derange that natural and most beneficial distribution of capital, Smith repeats.

The high profits of colonial trade thus force capital into channels in which it would not otherwise go. Overall trade did not increase. It just changed direction. New colonies always have less capital than needed. Ergo the great profits. Borrowing from the motherland satisfies in part this high demand for capital. But this is not a good thing. The colonies are far away. It takes a long time to receive payments. Slow payments mean less investment.

For Smith, the monopoly of colonial trade broke the natural balance between all branches of industry. Now a big single channel replaces many smaller channels. This big channel decreases security. It is like putting all the eggs in one basket. A bad idea. The economy looks like "a sick body with some overgrown vital parts", Smith depicts. A small blockage in a great vein that is artificially swollen is very dangerous. If a small vein busts, not much happens. But, Smith says, if a big vein breaks, we can have "convulsions, apoplexy, and even death"! So people now look at a possible break of this great vein of colonial trade with more terror than they would look at the Spanish Armada.

The artificially higher profits have an additional fatal problem, according to Smith. They destroy the natural parsimony of merchants. Because the lower ranked people look up and imitate the rich, they also will become less parsimonious. Capital will gradually decrease, and with it, productive labor will decrease too. Smith asks rhetorically: Have the exorbitant profits of Lisbon or Cádiz increased the capital of Portugal or Spain? Look at Amsterdam instead to see the difference.

So Smith accuses the monopoly of colony trade to be "mean and malicious", as it decreases everybody's industry. It benefits only a group of men at the expense of the general interest of the country. What today we call state capture is the problem: special interests capture the government. The empire is the "mean and malicious" product of special interests. "To found a great empire for the sole purpose of raising up a people of consumers is not a project fit for a nation of shopkeepers, it is the project fit for a nation whose government is influenced by shopkeepers. Such statesmen only would employ the blood and treasure of fellow citizens to maintain such empire". And Smith is not just saying "blood and treasure" for emphasis. All the recent wars have been fought to protect these monopolies. Even the very large naval force of Britain was built to guard against smuggling.

"The maintenance of monopoly is the sole and end of purpose" of the empire. The provinces have not contributed to either the revenue or the defense of it. They are a net loss for Britain. So much so that Britain would be better off without them and should voluntarily give them up. Yes, giving up the colonies is the best thing for Britain to do. It would immediately decrease its expenses. It would create a good friend with whom to have good terms in commerce and good alliances in wars. Unfortunately, Smith is well aware, this is unrealistic. It is contrary to the private interests of too many. It mortifies the pride of the nation, and it eliminates a place from which wealth and distinction is derived. Too bad.

Okay then, if it is not politically feasible to voluntarily give independence to the colonies, how about taxing them? Smith says that taxes could be imposed by their own assembly or by the British Parliament. It is unrealistic to expect that their own assembly will vote to increase taxes for the empire. They cannot even raise enough to pay for their own civil and military establishment. Even in Britain it was difficult to increase taxes. It was possible only by distributing offices. But the colonies are too far to manage. It would not work. And their distance is also an impediment to the knowledge of the needs of the empire.

They could be taxed by requisition then, meaning the British Parliament tells them how much it wants, and they can come up with the amount in the way they see fit, Smith suggests. But for Smith, this also is not going to work, because if Britain taxes its provinces without their consent, the provinces assembly loses importance.

Note that the incentives structure of Smith's analysis is based on psychological just as much as material motivations. Pride plays a fundamental role in human actions even if, as we would consider today, irrationally so. For Smith, men want to manage their own affairs because it makes them feel important. The key to a stable government is to preserve their feeling of importance. Smith is convinced that the colonists are so ambitious that they would draw their swords to defend their own importance. Not the most flattering description, but accurate.

No voluntary giving up, no taxation by requisition; is there another possible way to alleviate the burden the colonies cause Britain? Yes, Smith suggests. Give them representation in the British Parliament. By allowing representation, you can tax them. And, most importantly, you give them a new way to feel important. The presumptuous hope in their good fortune, which as we know every man in relatively good health has, and these colonists seem to have even more, will delude them into thinking that they can win great prizes in the lottery of British politics, Smith claims. They will feel so very important, much more than any subject of Europe. Smith believes that even now all of them, from shopkeepers to tradesmen and attorneys, think of themselves as statesmen and legislators, flattering themselves that they will become the greatest and most formidable country ever. If you do not give them something to be more ambitious with, they will die to defend their status.

For Smith, Britain flatters itself thinking it can sedate them by force, but their feeling of importance is too big to tame. Unless there is a union (like the one between England and Scotland), they will fight against the best of the mother countries.

A complete union with the colonies is thus Smith's most plausible solution. For this solution he does not think there are impossible problems, like the other two options. There are just some (insurmountable?) prejudices. Smith's union proposal is radical. And it gets even more radical.

Here is how Smith's explains it. The American colonies grow so much and so fast that, within a century or so, they will produce more than Britain, which means that their tax revenue will be more than Britain's. And because the seat of the empire tends to move to the part of the empire that contributes the most to it, the seat of the empire may very well move to America within a century or so after this union. How is that as a selling point to the British people?

Before describing the consequences of the presence of exclusive companies, such as the East Indies Company, Smith offers yet another condemnation of the modern colonization process: the natives got the short end of the stick; he says, "all benefits got lost in their dreadful misfortunes". The Europeans were able to create such empires, not because of anything intrinsic in their policies, but because of accidental circumstances. They happened to find natives who were militarily much weaker than them, which enabled the Europeans "to commit with impunity every sort of injustice". This may sound either like an apology for European powers, or as a condemnation of their arrogance in claiming greatness.

Now Smith's attention turns toward the East. The East Indies trade is cursed with exclusive companies. The typical features of the exclusive companies are their extraordinary waste, frauds, and abuses. Combine them with the extraordinary profits they manage to extract, and you have prices much higher than otherwise. This is one of the reasons why exclusive companies are always harmful.

The other reason why, according to Smith, they are harmful is that they derail capital from its proper course. Large parts of a country's capital could have been used in ways more suitable to the county's own circumstances rather than in long-distance trade. Instead, poor countries use more capital than they otherwise would and rich countries use less. Poor countries, like Sweden and Denmark would not have sent as many ships to the East Indies or any at all. Rich counties like Holland would have sent more, had there been freer trade.

The exclusive companies in the East Indies, combined with the fact that the indigenous population was not as defenseless as the one in America, are the explanation for the little progress we see in the East Indies, according to Smith. Africa is a bit better because it had more defenseless people and more trade with ships stopping by.

Smith declares that the exclusive companies are dreadful to both the home country and the colonies. Want proof? Look at the production of spices in the Dutch islands, and of opium in Bengal. If production exceeds what keeps Europe's high price, it is burnt. By destroying the extra, they make sure it will not be smuggled to Europe. The same happens with population. Wages are kept so low as to maintain only the number of people needed to supply the garrisons. Remember Smith's description of the hundreds of thousands of yearly deaths by starvation in Bengal in Book I?

Smith continues by claiming that the government of an exclusive company is a government subservient to the interest of monopoly. It is not by chance that the council of merchants can only command obedience with military force; it is a despotical government. Vain are the requests of moderation coming from the home country. "Nothing is more foolish than to expect the clerks at ten thousand miles distance and out of sight to follow orders not to make a fortune".

Look at it in this way, Smith tells us. The interest of the sovereign is in line with the interest of country, while the interest of the merchants is the opposite. If a sovereign wants to increase his revenue, he needs to increase the revenue of his people, which means to increase their produce, which in its turn means to decrease monopolies. An exclusive company acts as a sovereign but cannot think as a sovereign. It only thinks: buy cheap, sell high to increase profits; keep competitors out; and decrease production to raise prices high enough to have exorbitant profits. An exclusive company prefers temporary profits to permanent revenue.

Why? Because, for Smith, masters of countries are different from servants. A country belongs to its master, so a master has interest in it. If he oppresses it, it is out of ignorance: he does not understand his interest well enough. But the country does not belong to the servants. Their interest is, therefore, different. Even with perfect knowledge, they would have no incentives to stop its oppression. Think of the exclusive company as a government in which each member of the administration will leave, and will leave carrying his fortune away with him, Smith says. When they leave, they are, therefore, completely indifferent to the circumstance of the country, as if the whole country would be swallowed by an earthquake.

This image is powerful enough to describe the blunt indifference of the East Indies Company members. It becomes even more devastating when compared to what Smith writes about the possibility of a country being destroyed by an earthquake in his *Theory of Moral Sentiments*. In that book, he tells us that we care more about our little finger than about the destruction of a faraway country like China. If we know that we are going to lose our little finger tomorrow, we would not be able to sleep at night. But if we know that the entire population of China would be swallowed by an earthquake, we would snore placidly though the night. Yet, if asked to let the whole population of China die to save our little finger, we would not do it. We would not let China be swallowed by an earthquake. Nobody would. "Human nature startles with horror at the thought, and the world, in its greatest depravity and corruption, never produced such a villain as could be capable of entertaining it" (TMS III.3.4). With the exceptions of the people working in the exclusive companies! They would save their finger and impassibly let China be swallowed by an earthquake.

Yet, Smith cautions, as later on Public Choice scholars would also do, that we need to differentiate between people and incentives. People are all the same. A sovereign is as good or as bad as a clerk working in the East India Company. The destructive results of exclusive companies are not the results of bad people working in them. It is not that replacing bad people with good people would make a difference. All people are equally good or bad. Those clerks are just like you and me. That destruction comes from the perverse incentives that that institution generates. If you or I would work for the East India Company we would also walk away from our post, with our enormous fortune, without looking back to the devastating destruction we left behind. Human homogeneity remains. Institutional incentives are what matters.

BOOK IV, CHAPTER VIII: CONCLUSION OF THE MERCANTILE SYSTEM

This relatively short chapter summarizes Smith's concerns and accusations against the mercantile system. It lists several of the actual trade restrictions and their ferocious penalties, without holding back that they all come from the avidity of the private interests of merchants and manufacturers who are able "to extort" protection from the legislature.

These prohibitions and enormous duties not only are ineffective to prevent exports but also they are a violation of justice. The great price difference between the domestic and foreign markets is just a too strong to resist temptation for smugglers. With their exception, as well as the exception of the protected merchants and manufacturers, everybody would be better off with just a modest tax. It would give revenue to the sovereign and would save more burdensome taxes.

Smith points out that the prohibitions include also the one of movement of labor. Artificers are forbidden from leaving the country for fear that they would spread their knowledge to competitors abroad. This is a direct violation of their liberty. For Smith, their liberty is sacrificed to the futile interests of the merchants and manufacturers.

It is the merchants and manufacturers that can easily combine to gain monopolies because they are concentrated in urban centers. Most other professions have people dispersed in the territory making it impossible to collude. The consequences are unjust, Smith tells us over and over again: "To hurt in any degree the interest of any other order of citizens, for no other purpose but to promote that of some other, is evidently contrary to justice and equality of treatment which the sovereign owes to all his subjects".

This is even more absurd if we think, as Smith tells us, that consumption is the sole end and purpose of production. The interest of producers should be supported only insofar as it supports the interests of consumers. But the mercantile system, with its perverse avidity, reverses it. The interest of consumers is always sacrificed to the interest of producers, as if production was the sole end and purpose of industry and commerce. Which it is not.

Smith summarizes the conclusions of his previous chapters of Book IV: import restrictions benefit producers at the expense of consumers who have to pay higher prices. Bounties on exports benefit producers and hurt consumers who not only have to pay taxes for the bounty, but also have to pay a higher price because of the decrease in domestic supply due to the increased export. Treaties of commerce benefit producers who can sell with better terms in distant places, at the expense of consumers who are forced to buy more expensive and lower quality goods from those distant places rather than cheaper and better quality ones from closer places. Colonial management is the worst of all. "A great empire was established for the sole purpose of raising up a nation of consumers" obliged to buy from the mother country's producers. "For the sake of that little enhancement of price which this monopoly might afford our producers, the home-consumers have been burdened with the whole expence of maintaining and defending the empire".

Smith tells us again that "the cruelest of our revenue laws, I will adventure to affirm, are mild and gentle in comparison of some of those which the clamour of our merchants and manufacturers has extorted from the legislature, for the support of their absurd and oppressive monopolies. Like the laws of Draco, these laws may be said to be written in blood". He is not just offering a vivid image here. He explicitly accuses merchants and manufacturers to be solely responsible for the past two wars Britain fought. The wars' cost was human blood, and costs were much greater than the whole value of the colony trade.

The blame for the wastes and injustices of the mercantile system are unequivocally determined: "our merchants and manufacturers have been by far the principal architects".

BOOK IV, CHAPTER IX: OF THE AGRICULTURAL SYSTEMS, OR OF THOSE SYSTEMS OF POLITICAL OECONOMY, WHICH REPRESENT THE PRODUCE OF LAND AS EITHER THE SOLE OR THE PRINCIPAL SOURCE OF THE REVENUE AND WEALTH OF EVERY COUNTRY

In the last chapter of Book IV, Smith describes a theoretical system, which has never been put into practice, and therefore has never done any harm. This system is a reaction to the system that Colbert put into place in France. Colbert was a minister of Luis 14th. For Smith, Colbert fell into the trap of the mercantile system, and designed policies that gave extraordinary privileges to some industries and extraordinary restraints to others. In particular, in his attempts to promote the industries of the towns, he discouraged the one of the country. He wanted to offer cheap corn to the towns. He forbade the exports of grains, which, in conjunction with other restrictive regulations, ended up discouraging agriculture.

To counterbalance Colbert's actions, a group of French philosophers, led by Mr. Quesnai, articulated a system that ended up undervaluing the industries of towns.

In Smith's account, they thought that a society is divided into three classes: proprietors of land; farmers; and artificers, manufacturers, and merchants.

Whatever landlords spend to improve their land contributes to the annual produce of a country. Landlords are therefore a productive class. And to avoid giving incentives not to improve, their land should not be taxed until all its expenses are covered.

Farmers are also productive. They contribute to the produce of society by paying for the tools they use, including their seeds and cattle, and their annual expenses for the maintenance of their family, servants, and cattle and for the replacement of the wear and tear of their instruments of cultivation. Unless these two expenses are not regularly covered and profits are guaranteed, farmers cannot carry on their activities. So the rent they pay to their landlords is what remains after paying all the expenses. Farmers are productive because they are able to replace the original and annual expenses and to create a neat produce.

Artificers, manufacturers, and merchants, however, are unproductive and barren because they do not create new value. These French philosophers are called physiocrats (*physio* is nature and *crat* means ruling), for their desire to let nature rule. The labor of artificers, manufacturers, and merchants does not add any value to the whole annual amount of rude produce of the land, or so they claim.

Smith reports that for the physiocrats, the only way in which artificers, manufacturers, and merchants may increase the revenue and wealth of a nation is with parsimony, by depriving themselves of funds meant for their consumption. So, agricultural countries such as France and England can grow rich with enjoyment, while merchant countries such as Holland and Hamburg can grow rich only with privation.

Smith continues the description of physiocracy saying that, for them, the unproductive class, despite being completely maintained and employed by the productive classes, is very useful. It produces and buys domestic and foreign goods for the enjoyment of the productive classes, and it allows the productive classes to concentrate themselves on agriculture, rather than trying to produce manufactures themselves, which would waste productive resources. The unproductive classes, therefore, indirectly increase the productive power of labor by letting farmers be farmers.

It follows that it is not in the interest of the productive classes to restrict or discourage the activities of merchants and manufacturers. The greater their liberty, the more their competition, the lower will be the prices of their goods that farmers and landlords buy.

High duties would decrease the value of the surplus of the land by increasing the price of manufacture. They would give incentives to have more manufacture and less agriculture, decreasing productive labor and increasing unproductive labor. For Smith, Quesnai's economic tables represent how a violation of the natural distribution, which the most perfect liberty creates, would decrease the value, the annual produce, and the wealth of a society. Instead, to rival mercantile nations, a landed nation should continuously increase the surplus produce of land, which eventually will support artificers and manufacturers, and even foreign trade.

The best way for a landed nation to raise its own artificers, manufacturers, and merchants is, therefore, a perfect freedom of trade with all nations. In Smith's account of physiocracy, perfect justice, perfect liberty, and perfect equality is the recipe for the prosperity of all members of society.

Perfect, perfect, perfect. For Smith, this system requires a great deal of perfection. Too much. It implies, to use a physician image, as Quesnai was a physician after all, that unless we follow a perfectly healthy diet, we will get sick. But we know from experience, Smith reminds us, that somehow we remain mostly healthy even if our diet is not perfectly healthy. The political body, like the human body, does not necessarily prosper only under a perfect and perfectly followed regimen. Perfect liberty is nice, but Quesnai does not take into consideration the driving engine of human betterment for Smith: our natural desire to better our condition. Our effort to better our conditions is a remedy against many of the negative effects of oppressive policies. After all, Smith notices, if a nation could not prosper unless it had perfect liberty and perfect justice, no nation could ever have prospered. For Smith, the "wisdom of nature" offers remedies to the bad effects of the "folly and injustice of man".

The Oeconomists, the name by which the French philosophers were known, did make another serious mistake, according to Smith. They considered artificers, manufactures, and merchants as unproductive. Here are five reasons why they are wrong, according to Smith. First, artificers, manufactures, and merchants reproduce annually the value of their own consumption. They are like a couple who makes two children. They will maintain constant population. True, population will not grow, but that does not mean that they are barren. Second, artificers, manufactures, and merchants are not like menial servants, the work of whom perishes the moment of its performance. The labor of artificers, manufactures, and merchants instead fixes itself in the vendible good they produce. Then, it is wrong to say that the labor of artificers, manufactures, and merchants does not increase the revenue of society. The value of what each of them produces may be equal to the value of what he consumes, but the whole value of the goods in the market increases with his production. Furthermore, Smith reminds us, farmers also need to be parsimonious to increase the real revenue of society. Revenue increases only with improvements in the productive power of labor or with the increase in the quantity of labor. Manufacturing allows for more division of labor, therefore, for more improvement. So farmers, even more than artificers, manufactures, and merchants, need to save to improve. And finally, the revenue of a trading and manufacturing country is always more than the one who is not trading and producing manufactures. It is only with manufacturing and trade that one country can get more subsistence than what its land produces.

Also, recall Smith's defense of merchants in his Digression on the Corn Laws. That kind of defense would not be possible in the hands of a physiocrat.

Now, this system is not perfect, Smith tells us, but it is the one that gets closer to the truth. It understands that wealth does not consist of the "unconsumable riches of money" but of consumable goods. It also understands that if agriculture is to be preferred, restraining manufacturing and foreign trade is counterproductive, so it promotes liberty, even if perfect liberty.

For Smith, Quesnai and his followers did influence France's policies, which helped French agriculture recover a bit from its previous oppressions. Yet, Europe, generally, has had policies more favorable to manufacture and trade than to agriculture. Examples of nations that favored agriculture over manufacture and trade are China, Egypt, Indostan, ancient Greece, and Rome.

China has little respect for foreign trade and has little of it, according to Smith. But because it has a very large territory, with a many people, different climates and productions, and an easy internal navigation system, it was able to develop its own manufacture and division of labor without the need for foreign trade. But its closure to other nations, with the possible exception of Japan, prevented its improvement.

Egypt and Indostan also favored agriculture and disliked sea travel, so they discouraged manufacture, Smith tells us. Their developed agriculture tells us that, in a closed market, it is easier to support agriculture than manufacture.

Ancient Greece and Rome discouraged manufacture more than encouraged agriculture, according to Smith. We can see this in the price of their clothes, which was extremely high. When manufacture is little, clothes are very expensive and their variety is limited. With the improvement in manufacture, the price of clothes decreases, depriving the rich of a way of distinguishing themselves. The way they manage to keep their distinction is through the variety of clothing rather than through the expense of one dress.

The chapter ends linking the criticisms of the systems of political economy described in Book IV to the following Book V. Smith reminds us indeed that when a system of natural liberty is in place, every man, as long as he does not violate the rules of justice, is left free to pursue his interest in the way he sees best. If the sovereign does not have to be bothered with the impossible task of allocating labor and capital, a task for which "no human wisdom or knowledge could ever be sufficient", he can more easily concentrate on his three duties: defense against foreign violence and invasions; protection of his subjects from the injustice and oppression of some other of his subjects; and erecting and maintaining public works and institutions, which society needs but private interests would not create because they are deemed unprofitable. These, and the way to finance them, are the topics of the three chapters of the next and final book: Book V.

FURTHER READINGS

Groenewegan, Peter. 2009. "Adam Smith, the Physiocrats and Turgot", in *Elgar Companion to Adam Smith*, ed. Jeffrey Young. Cheltenham and Northampton: Edward Elgar. 135–140.

Pitts, Jennifer. 2005. *A Turn to Empire: The Rise of Imperial Liberalism in Britain and France*. Princeton, NJ: Princeton University Press.

Sen, Amartya. 2016. "Adam Smith and Economic Development", in *Adam Smith His Life, Thought, and Legacy*, ed. Ryan Hanley. Princeton, NJ, and Oxford: Princeton University Press.

Skinner, Andrew. 1979. *A System of Social Science: Papers Relating to Adam Smith*. Oxford: Oxford University Press.

Stevens, D. 1975. "Adam Smith and the Colonial Disturbances", in *Essays on Adam Smith*, ed. Andrew Skinner, T. Wilson. Oxford: Clarendon.

van der Haar, Edvin. 2013. "Adam Smith on Empire and International Relations", in *The Oxford Handbook of Adam Smith*, ed. Christopher Berry, Maria Pia Paganelli, Craig Smith. Oxford: Oxford University Press. 417–442.

10

BOOK V, CHAPTER I

BOOK V, CHAPTER I: OF THE EXPENSES OF THE SOVEREIGN OR COMMONWEALTH

PART FIRST: OF THE EXPENSE OF DEFENSE

Adam Smith is not an anarco-capitalist or a promoter of no government intervention, as we already saw. For him, the role of the government in society grows with society. The more developed a society, the more complex its needs and the more the government plays a role in it. Only in the first stages of development, in "savage" societies of hunters, do we see no government. But as soon as societies develop, so does government.

In this Book, Smith describes the three duties he believes a sovereign has (defense, administration of justice, and public works) and the ways to finance them (taxes and debt).

The first function that for Smith the government has is national defense: the duty to protect society against the violence and invasions of neighboring countries. This protection can be offered only with military force, the expenses of which vary from society to society.

Inspired by the tales about North American Indians, Smith believes that in the earliest stages of society, such as among hunters, every man is by necessity both a hunter and a warrior, given the nature of their subsistence. The cost of preparing and maintain an army is, therefore, minimal. But, what today we call the opportunity cost of fighting a war is quite high. Given the precariousness of their subsistence, if one fights, one does not hunt. It is thus rare to see an army of hunters larger than a couple of hundred men. Their wars tend to be short. They are no threat to a "civilized" (as in agricultural/urban, from *cives* -city – as we saw in the first chapter of this *Guidebook*) society.

Armies grow to a couple of hundred thousand soldiers with societies of shepherds, such as Arabs and Tartars. Armies of shepherds also grow to be a formidable threat for civilized societies. Among shepherds, as among hunters, every man has to be a soldier. But because of their nomadic conditions, when they go to war, the whole society goes to war. Nobody is left behind. They all move together, including their flocks, women, and children. Children play games that prepare them for war. Women are often worriers. Flocks move with them, providing subsistence even during wars. Shepherds can be worriers at little cost.

Agricultural societies, where farming is the norm, are more complex. People are fixed to the land. This implies that not everybody can go to war. Some people need to stay home to take care of their immobile possessions. But, as for hunters and shepherds, farmers are trained as soldiers by their daily occupation. Working the land exposes farmers to harsh weather and harsh conditions, making them accustomed to the life on a battlefield. The cost of training soldiers is, therefore, low for agricultural societies too. In addition, farmers can leave home between seeding and harvesting without losing much. So as long as soldiers can go back to their land to harvest, they are not very costly to maintain either.

Things are quite different in "advanced" societies. Shepherds have lots of free time, according to Smith. So they can practice martial exercises at no cost. Farmers have some leisure time. So they can practice military exercises, but not as much as shepherds. Artificers, however, have no free time. Each hour they do not work is an hour without their source of subsistence. With progress in manufacture and in the arts of war, it is therefore impossible for soldiers to support themselves when they are training and are in battle. The state needs to support the artificer when he goes to war. Thus, in civilized societies, the number of people who can go to war must be smaller than in the "rude" societies because soldiers need to be supported by nonsoldiers.

The implication is that civilized societies are incapable of defending themselves, and yet they are the societies with the strongest need of defense. Civilized societies, thanks to their division of labor, are the wealthiest societies. Their wealth is a temptation for their poor neighbors. The probability of a successful invasion from less wealthy nations is therefore quite high.

So far, Smith's logic is quite similar to David Hume's and most of his contemporaries. But when he offers his solution to the problem, Smith differs significantly from them. Among his circle of friends, especially the ones revolving around the Poker Club, one of the social clubs meant to offer avenues for discussion of current events, Smith stands out favoring a professional army, a standing army, as opposed to a militia.

His reasoning is as follows.

A militia implies that everybody participates in military exercises. It forces everybody to be a soldier. This is possible when soldiers make a living through jobs that give them enough free time to be able to exercise regularly.

In ancient Greece, the state could train soldiers at very little cost. Martial exercises were mandatory for all on state provided fields. *Campus Martius* in Rome is a Roman example of these fields. In feudal times, archery also did the trick. But then, military exercises were done less and less. So much less that in a civilized society the only way to perfect the art of war is to make it the sole or principal occupation of some men. In societies where division of labor is dominant, division of labor should include also the military, according to Smith. And because no individual would specialize in a profession that does not feed him, the state must provide for this specialized group.

In addition, before the introduction of firearms, Smith continues, the strength of an army depended on the strength and agility of its soldiers. But with firearms, what matters most is order and prompt obedience to orders. With firearms there is lots of noise and smoke in battle. Death comes in an invisible way. The skills needed in this kind of environment come from troops who train together over and over again.

For Smith, members of a militia do not have this kind of discipline because they practice once a week, not daily. They are also less ready to obey orders, for the same reason: they take orders only once a week, not every day, all day.

There are exceptions, of course, but these are exceptions that testify to the validity of the rule, according to Smith. Tartar and Arab militias are the best ones, but their members go to war under the same leader they obey in peace time. So they are accustomed to follow his orders. A militia that fights several successive campaigns is also an exception, because the duration of its engagement transformed it into a standing army. The exceptions go also in the opposite direction: a standing army can degenerate into an undisciplined militia, becoming incapable of resisting a well-trained militia.

History, for Smith, teaches us that the militia of shepherds is irresistibly superior to the militia of a civilized nation, but that a well-regulated standing army is always superior to any militia.

For Smith, that a standing army goes hand in hand with a civilized nation is testified not only by the fact that only a standing army can defend the opulence of a civilized society, but also that only the opulence of a civilized nation can afford its cost.

An additional benefit of a standing army, according to Smith, is that it is possibly the only tool to civilize and bring the law of the sovereign to some uncivilized and remote provinces of a nation, such as Peter the Great did in the Russian Empire.

The main objection to standing armies, as Smith knows well, is the fear that it could become a threat to liberty. But if the sovereign is the commander in chief and his nobles the chief officers, Smith replies, then the military force is in the hands of who has the greatest interest in preserving the civil authority, having themselves a large share in that authority. As a matter of fact, Smith emphasizes, if the sovereign has the support of the aristocracy and of the standing army, small remonstrations are not a threat to him, so he can safely pardon or ignore them. So a standing army allows a degree of liberty that may seem to approach licentiousness.

Smith's conclusion? Defending society from the violence and injustice of other societies becomes more and more expensive with the growth of society. The introduction of firearms also increases the expense of exercise and the discipline in war and peace. Arms and ammunitions, and even cannons and mortars are expensive tools of wars, not just more expensive to buy and use, but also more expensive to carry to the battlefield.

So, in ancient times, opulent and civilized nations had difficulties defending themselves against poor less civilized nations. But in modern times the opposite is true: poor and "barbarous" nations find it difficult to defend themselves against rich and civilized nations.

But here again Smith seems to remind us not to fall into *hubris*: the most important improvement in the art of war – the invention of gun powder – was a "mere accident".

PART II: OF THE EXPENSE OF JUSTICE

Violence and injustice can come from either outside or inside one's society, Smith tells us. The duty of the sovereign is to protect people against both. National defense is the first duty of the sovereign, the exact administration of justice is the second, according to Smith.

For Smith, just like national defense, the exact administration of justice has different costs in different kinds of societies.

Just like with defense, hunters face little or no cost to administer justice. Mostly because there is little or no justice to administer. Hunters generally do not have property, or have very little of it. What they hunt is highly perishable, so it makes sense to share it before it goes bad. The property they might have is generally not worth more than a couple of days' work. For Smith, the only injuries they may have are injuries to the person or to the reputation of a person. The injured suffers, no doubt, but the injurer does not gain from it, at least materially. Envy, malice, and resentment are the passions that generally induce these kinds of injuries. But, for Smith, they are not frequent. There is, therefore, no need to have magistrates and a regular administration of justice.

Things are different with the introduction of property. When there is property, there is inequality of wealth. And with property, the injurer benefits from the harm that is done to the injured. Combine the avarice and ambition in the rich, the hatred of labor and love of present ease in the poor, with envy and want and, for Smith, you have frequent and strong motivation to invade other people's property. The presence of a civil magistrate, thus, becomes indispensable. Without the protection of the civil magistrate, owners of valuable property "can [not] sleep a single night in security".

This is a striking point that Smith made previously in his lectures on jurisprudence when he taught at the University of Glasgow: without property there is no need for government. The civil government and the civil magistrate emerge from the need of the rich to protect themselves against the poor, for the defense of those who have property against those who do not.

Obedience to the civil magistrate needs to be explained. Using logic similar to his contemporaries and compatriots, such as Adam Ferguson, John Millar, and David Hume, Smith explains the causes of subordination to the authority of others, including eventually the civil government. His description of the gradual process of subordination can be read as an alternative to contract theory where individual deliberately submit to a government.

For Smith, the first source of superiority could be personal qualities such as strength, beauty, agility, wisdom, virtue, or moderate mind. These characteristics of an individual can give great authority, but cannot be easily defined. We need something more "plain and palpable". Superiority of age works. It is more difficult to dispute who is older and who is younger.

Among hunters, there is little or no inequality of fortune, Smith claims. They are too poor for that. Universal poverty means universal equality. Among hunters, therefore, age or personal qualities are the sole foundation for authority. But usually there is little authority and little subordination.

Another source of authority is, for Smith, superiority of fortune. This is very much the criteria of distinction in the "rudest" ages of society, where there is usually great inequality of wealth. Among shepherds there is possibly the greatest inequality of wealth, and it is where fortune gives the most authority. The authority of an Arabian sheriff is great; and the one of a Tartar khan is almost despotical. Picking up the description of precommercial societies of Book III, Smith reminds us that this is the case because men of great fortune can maintain thousands of people in a state of "servile dependency".

The final sign of superiority comes from birth, according to Smith. This presupposes an ancient superiority of fortune, though, because all families are equally ancient, being the family of a prince or of a beggar. Smith never relaxes his assumption of homogeneity of nature. We are born all the same, as he declared in Book I. Superiority of birth cannot be used by hunters because its prerequisite is ancient fortune, and hunters do not have much property. But it is very much used among shepherds, because not having luxury on which to dissipate their wealth, their wealth stays in the same family for generations.

For Smith, it is with shepherds, therefore, that we see the emergence of the civil magistrate. With shepherds, distinctions by fortune and birth are in full force. A great shepherd is also a great military authority. The people who are too weak to defend themselves look up to him for protection. He is thus the best person to compel the injurer to compensate the injured.

For Smith, therefore, distinctions of birth and fortune are the origins of judicial authority.

But this kind of judicial authority is not an expense; rather it is a source of revenue for the sovereign. The person who asks for justice is willing to pay and to give gifts to receive it. And the guilty person needs to pay compensation for having violated the peace of his lord.

The fact that judges were originally itinerant, meaning they would go around the country to hear complaints and bring justice, is a sign that they were sent, yes, to offer justice where the sovereign could not reach himself, but also to collect the revenue of the sovereign.

But when the administration of justice is a source of revenue for the state, Smith tells us, we should expect gross abuses. Indeed, the larger the present one gives to a judge, the more likely it is to receive a favorable judgment. A small present would bring something less than justice. Also, the judge has incentives to wait to deliver his judgment, just in case more presents arrive.

But if this is not bad enough, things can get worst, Smith tells us. The sovereign could hold in his own person the judicial power. Because there is nobody above the sovereign, corruption reigns as it did in all governments of Europe founded after the fall of Rome.

And yet, there is light at the end of the tunnel. Even if not by design.

Smith claims that as the expenses for national defense increase, the sovereign needs to find ways to get money. The rents from his private estates are no longer enough. Why not have people pay taxes for their own security? So we have taxes, offering "free" justice. Of course justice does not become free. One still needs to pay for the court and lawyers. But at least giving presents is forbidden.

Be it as it may, for Smith, as commerce increases, as improvements increase, the administration of justice becomes more and more laborious for the executive power. It requires undivided attention. The executive power cannot and does not want to provide that. So it appoints deputies, bailiffs, and judges. The unintended consequence of this is that it breaks the link that united the judicial and the executive power, which always forces justice to sacrifice to politics. And this is a good thing. A very good thing. The liberty of each individual depends fundamentally on the impartial administration of justice. And this is achieved, at least in Britain, according to Smith, again, not by design, not by conscious reason, but by a series of accidental circumstances.

At this point, though, Smith's narration becomes murky. The distinction between is and ought, between his historical account and his prescriptive account, is not always clear. He gives historical examples for all the parts of the story, but this does not necessarily make it into an accurate historical account, rather, it is a normative mixture of facts and suggestions. I will follow his narrative, without attempting to distinguish the "is" from the "ought" more than Smith does.

As gift giving is abolished, judges need another source of income. But because the office of the judge is very honorable, people do it with little monetary compensation. In Book I we were told that high monetary remuneration is needed only for jobs that give us a bad reputation. Compensation in approbation reduces monetary compensation, as in this case. Because being a judge is considered honorable, the expense to the sovereign is not going to be much, Smith claims.

As a matter of fact, the expense to the sovereign should be none. Justice could be financed by user fees, rather than by the general revenue of the state. The sovereign does not have to get involved with it, decreasing the opportunity for corruption. Judges must respect regulations. Sovereign may not. In addition, to give the right incentives to the judges, the fee should be paid to a clerk, who gives it to the judge only after he delivers the sentence. Smith indeed declares: public services are never better performed then when the reward comes after the performance and is proportioned to its diligence.

Now, because the court fees are the principal source of revenue for the court, each court has incentive to attract business to itself. How? Showing greater impartiality and speedier results. Competition does miracles in the administration of justice too.

Another way to raise revenue for the court, without tapping into the general revenue of society, could be a stamp duty upon law proceedings. This is risky, though. The judge may be tempted to multiply the proceeding to multiply the duties. This is what happened when the clerk of the court was paid by the number of pages written. They multiplied the words used.

Yet another way to finance the courts, for Smith, could be to use the rents of landed estates or the interest on loans.

But what matters the most is that the judiciary is completely separated from the executive power. It should be as much independent from it as possible, according to Smith. The caprice of the executive power should not be allowed to remove judges from office; and the regular payment of the judges' salary should not be dependent on the goodwill or on the finances of the executive power.

PART III: OF THE EXPENCE OF PUBLIC WORKS AND PUBLIC INSTITUTIONS

The third and final duty of the sovereign is to erect and maintain those works beneficial to societies but unprofitable for individuals. These public works and institutions are meant to facilitate commerce of society and the instruction of the people. Like the other two duties, the expense will vary with different kinds of societies. And like the administration of justice, these public works should be financed by tolls, or something like tolls, rather than by the general revenue of society.

ARTICLE I: OF PUBLIC WORKS AND INSTITUTIONS FOR FACILITATING THE COMMERCE OF THE SOCIETY

AND FIRST, OF THOSE WHICH ARE NECESSARY FOR FACILITATING COMMERCE IN GENERAL

Smith brings back his emphasis on good infrastructure. As he explained in Book I, division of labor is limited by the extent of the market. If we can facilitate the extension of the market with good infrastructure, we are facing a worthy expense. So, for Smith, good roads, bridges, navigable canals, and harbors are all examples of public works that facilitate commerce, the construction and maintenance of which should be considered as part of the duties of the sovereign.

Their expenses will vary with the kinds of societies they are in. For example, the expense of a bridge will depend on its strength, and its strength will depend on its use. If it is seldom used, because commerce is not very common, its cost will be different than if heavy carriages use it day in and day out as in societies where commerce is very much developed.

For Smith, these kinds of works, even if they benefit the whole society, do not necessarily require the use the general revenue of society. Small tolls can easily finance them. Seigniorage for coinage and fees of the post office, for example, finance their activities, and also generate substantial revenue. Times have changed.

Anyway, for highways and bridges, tolls in proportion to weight would make the payment in proportion to their wear and tear. Smith thinks there could be nothing more equitable than this. After all, the expense of the toll will eventually be passed on to consumers, who are the main beneficiary of the use of the highways and bridges. Unfortunately, Smith's understanding of the effects of tax incidence is not as lucid as one would wish. Yet, he continues, transportation costs will decrease thanks to the good highways and bridges, so the price of the goods carried on them will decrease. The combined effect of decreased transportation costs and increased costs due to the toll not only cancel each other out, but also will decrease the final price of the goods transported. Again, there are some issues with price elasticity missing, and lack of explanations of why the overall price would decrease rather than increase, but we can only take his word for it now.

Back to the toll analysis. Smith suggests that for transport of luxury goods, the toll should be higher than the proportion to its weight. This would be a way to have the "indolence and vanity of the rich to contribute to the relief of the poor" by making the transport of heavy cargos a bit cheaper.

Paying with tolls also allows people to build roads, bridges, and canals only where commerce needs them. A magnificent road through desert countryside where there is only the villa of a great lord, or a great bridge built just to embellish the view from a palace, would not be able to have enough funding for their construction and maintenance. We see these kinds of works only when they are paid for with other sources of revenue.

The tolls for canals, or duty locks, should belong to the person who cares for the canals. This sets the right incentive. If the canal is not well maintained, people will stop using it. So they will stop paying the toll. It is, therefore, in the interest of the person who manages it to keep it in good functioning order. If, instead, the tolls go to some commissioners, they will be less dependent on this revenue and, therefore, less attentive to the maintenance of the canal.

Things are different for tolls for high roads, according to Smith. These should not go to a private person but to commissioners. Why? Incentives again. A poorly maintained road is still usable. So the person in charge may not have incentive to keep it in good shape because he can get the tolls regardless. There is a better chance to have good maintenance if the tolls and the maintenance are in the hands of a commissioner.

"It has been said", Smith warns us, that the army should maintain the roads and the government should collect the tolls. Whatever is "commonly said" or "commonly believed" is usually wrong according to Smith, as we see throughout his work. Here we do not have an exception. What's wrong here? If the tolls are used to support the expenses of the state, they will increase with the inevitable increase in those expenses. But if the tolls do increase, they no longer facilitate commerce but become an obstacle instead. In addition, a tax on weight is very much equitable if used for the repair of the roads, but it becomes unequitable if it is used for other purposes. If the tolls are proportioned to weight, assuming again (even if incorrectly) that consumers will eventually face the whole burden of the tax, poor consumers will be taxed much more heavily than rich consumers. Poor people are more likely to consume coarse and bulky things. Rich people are more likely to consume precious but light things. In addition, if the government is in charge of repairs, and does not do them, it becomes difficult to have them fixed.

It is not by accident that in France, where road maintenance is in the hands of local magistrates one sees mostly ostentatious useless works and very few useful small works. Smith claims that a proud minister can show off the splendor of his works to the nobility in court. Small works go unnoticed. So why bother with them?

There are accounts that in China the executive powers care for roads and canals, and that they work magnificently. But these accounts, first, come from "stupid and lying missionaries" and, second, may be partially justified by the land tax that the sovereign collects there. For Smith, this land tax varies with the produce of the land. So it is in the interest of the sovereign to have good roads to transport that produce and to extend the market as much as possible. But in France there is no land tax. So that incentive does not exist.

Lesson learned? Public works should be done, maintained, and financed locally. Public works are always better maintained by local revenue and managed by local administration. The abuses of local administrations cannot be much, and can more easily be corrected than the abuses of a great empire.

OF THE PUBLIC WORKS AND INSTITUTIONS WHICH ARE NECESSARY FOR FACILITATING PARTICULAR BRANCHES OF COMMERCE

When we expand from domestic to foreign markets, commerce requires different conditions. In particular, if one trades with "barbarians and uncivilized people", one needs special protections. Warehouses generally need fortification. This is why both the English and the French East India Companies have forts.

But that was true also in the past. Ambassadors and similar consuls are also a consequence of this protection of trade with less civilized people. They helped decide disputes between natives and fellow countrymen. Embassies emerged from the need of commerce, not of wars. And their timing testifies to it. They started to be created in the fifteenth and sixteenth century, when commerce increased.

This protection of a particular branch of trade is different from national defense, and differently from it, it should not be paid by the general revenue of the state. It should be paid with a moderate tax on that particular branch of trade. There could be, for example, a fee to enter into a specific trade or a percentage duty on their imports and exports.

"It is said", again a warning sign that something is wrong, Smith tells us, that the duty of custom started as a way to pay for the protection from pirates and freebooters, and because the protection of trade is for the benefit of the commonwealth, the executive power should determine and collect that duty. But, as expected there is a "but", the protection of a particular branch of trade is in the hands of particular companies of merchants, who persuaded the legislature to give them the equivalent of military powers (which they exercised in the most unjust and capricious ways) and monopoly privileges over those trades.

For Smith, at the beginning these companies may fulfill a useful role because they try something that the state would not do, at their own expense. It is acceptable to give them a temporary monopoly to compensate them for the risk and expenses faced. The monopoly should be temporary though, like a patent for a new machine or a new book. When the monopoly expires, it expires. The government should buy the forts, and trade should be open to all.

If the monopoly is kept permanently, the people are absurdly taxed twice: for the higher price of goods, and from the exclusion from profitable trade. And why? "To enable the negligence, profusion, and malversation of his own servants" who cannot even generate a profit given how disorderly their conduct is.

There are two kinds of these companies: regulated companies and joint stock companies.

In Smith's account, the regulated companies admit anybody in them as long as they pay a fine. Each member trades with his capital at his own risk. They are like some sort of corporation seeking an enlarged monopoly. The Hamburg Company, the Russia Company, the Eastland, Turkey, and African Companies are all examples of regulated companies. They do not have or require forts or garrisons. Why? Members have no interest in the prosperity of the company. They are better off if there are fewer competitors. So if the general trade decreases, their own private one increases.

Smith describes joint stock companies instead, as requiring each member to share the profit or the loss of the company in proportion to his share in it. They do require and have forts and garrisons. Why? Because the directors have a share in the profit of the company and so it is in their interest that the company does well. The forts protect that profit. In addition, differently from regulated companies, the directors of joint stock companies manage very large capitals. Another difference from the regulated companies is that a member can sell his share at the market price, which may be different from the amount that its owner originally gave to the company. Furthermore, and most importantly shall we add, private copartnerships have unlimited liability while owners of joint stock companies have limited liability. The difference is that an owner of a copartnership is liable for the full amount of the debt of the company, not for the share of capital he put in originally. So if the company goes bankrupt, his personal asset is at stake. With limited liability instead, the owner of stock is liable only for the amount he contributed to the company. Add that the court of directors is controlled by the court of proprietors, but the proprietors do not understand what goes on with the company, and that the proprietors get dividends without trouble or risk, then you have a dangerous cocktail.

Joint stock companies attract many who would not dare use their fortune in private copartnerships. So they attract a great deal of capital. Just imagine: the trading stock of one of these companies, the South Sea Company, was three times larger than the capital of the Bank of England, Smith claims.

But the directors manage other people's money, not their own. So they are not as anxious about its correct use. For Smith, it is not by accident that "negligence and profusion" are typical of joint stock companies. They cannot compete with other companies. They cannot survive without exclusive privileges, and often not even with exclusive privileges! Without exclusive privileges, they would succumb to mismanagement. But even with exclusive privileges, they still succumb to mismanagement and, in addition, reduce trade.

For Smith, it is historically impossible to find a successful joint stock company. The incentives are just not there.

Look at the fate of the Royal African Company, Smith says. It went bankrupt and had to be dissolved by an act of Parliament. The South Sea Company does not have forts, so it does not have major expenses, but it has such an immense number of proprietors that it is subject to folly, negligence, and profusion. Only the Hudson's Bay Company seems to survive. But that is because it is very small and has no competitors. Its profits are so small that it does not even attract envy.

Look even, or especially, at the English East India Company, Smith continues. It attracts men of all kinds of fortune. They want a share in the company because they dream of the influence they may have with their one vote. They do not even care about the dividend or the value of the stock or the prosperity of the empire, or the fate of the people who live there. They just want to buy a share in the appointment of the plunderers of India. The company at the time of Smith's writing, in 1784 Smith tells us, is in as great distress as ever. It needed to ask yet again for assistance to prevent bankruptcy.

For Smith, joint stock companies may have a chance only with trades that are completely routinized, that is, trades where there is a uniform method that does not allow for variations. Such trades are banking, insurance, making navigable canals and cuts, and bringing water to great cities. All these four trades fit the bill that shows that the kind of trade is of greater utility than common trade and that it requires more capital than can be collected otherwise.

ARTICLE II: OF THE EXPENCE OF THE INSTRUCTION FOR THE EDUCATION OF THE YOUTH

Along with roads, canals, ports, and temporary monopoly powers to companies dealing with "barbarians" (the previous "article"), Smith includes the education of the youth (this "article"), and of people of all ages (next "article").

The institutions for the education of the youth, like the ones that facilitate commerce, generally should and do generate enough revenue to support themselves. If not, like the others, they should be funded by local revenue from landed estates or interests, but not from the general revenue of society.

As Smith explained when he described the incentives wages provide to workers, here he reminds us that the amount of effort offered in a job is proportioned to its pay. With competition, that effort has to be significant, given other competitors. Thus competition gives incentive to excel.

Apply this logic to teaching.

If an endowment pays for scholars and teachers, meaning if the teachers are on a fixed salary, the incentives to put great effort into what they do are not there. If the compensation of scholars and teachers is exclusively a salary, their remuneration becomes completely disconnected from their success or reputation. Their interest is opposite from their duty. They will neglect their duty and live an easy life. Because one is paid regardless of how he does his job, why bother doing it? And if forced to do it, why bother putting any effort in it?

And if he answers to the college or university of which he is a member, he and all his colleagues will cover each other's backs and they all will be negligent. Smith gives us an example of it from his personal life. He studied at Oxford, where the pay structure of professors is as he just described. His comment: at Oxford the great portion of professors "have given up even the pretence of teaching".

In France, professors answer to an external authority, such as a bishop or a governor, but things are not better. They may force professors to give some number of lectures, but they cannot control the quality of these lectures. The quality depends on incentives. Having none, lectures are horrible.

Other perverse incentives include forcing students to attend universities independently of the merits of their teachers; requiring that the privileges of graduation in arts, law, physics, and divinity are obtained only by residence for a certain number of years in a university; offering scholarships that attach students to specific colleges; and forbidding students from choosing or changing their teachers. They all decrease emulation, effort, and diligence in teachers.

Yet, if the teacher is a man of sense, he must feel uncomfortable in seeing that students do not attend his classes or when they do they are doing something else or make fun of him. He may then put a little effort in his work. Or may force students to attend his fake lectures.

The discipline of colleges, Smith declares, is not meant to benefit the students but the professors. If the professors do their duty, the students will do theirs. There is indeed no need to force attendance in a lecture that is worth attending. You may have to force young boys to attend, but after the age of 12 or 13 they can make their own decisions.

For Smith the best way to learn something is to study things for which there is no public instruction. Take dancing and fencing for example. They are taught only privately. You may not become the best dancer or fencer in the country, but you will surely learn how to dance and fence acceptably.

Similarly, the three basic parts of education – read, write, and account – are more successfully achieved in private than public schools.

In England, public schools are less corrupted than universities because the reward system is different. School masters are paid with fees and honoraria from students. And, to graduate, one needs to pass an exam, not to sit in school for some time.

"It is commonly said", red-flags Smith, that teaching in university may not be very good but at least there is teaching. If not, some subjects may not be taught at all. This is not a good thing for Smith. To the contrary. It is a sign that universities are not serving their purpose anymore, but they are serving some special groups instead.

The universities of Europe, after all, were created to educate the clergy and were under the authority of the pope. Their members were even under ecclesiastical rather than civil jurisdiction. The universities were meant to teach theology or whatever prepares to study theology.

Now, with the end of the Roman Empire, Latin loses ground to local languages, even if it would still be used in religious ceremonies. So there were two parallel languages in Europe: the language of the priests and the language of the people. The priests needed to learn Latin to understand the scriptures. Greek and Hebrew were not necessary because the Latin translation of the Bible was considered as much as the word of god as the original texts in Greek and Hebrew. So the university needed to teach Latin.

Note that with the reformation, there were claims that the Latin translation was wrong. People needed to look at the original texts in Greek. So Greek was introduced in the universities of protestant countries.

The Church affected the university curriculum more than with just Latin or Greek. In ancient Greece, philosophy was divided into three: natural philosophy or physics, moral philosophy or ethics, and logic.

Smith here picks up a theme he developed in a "juvenile" essay, on which he worked possibly until his death, one of the few things that he preserves from fire. In this essay, titled (for short) *History of Astronomy*, he explains the birth of philosophy. The great natural phenomena, especially the skies, excite fear and wonder. We start developing a system of explanation to try to satisfy our curiosity. So we go from superstitious explanations to science.

Natural philosophy is the first science to form. The beauty of systematic arrangements of our different observations of nature leads us to try to do the same for our observation of human conduct. This is how moral philosophy is born. But different people see things differently and create different systems. To show the inaccuracy in their argument, logic is born: the science of good and bad reasoning. It was generally taught before physics and ethics.

In European universities physics was divided into physics – the study of bodies – and metaphysics – the study of spirits. The comparison of the two disciplines created a third one: ontology. But, because theology was the primary interest of university education, the focus needed to be on how to achieve happiness in the next life, not in this one. So the curriculum required a different order: one would study first logic, then ontology, then metaphysics. Only after that, one would study the now-debased moral philosophy, and at last the superficial system of physics. This alteration of the course of studies was meant for the education of the clergy, not for the education of gentlemen and men of the world. Would that be so bad then, if some of the subjects would not be taught any longer?

Note a big difference from our times. Universities were not meant to provide education in the sense of technical knowledge that helps you in your profession. Universities were meant to create gentlemen, men of the world, and to teach men fashionable topics for polite conversation. And yes, as it is almost always the case in the *Wealth of Nations*, the gender bias is present and it is a reflection of the then-current state of the world. Women would not be educated in universities.

Women should and would be educated at home, according to Smith. Their education thus does not include "useless, absurd, and fantastic" topics, just what is considered useful for them.

Universities are also not necessarily the place of innovation and improvement. They are "sanctuaries in which exploded systems and obsolete prejudices found shelter and protection, after they had been hunted out of every corner of the world". And the richer the university, the more slowly and more adverse it is in adopting changes and innovation. Poorer universities do it faster because their teachers' compensations depend on their reputation, so they need to pay attention to the world. Smith does not explicitly say this, but he may have Newtonianism in mind. It took decades for Cambridge to teach Newton, even if it was where Newton originally taught. In Scotland, however, considered the periphery of civilization, Newtonianism was taught immediately.

Smith goes so far to say that the universities are so bad that the custom of sending children abroad for a few years, even if they return less disciplined than when they left, is a way for a parent "not to see his own son going to ruin in front of their eyes".

As to be expected, for Smith, different societies have different institutions for the education of their youth.

In ancient Greece, for example, education in music and gymnastic was mandatory for all. Gymnastics would harden the body and prepare for war. Music would humanize the mind for social and moral duties.

Ancient Rome had similar policies for martial education, but not for music. And yet, Smith claims, the morals of the Romans were superior to the Greeks, if judged by the behavior of factions in the two states. Studying music in Greece may have been a long-lasting tradition hard to shed. Music and dancing are indeed typical of "savages and barbarians," such as Africans, Smith declares.

Regardless. Both in Greece and Rome, the state did not pay for the teacher of gymnastics (and music). It did not even appoint them. It just required that all would practice military exercises and offered a public place to do it.

Learning to read, write, and account for the rich citizens was done at home with private tutors. For the poor it was done in schools with teachers for hire. In both cases, it was left altogether to the care of the parents.

Even with more refined times, when philosophy and rhetoric became fashionable, parents would send children to the school of the philosopher of choice. The state would not support any of those schools. As a matter of fact, they were barely tolerated, so much so that most teachers had to travel from place to place because the state would not welcome them. As demand increased, the school and teachers became stationary, but the state did not provide them with anything, not even a place to teach. There were no salaries and no privileges, just student fees.

In Rome, there were not even schools for studying law, the most important intellectual creature of it. If someone wanted to learn law, he must follow someone who understood it.

In Greece, law was not a science, while in Rome it was, and it gave a great reputation to those who understood it. The difference lies in the different justice systems in the two countries. In Greece the courts of justices counted between 500 and 1,500 people. The decisions were essentially random because the blame of a bad decision could not fall on anyone in particular. In Rome, however, decisions were made by a single judge. The responsibility and the reputational consequences of a bad judgment would fall exclusively on him. In doubtful cases, he would use examples and precedents. The superiority of characters of the Romans may thus be attributable to their better system of courts of justice.

Note how Smith again and again maintains his assumption. There is nothing naturally different between Romans and Greeks. Only their habits are different, and therefore their characters are different.

Similarly, there is nothing naturally bad about teachers. It is just that the set of incentives they have habituates them to bad behaviors. It is the disconnection of their remuneration from their success and reputation that corrupts their diligence. And because university teachers are paid by the endowment of the university, private teachers of subjects taught in university cannot receive a decent pay as they are competing against people who are subsidized. These poor private teachers are thus considered "the lowest men of letters". The consequence? One cannot find any good private teacher either.

Smith continues with his analysis. As with all other institutions, the attention the government needs to pay to education changes with times and circumstances.

In barbarian societies or even in agricultural ones, there is little division of labor, so each person has to do a variety of things, and to find solutions for all the problems he constantly faces. His mind, therefore, does not fall in that "drowsy stupidity of the inferior ranks of people of civilized societies". Everybody can form tolerable judgments, even if no one can have that deeper understanding that only few have in a civilized society. This means that every person is able to do what everybody else can do, that each person has breadth, even if not depth of knowledge.

This is why the education of the common people does not require the attention of the public.

In a civilized state, by contrast, a person does not do many things, but specializes in one or very few activities. The diversification of activities in the whole society seems infinite. The few people who can spend their time contemplating society can thus observe and make connections among what seems an almost infinite variety of things. Remember from Book I that in civilized societies there are people who specialize in observing everything – philosophers or scientists. But they are necessarily few.

The majority of the people are not able to observe their surroundings and make connections. They are stuck in their specialized activity that narrows, rather than broadens, their horizon.

With division of labor, the majority of the people do only a few simple things from a very young age. Their work is simple, uniform, and repetitive. They have no time to spend on education. The time they do not spend working is time for which they lose the opportunity to earn what is needed to survive. They, therefore, have no opportunity to develop what Smith calls "understanding", the ability to judge, to evaluate, and to find solutions to problems. Smith's words are strong and unflattering, to say the least. The division of labor causes a poor worker to become

> as stupid and ignorant as it is possible for a human creature to become. The torpor of his mind renders him, not only incapable of relishing or bearing a part in any rational conversation, but of conceiving any generous, noble, or tender sentiment, and consequently of forming any just judgment ... he is equally incapable of defending his country in war.

The specialized poor may gain dexterity, but he does it at the expense of his intellectual, social, and martial virtues. Because the laboring poor are the majority of the people, the education of the common people requires the attention of the public.

The situation is different for the people of rank or of fortune. They do not need the same attention as the common people do.

They do not need any attention at all, actually. People of rank start their professional activities at 18 or 19, as opposed to 6 or 8, as Smith told us also in Book I when he talked about nurture, not nature, causing differences among people.

Parents of children of rank are usually anxious about them getting a good education. If they do not get it, it is because of the negligence of the masters that Smith just described. In addition, the kinds of activities high rank people engage in are seldom simple and repetitive. Furthermore, their jobs are generally not strenuous: they have a great deal of leisure time that they can spend on "useful or ornamental knowledge". People of rank and fortune do not live in conditions that make them grow torpid.

So only the common people in commercial societies need the attention of the government. What kind of attention should it be?

Well, Smith tells us, "read, write, and account" can be learned at a very young age. Children can learn to read, write, and account before they can learn how to work. So they can, and should, be educated in that window of time. It does not cost much to do it. And it can easily be done in three ways: "facilitation, encouragement, and imposition".

The public can facilitate the education of the common poor, by establishing "little schools in each parish", like in Scotland. The public could contribute to the pay of the teacher. It should not pay the teacher 100 percent or he will lose incentives to do his job. Part of his pay should come from the parents of the children. The fee the parents pay could easily be moderate enough that any common worker can afford it. And if geometry and mechanics would substitute for Latin, the literal education of the common people would be complete.

The public can encourage education with small premiums and badges of distinction.

And it can impose upon it a mandatory exam requirement before anybody can enter a corporation or set up a trade.

This is how the Greeks and Romans did it. They facilitated education, which, remember, is gymnastics for martial preparation. They did it by appointing a place to practice, and by letting students pay their masters. They encouraged it with prizes (think of the Olympic Games). And they imposed a mandate to serve in the military.

Why should the government care, though? Smith here seems to engage with his contemporaries, making an argument that runs parallel to one with which they would be familiar. Remember that Smith was a lonely voice favoring a professional army, while most of his friends and contemporaries favored a militia? So here he tells his promilitia audience: you think that without government support we see a decline in military exercises and martial spirit, right? And even if this marital spirit would not be effective to defend a society, the government should still tend to it to prevent the "mental mutilation, deformity, and wretchedness of cowardice", right? Just like the government should give the most serious attention "to prevent leprosy or any other loathsome offensive diseases" even if neither causes mortal danger, right? Right. The government needs to give attention to things that may not have any other benefit but the prevention of a great public evil.

Well, the "gross ignorance and stupidity of the inferior classes of people" is one of those public evils. A man without the proper use of his intellectual faculties is more contemptible than a coward. "He is mutilated and deformed in more essential parts". So if the deformities and mutilation of cowardice need government attention even if the state does not derive any explicit benefits from it, it is even truer for the mutilations and deformities of the ignorance of the mind of the poor. And in case of the education of the poor, the state derives a considerable advantage: "The more instructed the people are the less liable they are to fall prey of delusion, enthusiasm, and superstitions, which are the roots of the most dreadful disorders of society".

In fact, instructed and intelligent people are more decent and more orderly than ignorant and stupid people. Because of their instruction, they feel more respectable and more likely to obtain respect from their superiors. And if their superiors respect them, they are more likely to respect their superiors. Because of their education, they are more able to understand the special interests that are at the base of the complaints and the seditions of factions. This means that they are less prone to be misled into unnecessary opposition to the government.

In free countries, the safety of the government depends on the favorable judgment of the people. This is why it is fundamentally important to educate the poor common people.

ARTICLE III: OF THE EXPENCE OF THE INSTITUTIONS FOR THE INSTRUCTION OF PEOPLE OF ALL AGES

The institutions for the instruction of people of all ages are religious institutions. They are not meant to prepare good citizens for this world, but to prepare people for the next one. Usually the teachers of these institutions depend on voluntary contributions or they receive a salary coming from something like a land tax. Needless to say, their effort and industry increases with the proportion of their salary that comes from voluntary contributions.

Smith claims that teachers of old religions tend to neglect their duties more than teachers of new religions. Why? Because old religions tend to be well endowed. The clergy of well-endowed religions are men of learning and elegance. They are no different from regular gentlemen. They stopped their instruction of the people. So, they lost their authority and their influence on the lower rank of people. Evidence? They need the civil magistrate to deal with their competitors. They call competitors disturbers of the peace and call for their persecution and destruction.

The Church of Rome survives because of the activities of its inferior clergy. They live on voluntary contributions from their churchgoers and from donations from confessions. The mendicant orders depend completely on donations, thus on their industry. Monks and poor parochial clergy are thus the ones keeping alive the spirit of devotion in the Church.

What should be the relation between a church and the state?

Here Smith offers a long direct quotation from David Hume's *History of England*, where Hume claims that the state should establish a state religion and pay directly the salary of the clergy. Hume uses exactly the same logic that Smith uses to justify why teachers should *not* have a fixed salary. A salary independent of merit takes away the incentive to be dutiful. By paying for the clergy, for Hume, the state would bribe priests into inactivity, eliminating the problem of fanatic sects and excessive zeal.

Smith thinks Hume is wrong. He thinks history proves Hume wrong. Usually the times of religious violence are times of political violence too. Political parties seek the support of religious sects and promise to favor whatever sect supports them. When one party wins, the religious sect associated with it demands its share of the spoils: silence of its adversaries and financial support. If political parties would not have had the opportunity to rely on some religious sects, they would have treated all sects equally and impartially, especially if there were many of them.

If one allows each man to choose their religion and their priests, one would see the multiplication of religions and priests. This implies that nobody would have a great success, and zeal would be avoided. Zeal becomes innocent if divided among two or three hundred or even thousands of sects because nobody is powerful enough to disturb public tranquility. Smith, forgetting his own argument on the inactivity induced by the pay structure, claims instead that if zeal is concentrated in the hands of one sect, or a couple of great sects, it becomes quite dangerous.

However, Smith continues, with more enemies than friends, one needs to learn moderation and to give concessions to reach what is mutually agreeable. So much so that religious doctrines would evolve into rational religions. If there are only a few great sects instead, one sees only the veneration of his followers and admirers, which promotes extremisms.

Note this argument is potentially as unrealistic as it is similar to his description of moral development in *The Theory of Moral Sentiments*. There, Smith tells us that if we surround ourselves only with family and close friends, they will let us indulge in our biases, slowing down our moral development. To reduce our innate egocentrism, we need to be surrounded by strangers, by people who do not care about us. Only then we can realize we are just one in a multitude, thus constantly adjusting the pitch of our passions to the level that is acceptable and agreeable to the people around us. This constant adjustment of the pitch of our passions is the training ground for our moral development. So, just like in *The Theory of Moral Sentiments*, here too Smith tells us that the realization of being one in a multitude of sects is what gives moderation.

Smith goes on to analyze the social importance of religion. He claims in that in civilized societies, where there is a notable distinction of ranks, there are also two parallel moral systems: an austere one for the poor and a loose one for the rich.

The loose or liberal system of luxury for the people of fashion tolerates intemperance and great indulgencies, and even breach of chastity if not followed by "great indecencies". In fact, the liberty of indulging without disapprobation is seen as a privilege of people of fortune and status. Why? Because they can. ... People of fortune can engage in years and years of extravagances without major consequences.

A few days of excesses, however, are fatal for the poor. This is why the austere or strict system of the common people, instead, sees all excesses with "utmost abhorrence and detestation". Again, this makes sense. Even few excesses and extravagances inevitably ruin a poor person. A few days of dissipation will destroy a poor man forever, leading him even to possibly commit great crimes.

This is also why austere systems of morality are typical of religious sects that appeal to common people. The more rigorous the system of morality of the sect, the more common people respect and venerate it.

Small sects are thus more important checks for the morality of common people than established churches.

If a man of low condition lives in a country village, he will be under the eyes of all his fellow villagers, so he will be forced to behave well. But when he moves to a big city, he moves into anonymity. Nobody knows him, nobody cares for him. He will let himself go and fall into vices, which will ruin him. But if he finds a small sect, he will be saved. Now his fellow sect members will always keep an eye on him. If he creates scandals, he will be expelled and excommunicated, which is one of the most severe punishments for him.

The negative side of these super rigorous religious sects is that the rigor of their morals can be excessive. But here is where the state can intervene and can do it without violence. The state can offer a couple of remedies against this "unsocial and disagreeable" moral rigor: it can impose the study of science and philosophy, and it can offer frequent cheerful public entertainments.

Science is "the great antidote to the poison of superstition". Requiring a mandatory exam before entering any profession means, in practice, imposing mandatory universal education. And by letting people choose and pay for their teachers, it would assure that some education is achieved. Public diversions "dissipate melancholy and gloomy humor" that feeds superstitions. The state should thus give full liberty to anybody to engage in the arts, painting, poetry, music, dancing, or dramatic representations. Note again this is not a call for a subsidy, but for freedom of entry.

The other advantage that Smith sees in not having the state favoring any religion is that religion will not depend on the executive power. Which, in a twisted way, means that the executive power will not depend on an established religion. Why does it matter? Because with an established religion, with a state religion, the sovereign will never be safe.

The interests of the clergy and of a state religion are different, are opposite, from the interests of the sovereign. The clergy wants to maintain authority with the people. If the sovereign doubts even the most trivial part of the church's doctrine, or if he protects those who do, he will be blasphemous. And the church will use all its religious powers to "transfer its alliance to a more orthodox and obedient prince". If the prince rebels, it is even worse: he will be considered a heretic. And because the authority of religion is superior to all authorities, the only ways for the sovereign to maintain power is either to submit without questions to the church, or to use violence. But, soldiers may also bow to their spiritual leader more than to their temporal one. Furthermore, persecutions with violence render the sect and its doctrine "ten times more popular", thus "ten times more dangerous". The use of violence against a popular church is thus a path to disaster. This is why the sovereign is always in a precarious situation and always unsafe when there is an established church.

Does history confirm this analysis? Yes. In the ancient Christian church, the clergy elected its bishops, who became a "spiritual army" independent from the temporal sovereign, but dependent on a foreigner sovereign: the pope. Its power was "formidable" because it combined spiritual authority, with the influence that the great wealth of the church had on the common people and on some knights of low fortune, and with the liberality in hospitality and charity, which created respect and veneration among the poor.

The king was not even able to adjudicate disputes involving the clergy. It was too dangerous for the king to punish a clergyman. So he would leave him to the ecclesiastical courts, which very much cared to punish whoever may endanger the honor of the church.

The Church of Rome created thus "the most formidable power" ever formed "against the authority and security of the civil government, and against the liberty, reason, and happiness of mankind". Note how Smith builds up the power and authority of the church. It is an impenetrable and unshakable power as it combines the "delusion of superstition" with private interests. If reason could maybe crack superstition, reason remains impotent against private interests. Had it been attacked only by human reason, the temporal power of the Church of Rome would have lasted forever, Smith believes. The more unconquerable and indestructible the power of the church was, the more shocking its collapse became.

And the power of the Church did collapse. But not by armies or reason. Instead, it was by the gradual improvement in the arts and manufactures. The gradual and silent revolution of commerce, not only destroyed the power of the great barons, as shown in Book III, but also destroyed the otherwise indestructible temporal power of the Church.

The clergy, like the barons, started to spend their revenue on themselves, as soon as they could buy manufactures and luxuries. They also had to grant long-term leases to their tenants, who then became independent. In addition, they decreased their charity and hospitality, decreasing their spiritual authority. Their vanity, which made them spend on themselves what was meant for charity for the poor, disgusted the common people.

The reformation filled the vacuum of authority that the Church of Rome left open, offering that austerity that attracts common people, Smith tells us.

Because there was no general tribunal to settle internal disputes among Protestants, there were divisions. The followers of

Luther favored peace and order. They were willing to submit to the civil sovereign to avoid conflicts. This split the people of rank and people of lower rank. The clergy wants the influence on the sovereign and neglects the influence on the lower ranks of people.

The followers of Calvin kept both the right to elect their pastors and equality among the clergy, but fanaticism emerged. To maintain the peace, the magistrate took the right to fill vacancies himself. But parishioners managed to get it back by buying it from the magistrate. This means that now they cannot expect any favor from the state. And given that the only way left to distinguish themselves is through exemplary morals, the clergy is kind to the people and, in response, the people are kind too. This is why the Presbyterian clergy has the most influence among common people and is able to convert them without violence, according to Smith.

If you think back to what Smith said when he offered an alternative system to the one proposed by Hume, this is what Smith was proposing: a system like the Presbyterian Scottish system.

He sees two additional advantages to a competing system of religions in which the state does not get involved. First, when the church receives state benefits, it attracts men of letters away from the universities, like in Catholic counties and England. When the church does not receive and give great benefits, the universities can choose the best men of letters, as in Geneva, Germany, Holland, Hamburg, Sweden, Denmark, and ... Scotland.

This means that like the ancient philosophers, men of letters will have to teach. And teaching makes people masters of their subject, additionally increasing the quality of both education and knowledge.

Second, not having an established church frees state revenue, which can now go to defense, making the sovereign and the people both richer and military stronger.

In private correspondence, Smith described *The Wealth of Nations* as a severe attack against the mercantile system, the universities, and the church. He was correct in his judgment.

PART FOURTH: OF THE EXPENCE OF SUPPORTING THE DIGNITY OF THE SOVEREIGN

There is a last expense of the sovereign, which is not a duty but a public good needing financing from the general revenue: the dignity of the sovereign.

This is the only other expense, with national defense, for Smith, to call for financing from the general revenue and not from tolls, fees, or local revenue.

Like all other expenses, the amount of expense will vary with times. The sovereign must follow the fashion of the time, which means he cannot be less magnificent than a magistrate. So the expenses for the dignity of the sovereign will increase with the increase of wealth, as he needs to have more splendor than his inferiors.

CONCLUSION OF THE CHAPTER

The only two expenses that should be funded from the general revenue of society are defense and the dignity of the sovereign. They are the only two expenses that truly benefit everyone.

The administration of justice also benefits the whole society, but it benefits more the parties involved. So it should be financed by the parties involved, with fees.

All local benefits should be financed locally. It would be unjust to make all pay for something that only benefits some. So it is true that good infrastructure benefits all, but some benefit more than others, so those are the ones to pay. Similarly, the institutions for the education of the youth and for religious education benefit all, but some receive a more direct and immediate benefit, so they are the ones who should pay for that benefit with voluntary contributions.

Is there a general principle to direct us? Yes. If the institutions or the public works benefit the whole societies and, if and only if the people who immediately benefit from them cannot maintain them, then and only then, their maintenance may come from the general revenue of the state.

The state does play a fundamental role, thus, in Smith's system. Yet, that role is constrained by the right set of incentives and by justice.

FURTHER READINGS

Anderson, Gary M. 1988. "Mr. Smith and the Preachers: The Economics of Religion in the Wealth of Nations". *Journal of Political Economy* 96.5: 1066–1088.

Iannaccone, Laurence R. "The Consequences of Religious Market Structure: Adam Smith and the Economics of Religion". *Rationality and Society* 3.2: 156–177.

Montes, Leonidas. 2006. "Adam Smith on the Standing Army versus Militia Issue: Wealth over Virtue?" in *Elgar Companion to Adam Smith*, ed. Jeffrey Young. Cheltenham and Northampton: Edward Elgar. 315–334.

Paganelli, Maria Pia. 2017. "Adam Smith and the Scottish Model of Education". *The Adam Smith Review* 10: 92–104.

Paganelli, Maria Pia and Reinhard Schumacher. 2019. "Do Not Take Peace for Granted: Adam Smith's Warning on the Relation between Commerce and War". *Cambridge Journal of Economics*. 43. 3: 785–797.

Sher, Richard. 1989. "Adam Ferguson and Adam Smith and the Problem of National Defense". *Journal of Modern History* 61. 2: 240–268.

West, E. G. 1977. "Adam Smith's Public Economics: A Re-Evaluation". *The Canadian Journal of Economics* 10.1: 1–18.

11

BOOK V, CHAPTERS II–III

BOOK V, CHAPTER II: OF THE SOURCES OF THE GENERAL OR PUBLIC REVENUE OF THE SOCIETY

After analyzing the expenses of the government, most of which can be financed with user fees, as Smith explained in the previous chapter, we are left with the question of how to finance the expenses that cannot be funded with user fees or similar mechanisms: national defense and the dignity of the sovereign. Smith's answer is to fund them with the general revenue belonging to the sovereign or with taxes.

Let's analyze these two sources of revenue.

PART I: OF THE FUNDS OR SOURCES OF REVENUE WHICH MAY PECULIARLY BELONG TO THE SOVEREIGN OR COMMONWEALTH

What are the sources of revenue of the sovereign? In Smith's account, the sovereign has capital, which he can either use and earn a profit or he can lend it and earn interest. And he has land.

For Smith, the sovereign uses his capital to generate significant revenue generally only in "rude" societies. In "advanced" societies, when a sovereign engages in financial adventures, he uses the skills he has: profusion. If he uses agents, they also use profusion. The capital is not theirs after all, so they act as if the wealth of their sovereign was infinite.

Trading and ruling are incompatible, Smith believes. A sovereign makes a bad trader, and a trader makes a bad sovereign. The only examples of successful direct use of the fund of the sovereign may be seen in small republics: Hamburg, Venice, and Amsterdam. They seem to have successful state banks. The post office also seems to generate revenue for the state. But that is about it.

The sovereign does not have to use his capital. He can lend it out, at an interest. But this is not a common practice. If the state has a treasure, part of that treasure could be lent out to citizens or foreigners, rather than letting it lay idle in the treasury. But as far as Smith knows, only Berne lends to foreigners, and Hamburg lends domestically, like a pawnshop. The North American colony of Pennsylvania lends to its subjects, even if without a treasure. But they use paper bills of credit. These advances bear an interest, are transferable, and are legal tender. They are accepted because there is a demand for an instrument of commerce other than gold and silver, because the government has good credit, and because they are equivalent in quantity to the quantity of gold and silver that would be in circulation, if gold and silver were to be used. But because of its unstable nature, this cannot be the primary source of revenue of a great nation, Smith claims.

Land is more permanent and stable and a more reliable source of revenue, in Smith's view. Indeed, it is not by accident that the rents of public lands are generally the principal sources of revenue for governments of precommercial societies.

In precommercial societies, the rent of the sovereign's lands is generally enough to cover the expenses for wars and preparation for wars, and the maintenance of the sovereign's family. But, for Smith, this is not because the revenues are high, but because the expenses are low. In precommercial societies, all citizens are soldiers, so defense expenses are quite minimal. And the administration of justice, as Smith told us earlier, is a source of revenue, rather than an expense.

Things are not the same in civilized monarchies. In civilized monarchies, the rents barely cover the expenses in time of peace, mostly because of its inefficient use. Smith tells us that the lands of the crown in Great Britain give less than a quarter of what they could give if they were in private hands. But Britain is not an exception. No European state receives great revenue from land rents. Yet a great deal of land belongs to the state. The revenue from the crown lands costs more than any other revenue in society. For Smith, crown lands are a loss for the country.

It would make more sense to divide the land and have a public sale, Smith suggests. The sale would generate a large sum of money, which can be used to pay down the public debt. And this is a benefit larger than the lands could ever produce. In addition, in private hands, these lands would be improved and cultivated, which means that the produce would increase and, as a consequence, population would also increase, and with it, consumption and thus public revenue would increase too! Remember, not accidentally, Smith's position on primogeniture: having too much land concentrated in one person's hands incentivizes waste and higher prices. Ending primogeniture would allow the sale of land, making it cheaper and more available to more people, which would be a great economic stimulus. The same logic applies here.

Only parks and gardens should remain in the crown's hand, but they should count as expenses, not as sources of revenue.

To sum up: the sovereign has capital and land to generate public revenue. But he uses them both improperly and inefficiently. He thus needs private revenue to contribute to public revenue: he needs taxes to cover his expenses.

PART II: OF TAXES

And so on to taxes. Smith tells us that taxes come from the private revenue of individuals, which in their turn take the form of rent, profit, or wage, or a combination of them.

Smith offers us four maxims of taxation, four characteristics of taxes that ought to be present to have a good tax system.

First, Smith claims, taxes must be in proportion to the revenue of the individual taxed: they must be as much as possible in proportion to the ability to pay of each contributor. If a tax falls only on one kind of revenue, the tax becomes unnecessarily unequal.

Second, for Smith, a tax ought to be certain and not arbitrary. One needs to be sure about the time, the manner, and the quantity of the tax payment. If not, the tax collector will have extortion powers. Uncertainty in taxation is also the most odious defect of a tax. It is less accepted than inequality.

Third, according to Smith, a tax ought to be levied at a time and in a manner that is convenient to the contributor. For example, taxing little by little, as a consumer buys a good, is generally more convenient than paying a large tax all at once.

Fourth, Smith continues, collecting taxes should be as cheap as possible. If to levy the tax, one needs many officers, their salaries will eat up a large part of the tax, which induces the tax to be large. But a large tax discourages industry and encourages evasion. Smuggling may then prevail. And to prevent smuggling, penalties may increase, which creates a set of incentives contrary to justice. Furthermore, frequent visits of tax collectors become odious and synonymous with oppression.

Yet again, Smith reminds us that different societies have had different successes in applying these maxims.

What follows is a problematic part of the *Wealth of Nations*. Smith's analysis of tax incidence is inconsistent and, more often than not, incorrect, given today's understanding of price elasticity of demand and supply, that is, given our understanding of how much consumption and production change given taxation. This matters because it is the source of how much consumers and producers share the tax burden. Smith does understand that who is legally obliged to pay a tax may not be the one paying the tax. Yet, he finds himself at a loss to explain tax incidence in a way that makes sense to us today. So, bear with him.

ARTICLE I: TAXES UPON RENT; TAXES UPON THE RENT OF THE LAND

Taxes on rent can take two different forms, either a fixed tax or one that varies with the fluctuation of the rent and production.

The fixed tax is equal for all when it is established, but it becomes unequal over time because the productivity of different lands will vary over time. For Smith, the positive aspects of this tax are that it is certain, cheap to levy, and conveniently collected with rent. It also does not create perverse incentives that may lead to a decrease in industry. But because of its fixity, this tax cannot capture improvements in production. Landlords pay a fixed amount, whether their rent increases or decreases. So when the rent increases, they keep the higher profits. They are better off, but the sovereign is not. In times of economic downturns, instead, this fixed tax may benefit the sovereign at the expense of the landlords. Furthermore, if the payment is required in money, and if the value of silver increases, the tax may become oppressive. However, if the value of silver decreases, the revenue of the sovereign will decrease with it. This variability of benefits with their circumstances makes the fixed tax problematic, as a tax should be convenient in all circumstances, not just in some.

A tax that varies with the variations of rent, instead, changes with improvements, Smith claims. Smith claims also that the French economists recommend it. It may be more equal than a fixed tax, but it is more uncertain and more expensive to assess and collect. A possible way to reduce uncertainty would be to record each lease in a public registry. But this may encourage landlords to ask for fees rather than increasing rent. The practice is also deleterious because it requires a relatively large sum of ready money, which reduces capital and thus reduces the ability to cultivate the land.

Some landlords may believe they have better knowledge than their farmers. But Smith believes that most likely that is not the case. Nevertheless, they may dictate in the terms of the lease the kind of cultivation to be done and the methods to use. This is like asking for an additional rent, in service rather than in money. It is a practice to discourage. A higher tax for these kinds of leases may do the trick.

Some other landlords may require payment in kind. Tenants are always hurt more than landlords benefit. The poverty of the tenants where there are these leases is evidence of it. These leases should also be discouraged with higher taxation.

Finally some landlords occupy part of their lands. For Smith, they encourage cultivation because they have more capital available than their tenants so they can afford experimentation. If they fail, it is a small loss to them. If they succeed, everybody benefits from the improvement. But too much of a good thing can become a bad thing. Landlords should not try to cultivate all their lands themselves. They would displace the sober and industrious tenants, decreasing the revenue not just for themselves but for society too.

Additionally, a tax that varies with the variation of rent is expensive to collect. But Smith views the most powerful objection as that this tax would discourage improvement. A possible way around it is to reimburse the expense of the improvement and also to try to offer a larger market for the produce of these improvements.

Yet, a tax that varies with rent has the advantage that it varies with the changes of society, with its improvements, and with variations in the value of silver and the standards of the coin. This tax adjusts itself to changes of circumstances without much attention from the government.

Now, Smith continues, regardless of a fixed or variable tax, which rents should we tax? Some states require the registering of leases; others require a laborious and expensive survey and valuation of lands. Chances are that the lessor and the lessee combine to defraud the public. The problem is that even a land tax assessed according to general survey and evaluation becomes unequal over time. It needs continual and painful attention from the government, causing more pain than benefits to the contributors.

One last thing that Smith notes is that the lands of the church are treated differently from the lands of regular landlords. In some states they are not taxed at all; in other states they are taxed more lightly than the land of private individuals.

TAXES WHICH ARE PROPORTIONED, NOT TO THE RENT, BUT TO THE PRODUCE OF THE LAND

Here we can't escape seeing the unfortunate problem that Smith incurs in explaining actual tax incidence. For Smith, these taxes on the produce of the land are still taxes on rent. The farmers may be paying them at first, but the landlord is the one having to pay them in the end. The price of produce will not change and the wage of the worker will not change, so rent will. Only rent will decrease – by the amount of the tax.

An example of tax on produce that Smith gives is the tythe, usually a tenth part of the annual produce collected by the church. This type of tax might seem equal but in reality is not. In very poor places, cultivating is quite expensive. Paying a tenth of the produce in taxes may easily decrease capital. The tythe is thus unequal, and it discourages improvement and cultivation.

In theory the church's tythe is similar to the Asian land tax. In Asia, Smith reminds us, it is in the interest of the sovereign to extend the market with good roads and canals: if agriculture improves, he collects more taxes. But the taxes in Europe are used to support the church, not good roads. Thus, there are no benefits in having a tythe.

Taxes on the produce of land can be levied in kind or in money. Smith sees that if the landlord has a small estate, payment in kind is better because it is easy to see and check the quantity collected. If the estate is large, and if he lives away, paying in kind means frauds, with great losses to the sovereign too. The servants of the most careless private person, Smith tells us, are more under the eye and control of their master than the one of a very careful prince. The public revenue collected in kind is, therefore, always mismanaged by its collectors. Remember that the Mandarins are abusive and extortive, in Smith's account of the stationary conditions of China? Guess how they collect taxes? Yes, in kind.

More evidence? A tax levied in money is always in proportion to the value of the produce, varying with the variations in market prices and the value of precious metals, Smith says. If the tax is equal to a certain sum of money, such as the land tax of England, it will not change with the changes in rent or improvement. This means that as the economy improves, tax revenue remains the same. So, some servants in the East India Company, under the pretense of restoring public revenue to the previous value, petitioned and obtained changing the payment into an in-kind payment. Not surprising, cultivation declined, abuses increased, and revenue dropped.

TAXES UPON RENT OF HOUSES

The rent of a house, for Smith, is divided into two kinds: the building rent and the ground rent.

The building rent is the interest or profit of the capital spent in building the house. Because capital can be either lent out at interest or used to build a house, the rent is the same as the forgone opportunity of receiving interest had the money been lent. In addition, it includes the costs of repairs of the house. If not, the building would not be there. This is why, for Smith, the interest of money regulates the building rent.

The ground rent, instead, for Smith, is what is left after a reasonable profit. It is the price paid for some real or imagined benefits. So, for example, ground rent is usually higher in the capital or where the demand of housing is higher.

Smith goes on explaining: a tax on the house rent does not affect the building rent. If the builder does not get what is considered a reasonable profit, he will not build the house. The demand for buildings will thus increase, bringing profits back to the level of the profits in other trades. As a side note again, that differentiation between changes in demand and changes in quantity demanded are still to be desired at this time, and yet here he seems to have some visions of shared tax burden. He indeed continues by saying that this tax will not fall on the ground rent but will be divided between who lives in the house and the owner of the ground. The inhabitants of the house will pay part of the tax in the form of smaller homes with fewer conveniences. By looking for a smaller place, they reduce competition for larger houses, decreasing their prices. The owners of the ground, receiving a lower rent, will pay part of the tax by ways of the lower revenue received.

This tax on house rent has an unintended benefit: it falls more heavily on the rich. Again, here we need to follow Smith in his logic. Rich people, Smith tells us, spend more on housing than poor people (in absolute, not relative terms). Homes are conspicuous consumption goods, to use a term made famous later by the economist Thorstein Veblen – they are goods meant to show off status and wealth. The poor, being poor, spend most of their income on food, trying to survive. Housing, let alone fancy housing, is not as much a priority as food. So because the rich spend more on housing than the poor, the house rent tax will fall more on the rich than on the poor. And this is not a bad thing, to Smith.

A house rent tax is different from a land rent tax, as Smith explains. The land produces the means to pay for its taxation. For a house rent tax, the ground on which the house stands does not produce anything. So the means to pay the tax must come from other sources of revenue, more or less like a tax on consumable commodities. This means that the tax on house rent falls equally on all kinds of revenue, in this way fulfilling one of the maxims of good taxation.

But as for all taxes, if this one is too high, it will incentivize evasion and substitution toward other possibly less comfortable housing options.

Smith offers two final suggestions: a house that is not inhabited should not be taxed. And a house inhabited by its owner should be taxed as if it was rented out.

For Smith, ground rents are a more proper subject of taxation than rents. The ground-rent tax does not increase the rent of the house. It simply, well not that simply, but simply for Smith, falls on the owner of the ground. The owner of the ground is like a monopolist, and he can extract the highest rent possible from his tenants. But the more one has to pay in taxes, the less one is willing to pay for the ground. This is why the final payment falls on the owner of the ground rent and not on the tenant.

The ground-rent and rent-of-land taxes are special because they create revenue without discouraging industry, according to Smith. This seems to be because they do not affect the price of the good. But in Europe it is difficult to find ground rents separated from building rents so it is difficult to separate which is which to tax them separately.

Other taxes, all odious, include a heart tax, a dwelling tax, and a window tax. A heart tax is a tax on each heart beating in a house. This implies that the tax collector needs to inspect regularly all the rooms in a house. A dwelling tax is a tax on the number of windows in a house. It is less invasive because one can count them from the outside. A window tax is a tax that increases with the number of windows in houses. Countryside houses tend to have more windows than city houses, and poor people tend to live in the countryside while the rich reside in cities. So this law unequally punishes the poor. But at least it is easy to collect, certain, and conveniently paid.

Lesson learnt? For Smith, rents decrease as taxes increase. Can we prove it? Yes, we can look at the data on rents and taxes. But if we do, we see the opposite! Rent generally increases as taxes increase. But Smith reminds us once again to look with care at what goes on. There may be what we call today a missing variable. And indeed there is. At the same time, and for independent reasons, the demand for housing increased. The higher demand increased rents more than the increased taxation decreased rents. Without taxes, rents would be much higher. Too bad for the landlords who are losing out. And, Smith seems to tell us again and again: when you look, be careful to look at the right thing before drawing any conclusions.

ARTICLE II: TAXES UPON PROFITS; OR UPON THE REVENUE ARISING FROM STOCK

Smith recalls that capital creates a surplus to pay for its interest. This surplus is not taxable directly. It is the compensation for the risk and trouble for using the capital. If taxed directly, it would either increase profits or reduce interest.

If it increases profits, the capital owner simply advances the tax. In reality, the tax will be paid either by the landlords, in case the tax increases the price of produce and thus decreases the rent of land, or by consumers, if the tax increases the prices of goods. If the tax increases profits, it will decrease interest.

The interest of money seems to be taxable directly like the rent of land, according to Smith. But what it seems is not what it is, as it is often the case for Smith. The quantity of land one owns is not a secret. The amount of capital stock is. In addition, capital stock varies constantly, almost from day to day. An inquisition over the private circumstances of individuals would create an unbearable burden.

Another difference between land and capital stock is that land does not move. Capital does, and easily so. The owners of capital are citizens of the world, in the sense that they are not attached to any countries. They are willing to abandon a country if that country proves too intrusive. If they move their capital, the industry will suffer, and with it the revenue of both the sovereign and of all people because both rents and wages will decrease. The only way to prevent this disastrous situation is to use extreme moderation in taxing capital, to the extent of taxing it below its earned revenue.

In England, for Smith, the tax works because the tax assessment is very old; because the economy grew over time, the tax decreased over time. In Hamburg, to avoid an inquisition, there is a system of self-declaration of wealth with anonymous contribution to the public revenue upon oath. In a canton in Switzerland people publicly declare their wealth by oath and pay a percentage of what they declared. But these systems would not work elsewhere. In particular, they would not work where there are many merchants engaged in risky business. Sober and parsimonious people do not feel the need of secrecy, but merchants of risky trades are terrified to declare publicly the state of their finances. Their credit could be ruined and their projects decrease.

TAXES UPON THE PROFIT OF A PARTICULAR EMPLOYMENT

In some countries, Smith tells us, there are extraordinary taxes on profits of particular branches of trade or agriculture.

One form of this extraordinary taxation is a license fee. Now, the tax on profit of capital employed in trade falls on consumers, as the prices of goods increases with the tax, so Smith claims. This tax is equal because each consumer pays the tax in relation to how much he wants to consume. But a fixed license fee to sell something is unequal. It is the same for small and big businesses. It can thus be oppressive for smaller businesses. If it is moderate, this inequality becomes less important. But if it is considerable, it will put small dealers out of business.

Furthermore, taxes on profits in particular employments do not affect the interest on money. If they did, nobody would lend to the employment that is taxed.

Smith here lists a bunch of activities with these extraordinary taxes. For example, in England there is a special tax on hawkers (a sort of street vendor), peddlers (a sort of travelling seller), or keeper of alehouses (a sort of bar). They all have to pay a license to work.

There is a tax called taille, which is a tax on the profits of capital used in agriculture, Smith tells us. It probably originated from the jealousy of great landlords who see their former dependents now owning land. They convinced the king to tax them out of envy. This tax takes two forms: the real taille, which is a tax on the lands held by "ignoble tenure", which is very unequal; and the personal taille, which is a tax on the profits of each farmer, which is very unequal and very arbitrary.

In the case of a tax on the profits of particular trades, traders bring to market only the goods they can sell at a price high enough to cover the tax. Ergo the tax falls entirely on consumers. Yes, that is not right, his lack of marginal analysis tools forces him to consider the shift an all or nothing shift, rather than a sharing of the tax burden, but let's just follow Smith's logic. In the case of a tax on agricultural profits, Smith says, farmers have incentives to bring to market all their produce, just like before. They pay taxes on land, so if they reduce the quantity sold, they may no longer be able to pay rent or taxes. Ergo taxes here do not increase the price of produce, but decrease the rent the farmer pays to the landlord. If farmers see their profits decrease, they will stop cultivating land and switch jobs.

With a personal taille, a farmer is assessed in proportion to the capital he appears to employ. He will, therefore, fake poverty. But to show how hated this tax is, Smith tells us that farmers will most likely lose more by the reduction in production than what is saved in taxes. In addition, their actions will make everybody else suffer too because of the reduction in production.

Finally, in North America there is a special tax called poll tax on African slaves. Paying it is a sign of freedom because if one has property to be taxed, he cannot be property himself. In Holland, instead, there is a tax on servants. But this is more correctly an expense tax.

APPENDIX TO ARTICLES I AND II: TAXES UPON THE CAPITAL VALUE OF LANDS, HOUSES, AND STOCK

Taxing transfer of property often results in a tax on its capital value. For Smith, to transfer from the dead to the living, or to transfer immobile property, direct taxing is generally easy because the transfer cannot be hidden for long. Taxing the transfer of capital or movable property when it implies lending of money is instead not easy because it is possible to keep it secret. Thus, taxation needs to be indirect, such as with a deed on paper with a duty stamp, the absence of which would invalidate the deed, or with a record in a public or secret registry with a duty of registration.

Stamp duties and duties of registration are now used for all transfers of property, Smith tells us, even the ones that can be taxed directly. Why? Because it is easy to do. And, not holding punches, Smith comments that governments learn very quickly how to drain money from people's pockets. The implication seems to be that governments do not learn as quickly how to prevent special privileges from hindering the economy.

Here Smith offers a hint of intuition that price elasticity of demand and supply may have an effect. So Smith claims, uncontroversially, that the tax for the transfer of property from the dead to the living falls, of course, on the living. Then he claims that the tax on the sale of land falls on the seller because the seller needs to sell more than the buyer needs to buy. The tax on the sale of newly built houses falls on the buyer because the builder must have his profits or he would not build. The tax on the sale of old houses falls on the seller, as he needs to sell. Smith can see this also because the number of newly built houses brought to market depends on demand, while the number of old houses brought to market is independent of demand. Finally, the tax on the sale of ground rents falls on sellers like the tax on land and on old houses. The stamp duties and the duties of registration for borrowed money fall on borrowers. The problem here, again, is the incomplete understanding of price elasticity of demand and supply, and thus an all-or-nothing analysis.

Now, for Smith, if taxes on property transfers decrease the capital value of the property, we increase the revenue of the sovereign, which maintains mostly unproductive labor, at the expense of the funds that maintain productive labor, which now decreases. Despite this negative effect, this tax is, yes, unequal, but it is not arbitrary. It is also convenient and inexpensive to pay.

The registration of mortgages is beneficial, in Smith's account. It gives security to both creditors and debtors. Other deeds, unfortunately, are inconvenient and do not offer any significant benefits to the public.

Finally, Smith believes that stamp duties on cards and dices, on newspaper and periodicals, are consumption taxes, that a consumer pays in proportion to his desire to consume them.

ARTICLE III: TAXES UPON WAGES OF LABOR

As Smith reminds us here, the wage of a worker depends on population and on the price of subsistence goods. If the price of subsistence goods increases, wages have to increase too. Workers have to have enough to live. So a direct tax on wages will have the effect of increasing wage, and of doing it more than the tax. I use a numerical example, even if Smith does not, to clarify his reasoning. Let's say a worker needs a wage of 100 to live and the tax is 10 percent. Ten percent of 100 is 10, but if you pay him 110 and tax him at 10 percent the tax paid is 11, and he will have only 99 left to eat. This is why the raise in wage has to be more than the tax. The worker still needs to have 100 in his pocket after the tax is paid, or he will not survive.

If the direct tax on wage does not affect wages, it is because landlords and consumers paid it, thus decreasing the demand for labor. The decline in industry and employment of the poor will follow, as well as the decline in the produce of the land.

A tax on wages of country labor will increase the price of rude produce and will be like a tax on the farmers' profits, Smith explains. It is absurd and destructive and yet adopted by many countries.

The tax on the recompense of "ingenious artists and men of liberal professions" increases their wages so that the after-tax wage is as it was before the tax, or people will quit these activities.

Wages of office are often higher than what they would be if there was competition like in other professions, Smith states. But there is not competition, so wages are higher. These are good wages to tax. And because they usually generate envy, a tax higher than others would be popular. Passions always play a role in Smith's analysis.

ARTICLE IV: TAXES WHICH, IT IS INTENDED, SHOULD FALL INDIFFERENTLY UPON EVERY DIFFERENT SPECIES OF REVENUE

Capitation taxes and taxes upon consumable commodities do not target any specific revenue, for Smith, but are paid indifferently from whatever revenue one has.

CAPITATION TAXES

Capitation taxes, also known as "head taxes" are a catch-22: one cannot win. If you gain on one margin, you lose on another; if you make them equal, they become arbitrary and uncertain; and if you make them certain, they become unequal. So, Smith tells us, if capitation taxes are in proportion to the fortune or revenue of individuals, they are arbitrary. In addition, because fortunes can and do change frequently, capitation taxes require an "intolerable inquisition", as Smith calls it. This makes the tax arbitrary because its assessment will depend on mood of the assessor. Even if you make them proportioned to the rank of individuals, you make them unequal because there is a wide variance of fortune within each rank.

For Smith, uncertainty is always a problem. Inequality is more acceptable when taxes are light, but it becomes intolerable when taxes are high. A capitation tax does not cost much to levy, and it provides sure, even if modest, revenue for the state.

TAXES UPON CONSUMABLE COMMODITIES

The impossibility to tax people in proportion to their income with a capitation tax led to the creation of a new tax: a tax on consumption. Smith explains that when one's consumption is proportioned to one's revenue, this tax on consumption is proportional to revenue. In addition, taxes on consumable commodities are generally certain: one knows how much and when to pay them; they are generally paid piecemeal, which is also a plus. The problem is that they are costly to administer. They need a large number of customs officers. This discourages industry because the tax increases the price of the goods, and an increase in price induces a decrease in quantity demanded and supplied of all other domestic products too. As productive labor decreases, it alters the national industry in a direction that is less advantageous.

Consumable goods are of two kinds, according to Smith: necessity and luxury. He defines them both.

Necessities are those things that are seen as indispensable to support life and decency, so that even people of lower ranks cannot go without. Note that the definition includes decency, and standards of decency are something that vary from culture to culture and from period to period. Indeed, Smith immediately tells us that in his time in Britain, a linen shirt is a necessity, not a luxury. Why? Because even a day laborer would be ashamed to go around without wearing one. But while leather shoes are seen as a necessity in England, they are not for Scottish women or for both man and women in France, who are perfectly unembarrassed to go around barefoot.

Luxuries, for Smith, are those goods from which one can abstain without reproach. Beer and ale are, for instance, luxuries in Smith's account because one can live without them and still be considered a decent person.

We already know that the wage of labor depends on its demand and on the average price of necessities. And we already know we need to ignore our knowledge about tax incidence and follow Smith's logic, even if imprecise. So, the consumption of necessities, being necessities, will be unaffected by a change in their price. The change in their price will be picked up by wages, which will change so that real wage (how much you can buy) stays constant. This implies that taxing necessities will increase not just wages, but also the price of all manufactures, which will eventually decrease consumption. So, for Smith, taxing necessities works like a direct tax on wages: the final payment of the tax will fall on rich consumers of manufactures because the employer will charge a higher price to maintain the same level of wages and profits. And if the employer is a farmer, the final payment will fall on the rent that the landlord receives. If an increase in wage does not compensate the average increase in the price of necessities, the supply of labor will fall because the poor will not be able to bring up children.

If only the people of superior ranks understood their interest, laments Smith. They would never favor a tax on necessities or direct taxation of wages. But we know from Book I that they do not know their own interest, even if it is an interest that aligns with society's interest.

The other reason why necessities are taxed, according to Smith, ignorance aside, is that they do generate considerable revenue for the government, and it is almost impossible to find a suitable substitute.

In Britain, during Smith's time, Smith tells us, the principal taxes on necessities are on salt, leather, soap, and candles.

Taxes on luxuries work differently, Smith explains. They will not affect the wage of labor, nor will they affect the ability of the lower classes to raise a family. They are more like sumptuary laws: they induce the industrious poor to refrain from consumption, maybe even increasing their ability to raise a family, given the extra money saved from the decreased consumption. The dissolute poor, however, will continue with his indulgencies. This will not change his inability to raise a numerous family, as usually his children perish from neglect anyway.

Taxes on luxuries will also not affect the prices of other goods and will be paid by consumers, independently from the source of their revenue, Smith tells us. They may not be proportional to their revenue, as they are proportional to their expenses. If expenses are not proportioned to revenue, then they are not taxes proportioned to revenue. For example, two people may have the same revenue, but one is more frugal than the other. The frugal will pay fewer taxes than the other, despite having the same revenue.

But at least this tax is a voluntary contribution because one chooses to consume the taxed good. Furthermore, the payer eventually will get accustomed to the tax and will assimilate it with the price.

Now let's figure out how to pay for these taxes. There are two ways, Smith tells us. One is to pay an annual sum, usually for non-perishable goods. The other is to pay the tax while the goods are with the dealer, before they are delivered to consumers, usually for perishable goods. So for example, taxes on houses are more conveniently paid in small annual installments than combined in one single payment at the time of the sale of the building.

The other form of taxation is a sort of license to consume, which could substitute for import and export duties, in Smith's mind. But this fee would make the tax unequal because it would not be in proportion to consumption. If people have to pay the same amount to buy drinks, a man who drinks lightly and occasionally would be taxed more heavily than a drunk. This fee would also lose the convenience of paying taxes a bit at the time and add the distress to have to pay it all at once. It would also lose the function of a sumptuary law as, once the tax is paid, it will not matter if one drinks a great deal or a little. It is not a good idea.

What about excise and customs duties? Excise duties on domestic goods meant for domestic consumption are similar to taxing luxuries. Duties on customs seem to have ancient origins. Smith claims that "customs" in customs duties refer to the practice of "customary payments", or customary taxes on the profits of merchants. Merchants generated envy for the nobility, and because foreign merchants were disliked even more than domestic ones, they could be taxed more heavily. Again, note how Smith uses psychological motivations to explain "the spirit of monopoly" that afflicts society.

Probably Smith's experience at the customs house in Edinburgh motivated this sort of back hand praise of smugglers. Smith claims that the ancient duties were levied equally on all goods. While in Smith's time, it is altogether prohibited to import several goods. The prohibition makes smugglers into the main importers. And smugglers do not give any revenue to the state. This is also true for high duties. They encourage smuggling, decreasing the revenue of the state. Smith cites Jonathan Swift: with customs two plus two makes one more often than four. Hume cites the same passage in his accusations of mercantile policies.

Criminalizing imports, for Smith, makes something that is natural into a crime. It creates a group of hypocrites: those who pretend to be concerned about buying smuggled goods. And it wastes productive resources attempting to stop smugglers, thus decreasing the capital of society.

Then there are bounties on exports of domestic products, which are export subsidies, and drawbacks on reexportation, which are tax rebates for imported goods that are then exported, as described in Book IV. For Smith, the combination of the two is a destructive cocktail of fraud that damages the public finances. The goods are sent at sea to collect either the bounty or the drawback, and then are smuggled back in to be resold in the domestic market. But on the books of the customs house, they show up as exports, so it looks like the balance of trade is better than otherwise. What comfort politicians get from these frauds! Frederic Bastiat, a French pamphleteer of the following century, will repeat this argument in a similar way in his accusations against mercantilists: if one cares only about a favorable balance of trade, the only thing that matters is that ships leave domestic ports full of domestic goods. Whether the ships sink immediately after departure or arrive safely is irrelevant: the customs books note the increased exports and all is well.

Following Smith, all imports are somewhat taxed according to some uncertain classifications. This uncertainty makes import duties inferior taxes compared to excise taxes.

It is not necessary to tax all imports, Smith says. It would be more effective to tax just some, decrease those taxes left, and eliminate all the prohibitions, if you care about state revenue, that is. If you care about restricting competition of foreign producers on domestic markets, then all these high duties and prohibitions make more sense.

So what exactly should one do to increase tax revenue? Smith believes that the only solution is to decrease taxes. Lower taxes will decrease the temptation to smuggle. Substituting excise taxes for customs duties and eliminating bounties will also allow for a more effective system. The problem is that excise duties require more checks and visits from the odious tax collectors, making both excises duties and their officers more unpopular than customs duties and customs officers. Yet, for Smith, a solution could be that some, not all, imported goods could be stored in public warehouses and duties could be paid on storage. Public revenue would see no losses and trade and manufacture would benefit. The free circulation of goods and the decrease in price of raw materials would decrease the money price of necessities, which would decrease the money wage of workers, so that the price of manufacture would also decrease, bringing benefits both to foreign and to domestic markets.

But factions and the interests of smuggling merchants are too strong to implement these changes. So British people of middling and higher ranks keep paying duties on imported foreign luxuries, and all rank of people keep paying duties on cheaper luxuries.

The same logic of changing customs duties into excise duties may be applied to reform the current excise duties system with the same result of increasing tax revenue. Smith offers as an example the then-present tax on malt, beer, and ale. Malt, beer, and ale are luxury goods for Smith. They are also popular items of consumption and taxation. In the mid-eighteenth century their taxation is the source of riots in Scotland. Like for import taxes, Smith suggests decreasing the tax on malt – the prepared grain used to make beer, ale, and spirits. And similarly to the "warehouse" solution for imports, taxing malt rather than the distillery would also decrease the incentive to smuggle, which would be otherwise high.

With an analysis of equilibrating forces, Smith reminds us, a tax cannot reduce the profits of a trade for long. The profits of each trade must be kept at the level of other trades or people will quit. Similarly, Smith explains that the demand for barley would most likely increase with the decrease in taxes. Yet the rent and profit of barley would stay more or less the same as the rent and profits of other equally fertile lands. If they were less, less barley would be produced as the field would be used for other produce. If it is larger instead, more land would switch into barley cultivation.

For Smith, the only real sufferer from this change in taxes would be the people who brew for private consumption. If the consumption tax is levied at the retail level, private brewers do not pay it. If the tax is levied on malt they do. The people who brew at home in Smith's time are people of higher ranks. This change would not be that bad, after all, because higher rank people can enjoy many exemptions from taxes, which is unjust and unequal. So it would only be fair that they pay this tax, like others do. Fairness should have priority, but it succumbs to private interests instead. Here, as it is often the case, the interests of the superior ranks of people stand in between the possibility of change that would increase revenue and bring relief to the poor. The consistency of Smith's arguments is not always as solid as one wishes. While before people of higher rank did not understand that it was in their interest not to tax necessities because they would end up paying for those taxes, and thus letting necessities being taxed, here they do know what their interest is, and try to prevent this form of taxation that would hurt them directly.

There are other kinds of taxes on consumable commodities. Most are disruptive, according to Smith. The duties of passage are additional unequal duties that the sovereign collects to increase his revenue, rather than for the maintenance of the transportation system. These inland customs are generally not on bulk but on value because they are not meant to maintain roads. They obstruct the most important of all branches of commerce, which is the interior commerce of a country. In some smaller states there is a version of these duties, called transit duties. They are duties collected to transport goods across the small states. Foreigners are the ones paying them.

So for Smith, the system of taxation in Great Britain is far from perfect, but is far from being the worst system either. It is uniform for the whole interior of the country, and the inland and coastal trade is almost entirely free. Smith goes so far as to claim that this freedom of interior commerce and the effect of the uniformity of the system of taxation is probably one of the main reasons why Great Britain achieved prosperity.

By comparing the system of taxation of Britain with the French, one will see the point clearly, in Smith's view. In France the government appoints the officers who levy taxes on consumable commodities. These officers are directly accountable to the government. Taxes are also levied by "farmers", agents that substitute the government officers in collecting taxes. "Farmers" receive the right to collect revenue in exchange for a rent that they pay to the state. But because very few people can become "farmers of public revenue", the competition among them is limited and it is easy for them to combine. They thus can offer close to no rent or something much less than the real value of the tax.

Smith concludes with one of his paradoxes: the sovereign is compassionate toward his subjects because he knows that the prosperity of his family depends on the prosperity of his people, so he will never knowingly ruin his subjects. The "farmer", however, is a monopolist. He extracts two kinds of exorbitant profits, one as a farmer, and one as a monopolist. Because "farmers of public revenue" do not have reason to care about what happens to the subjects after their "farm" expires, they try to extract as much revenue as they can. So, to them, the law is never severe enough. They constantly push for more rigorous revenue laws.

This is a testable hypothesis. And Smith indeed tests it. Revenue laws should be the most sanguinary where there is "farming" of revenue and the mildest in the areas under the direct control of the sovereign. Not surprisingly, we see that with "farming", the blood of people is nothing compared to the revenue of the prince: smuggling salt and tobacco sent several hundred people to the galleys (a death sentence to row to death on war ships) and to the gibbet (a death sentence to be hung in a public space).

Thus, Smith thinks that the British system of taxation, with all its imperfection, is superior to the French one.

One last topic is left to Smith's analysis: what happens if all the proper and improper forms of taxation are exhausted, and one country faces a war that is so expensive that no tax revenue would be able to pay for it? This is the topic of next chapter in the *Wealth of Nation*: the great debts of the state.

BOOK V, CHAPTER III: OF PUBLIC DEBTS

Smith has been telling us that the size and the nature of government expenditure as well as the revenue used to pay for those expenditures vary with the different historical circumstances of a nation. To understand the current circumstances, we need to compare them with others. And this is how the last chapter of the *Wealth of Nations* starts.

In "rude" states of society, a sovereign has nothing to spend his revenue on but to maintain people. What Smith calls rustic hospitality is thus the principal expense of the rich and the great. As we were told in Book III, it is unlikely that one ruins himself by feeding and clothing others. Evidence of this, for Smith, is the length of time an estate remains within a family. In precommercial societies, estates stay within the same family for generations and generations. If the surplus of the estate, say wood or raw hides, could be sold for money, people would hoard the money, in part because there was nothing interesting to buy, and in part because it was considered a disgrace for a gentleman to engage in trade or to lend at an interest. Plus, in times of violence and disorder, having some money at hand was convenient. If people had to escape they could have some valuable things to take with them. But that same violence also provides incentive to hide the hoarded money, Smith claims. Evidence of this? Smith cites the frequency of treasure troves, of treasures buried or hidden away, which are later found. In the past they were a considerable source of revenue for the sovereign. In Smith's day all the treasure troves of the country would not make a dint in the revenue of a wealthy person, let alone of a country. This is not necessarily to say, even if Smith leaves it unexplained, that treasure troves are less frequently found in Smith's time, but that wealth has significantly increased. So, in ancient times, the disposition to save and the lack of things to buy, and the absence of standing army and of other expenses was such that ancient sovereign would build a treasure.

In commercial societies, there are expensive luxuries and trinkets to spend money on, Smith reminds us. And the sovereign as well as the great lords do spend their revenue on trinkets and baubles. They will eventually dismiss their retainers and give independence to their farmers to pay for these "childish vanities", to bring back the words Smith uses in Book III, where he fully describes the process of emergence of commercial societies.

The ordinary revenue of the sovereign is now barely enough to cover his ordinary expenses, in Smith's account. There is nothing left to amass in a treasure. So when the sovereign faces extraordinary expenses, he has no other option than to ask for extraordinary help. Smith's claim is that the lack of parsimony in times of peace forces the sovereign to contract debts in times of war. But even if there was something in the treasury, war expenses are three to four times more than peace expenses. It would be impossible to cover those expenses with only the treasure and tax revenue. And even if one increases taxes, Smith tells us, the revenue comes in around a year after the tax is imposed. How does the sovereign pay for his troops? Borrowing is the only option. And so borrowing it is.

For Smith, borrowing is possible because the same commercial state that brings the need to borrow to the sovereign brings the ability and willingness to lend to his subjects.

If people are not confident in the justice of their government, Smith explains, they would doubt the enforcement of contracts and payments of debts. They would only reluctantly engage in trade and manufacture. But if they believe their government would protect their property, they would also trust the government with the use of their property. And it does help that, given the pressing need of the government to borrow, it generally offers lenders advantageous terms. And, the general confidence in the justice of the state often allows government debt to sell for more than what was originally paid for it. So, for Smith, traders happily lend because they can increase their trading capital. And the government, knowing it can easily borrow, does not save anymore.

In "rude" societies the opposite is true. For Smith, hoarding is a sign of the distrust that people have in their government. They hide their treasure for fear of government's plunders. Nobody would be willing to lend to these governments. And so these governments, foreseeing the almost impossibility of borrowing, save.

All great nations of Europe are now borrowers, Smith states. They start borrowing on "personal credit", without assigning or mortgaging (collateralize, that is) any particular funds for the payment of the debt.

When this credit is exhausted, sovereigns have to borrow offering collateral: future tax revenue or, as it was called at the time, by mortgaging taxes. The future tax revenue would go to pay this debt. The mortgaging of tax revenue could be of two kinds: for a short period or in perpetuity. Smith explains that a short-term mortgage of taxes implies that the fund should pay both the interest and the principal within the amount of time specified. Because the debt is issued in anticipation of the future tax revenue, this technique is called "raising money by anticipation". A mortgage of taxes in perpetuity would instead create a fund for paying only the interest, not the principal, and the government could redeem the debt at any time by paying back the principal. This is called instead "by perpetual funding" or just "funding".

Smith describes that in Great Britain the annual land tax and malt tax are anticipated every year. The Bank of England advances them at interest, and it receives payments as the tax revenue gradually arrives. Should this revenue not be enough, as it never is, the incoming revenue covers it. So the only tax revenue not yet mortgaged is spent before it appears.

Perpetual funding seems to have been present with three major funds, Smith explains. The South Sea Fund was created to pay the interest on the money that had been anticipated to the government by the Bank of England and the East India Company to create a land bank, which was never created. The Aggregate Fund brought together several funds of mortgaged taxes that were now made in perpetuity to pay the Bank annuities and several other annuities. Then, several more taxes were made into perpetuity forming the General Fund. By now the greater part of taxes previously anticipated for short terms are perpetual ones, paying only the interest of the debt. For Smith, this is the birth of the most ruinous practice of perpetual funding. Nobody will ever care to "liberate public revenue", meaning to free the tax revenue from paying the interest of the public debt and use it for other purposes.

Then, Smith's narration continues, the legal rate of interest was lowered from 6 percent to 5 percent. So 5 percent was declared as the highest rate that was legally possible to receive for lending money. How convenient! Soon after the perpetual funds were created, the creditors of the South Sea Fund, General Fund, and Aggregate Fund were forced to accept an interest rate of 5 percent rather than of 6 percent. This is a saving of 1 percent, which left a considerable surplus from the taxes accumulating into the funds. By 1757 the legal interest dropped to 3 percent, creating an even more significant increase in this surplus.

The surplus of the three funds formed a "sinking fund", a fund meant to pay old debts. In reality the sinking fund facilitated contracting new debts instead. The sinking fund is inadequate to pay off the debt, especially war debts. It is easier to use it for other things. Raising taxes or creating new ones always generates loud complaints. It is difficult. It is much easier to borrow from the sinking fund. And so it is done, Smith tells us.

Borrowing took different methods: upon anticipation or upon perpetual funding, upon annuities for a term of years or for life. If the annuities were for life, they could be upon separate lives (when a person dies, their annuity stops) or upon lots of lives (when a person dies, their annuity goes to the survivors; the last survivor gets the annuities of all the subscribers, which at times can be 20 or 30 people). These last annuities, the one with rights of survivorship, are worth more than the sum of equal annuities on separate lives. Smith's explanation? The good confidence each man has in his own good fortune, the same overconfidence that every man in relative good health has in his probability of success which we met in Book I. That overconfidence that induces people to play the lottery or to become soldiers. Governments prefer these annuities too, Smith claims here, because they raise the most money, even if they are not the ones that enable the fastest liberation of the revenue.

Here Smith describes another difference between France and Britain: an implicit reminder that people are all the same and if they behave differently it is just because they have different constraints not because they are different. So, Smith goes, in France the annuities for life (as opposed to annuities for a term of years) are more popular than in England. Why? Well, the interests of the lenders are different. In England the seat of the government is in the greatest mercantile city in the entire world. Merchants advance money to the government because they want to increase their capital. When they subscribe to a loan, they expect to sell it and to make a profit. However, annuities on one's own life always sell at a loss because you would not pay the same amount for an annuity on the life of another person of similar age and health as for one on your own life. As we see again here, Smith believes we prefer what is close to us than what is farther away. And what is closer to us than ourselves? So, these annuities are not good transferable stock as perpetual annuities. But in France, the seat of the government is not a great mercantile city. The receivers of taxes are tax farmers or court bankers. They are commonly men of low birth, good wealth, and great pride. As a matter of fact, for Smith, their pride is so great that it prevents them from marrying their equals, who would be now deemed inferior. But "quality women" look down on them. So the number of unmarried men is greater in France than in Britain. Unmarried men do not care about posterity because they will have none, so they are happy to exchange their capital for revenue that lasts just as long as their own life and that allows them to live a life of splendor. Smith's explanation is, as usual, a mix of passions and incentives.

Back to the government. Why does the government need to borrow so much again? For war, Smith answers. Wars in commercial societies are extremely expensive as we saw in the first chapter of Book V. The government has no way to increase its revenue as fast and as much as its expenses. The sovereign is afraid that raising taxes so much and so suddenly would "offend people" and disgust them. The ease of borrowing eliminates these fears. Borrowing, especially if with perpetual funding, allows raising money to pay for war with the smallest possible increase in taxes. And, Smith states, the people who live in the capital, away from the dangers of wars, enjoy reading in the newspaper the adventures of their troops! They can dream of the greatness of their empire. When peace comes, they are disappointed because their amusement ends and with it their visionary hopes of national glory. Smith here gives us a very novel understanding of the relation between debt and war: debt reduces the perceived costs of wars and can transform wars in a form of entertainment for the people not directly involved.

The decrease of debt in peace time does not even remotely make up for the increase in expense during war, Smith declares. The enormous debt Great Britain accumulated with recent wars could never be paid off. Expecting that public debt is completely paid off is daydreaming, if one relies only on current ordinary revenue.

Arguing against Melon (1734), a supporter of public debt, Smith reminds us that the capital advanced to the government is capital that generally goes from maintaining productive labor to maintaining unproductive labor. It is wasted capital. The only beneficial use of funding – paying only interest on debt – is during wars. If people feel the complete burden of wars, they would soon grow weary of them, and wars would not be accepted so carelessly and would end faster.

Furthermore, Smith tells us, if taxes become very high, capital owners would take their capital where they can buy more with it because of the lower taxes. And if tax collectors constantly trouble merchants, merchants will move too. Industry would thus decline, as well as trade and manufacture and agriculture.

Now, Smith notes that half a century earlier no one would have thought Great Britain could withstand her current debt burden. But this does not mean that it can support any burden, or even more than the present one. Indeed, chances are that if the national debt rises above a certain threshold, it becomes impossible to pay it, Smith worries. The only way to liberate public revenue, Smith claims, is with bankruptcy, or "pretended payment". Pretended payment is either raising the denomination of the coin or adulterating the coin.

Raising the denomination of the coin (the same coin was before, say, 10 and now, say, 20) is a common expedient to hide bankruptcy by pretending to pay the debt, as Smith explained earlier. In reality creditors, both private and public, are defrauded. Raising the denomination of the coin has the effects of what today we call inflation. It is the "most general and pernicious subversion of fortunes of private people". It enriches the idle and profuse debtors and punishes industrious and frugal creditors. Capital goes from one who can increase it to who dissipates it. Almost all states from antiquity to modernity have used this trick. The direct raising of denomination of the coin (a small weight coin is now called by the same name as a big weight coin) is an unjust operation, but at least it is an open and known operation, Smith tells us.

Adulterating the coin works in the same way. But in adulterated coins precious metals are mixed with a greater quantity of alloy, thus reducing the quantity of precious metals in the coin. Smith explains that the French call this process "augmentation" of the coin. Adulteration, different from the direct raising of denomination, is a secret operation. The coin has the same denomination, the same look, but less metal in it. It is an unjust operation and a "treacherous fraud". When it is discovered, it causes great protests. So much so that coins have to be brought back to their original fineness.

Back to the debt of Great Britain. According to Smith, it is too big to pay off unless one of two of the following things happens.

Remember the *Wealth of Nations* was first published in March 1776 and in Book IV Smith already told us he favors a complete union of the colonies with Britain, just like Scotland did with England, or letting the colonies go. Or else a war will happen.

Smith suggests that Britain could extend taxation to the colonies. This would raise enough revenue to take care of the debt. The problem is that it cannot be done without offering the colonies representation in the British Parliament. And private interests and prejudices would make the change impossible. Yet, it is something worth exploring, even if just as speculation. A new utopia, Smith states.

Land tax, stamp duties, customs, and excise are the four principal taxes of Britain. Ireland as well as both the North American and the West Indian plantations are able to pay a land tax too. Stamp duties can be requested with the deeds of the transfer of property everywhere, just like in Britain. The extension of customs duties to Ireland and to the plantations, combined with the freedom of trade, would benefit everybody: when all the invidious restraints to trade are removed, there would be an immense internal market. For Smith only the excise duties need some modifications, mostly because consumption patterns are not the same in all British territories. Yet we can say that sugar, rum, and tobacco are not necessities of life even if they are universally consumed. They are thus the proper object of taxation and should be taxed before they go out of the hands of the manufacturers and growers, or deposited in public warehouses and taxed there.

It is difficult to estimate the exact increase in tax revenue this union would bring, Smith admits, but it could well increase the sinking fund enough to pay off the whole debt in a few years, and relieve some of the more burdensome taxes too. This would increase the standards of living for the laboring poor. The price of their goods would decline, and thus the demand for them would increase (Smith is unfortunately but understandably always sloppy in distinguishing between changes in demand and changes in quantity demanded, so bear with his imprecision). The demand increase would increase the demand for labor, which would increase population and the standards of living of the working poor. Their consumption would increase, and thus also the public revenue from the taxes on consumption. Everybody is better off.

Objection: Americans do not have gold and silver money. So they would have issues paying taxes, which are required to be paid in gold and silver. Smith's answer: the absence of gold and silver money is not a sign of poverty. Rather, it is a sign of the entrepreneurial spirit and of the desire to employ all stock productively. Using paper money saves the expense of using gold and silver money, which as described in Book II is a much more expensive form of money. The objection is irrelevant: it is not poverty that makes their payment irregular and uncertain, but their eagerness to become rich.

Objection: it is unjust that Ireland and North America contribute toward the discharge of the debt of Great Britain. Smith's answer: on the contrary. That great debt was contracted to support the government that gave Ireland security and liberty, and gave the American colonies their charter, that is, their present liberty and security. The debt was not contracted to defend Britain, but to defend the provinces of the empire. Actually, if one wants to be precise, the last two wars to defend the North American colonies are the causes of this immense debt.

Objection: both Ireland and North America would face higher taxes in the case of a complete union with Britain. Smith's answer: true, but if the debt is indeed paid off, those higher taxes would not be there for long.

The union should also include the territories of the East India Company, according to Smith. They are fertile and populous. They would generate great revenue. Their taxes, though, should not increase. They are already too high. They should decrease.

This is a first solution.

Solution two: if it proves impossible to tax the colonies and to incorporate them in full into the British Parliament, the only other solution is to decrease the expenses of the government, Smith declares. And the only way to do it is to eliminate the expenses for the defense of the colonies. Had it not been for those wars to defend the colonies, the debt would probably have been paid off. And had it not been for those colonies, there would have been no war.

So, for Smith, if the empire cannot sustain the expense of keeping the colonies, it should let them go; if it cannot have revenue that covers its expenses, it should reduce its expenses to match its revenue. Smith states loud and clear: the British Empire is an "imaginary empire", it is a "project of empire", it is a "golden dream" that cannot be realized. Give it up.

The first edition of the *Wealth of Nations* was published on March 9, 1776. July 4, 1776 proved to Britain it should have listened to Smith's advice.

FURTHER READINGS

Kennedy, Gavin. 2008. *Adam Smith*. London: Palgrave Macmillan.

Paganelli, Maria Pia. 2006. "Vanity and the Daedalian Wings of Paper Money in Adam Smith", in *New Voices on Adam Smith*, ed. Eric Schliesser, Leonidas Montes. London and New York: Routledge. 271–289.

Paganelli, Maria Pia and Schumacher, Reinhard. 2019. "Do Not Take Peace for Granted: Adam Smith's Warning on the Relation between Commerce and War". *Cambridge Journal of Economics* 43.3: 785–797

Peacock, A. T. 1975. "The Treatment of Principles of Public Finance in the Wealth of Nations, Disturbances", in *Essays on Adam Smith*, ed. A. Skinner, T. Wilson. Oxford: Clarendon. 553–567.

Stigler, George. 1973. Adam Smith's Travels on the Ship of State. *History of Political Economy* 3: 217–230.

Viner, Jacob 1928. "Adam Smith and Laissez Faire", in *Adam Smith 1776–1926*, ed. J. M. Clark. Chicago: University of Chicago Press. 116–155.

12

LEGACY

The *Wealth of Nations* is an old book. It was published in 1776. One of the most famous editors of the book, Edwin Cannan, described it in the following terms during the celebrations of the 150th year of its publication:

> Very little of Adam Smith's scheme of economics has been left standing by subsequent inquirers. No-one now holds his theory of value, his account of capital is seen to be hopelessly confused, and his theory of distribution is explained as an ill-assorted union between his own theory of prices and the physiocrats' fanciful Economic Table. His classification of incomes is found to involve a misguided attempt to alter the ordinary useful and well-recognised meaning of words, and a mixing up of classification according to source with classification according to method or manner of receipt. His opinions about taxation and its incidence are extremely crude, and his history is based on insufficient information and disfigured by bias.
>
> (Cannan, 1926, p. 123)

Cannan was right. The book is not just old. It is dated. Yet, with Karl Marx's *Das Capital*, it is to this day the most important and famous book in economics. It is also a book that draws scholars from different disciplines. Why? Why is the *Wealth of Nations* still read and important even today?

I do not have a specific answer, but I shall suggest some possible reasons for why the *Wealth of Nations* is considered a classic and part of the great books that shaped Western thought.

First, Adam Smith is a philosopher, in his own meaning of the term. He is someone who specialized in observing, making connections, and systematizing the observations he collected. He follows an implicit yet rigorous method, the same scientific method we use today in scientific analysis. He may have borrowed this method from the natural sciences and applied it to the moral sciences, or social sciences as we would say today. His contemporary, compatriot, and friend David Hume more explicitly called for the development of a "science of man". Adam Smith may have picked up on Hume's challenge and developed this science.

As we saw in the introduction of this *Guidebook*, in an essay on metaphysics, published posthumously, Smith claims that the object of science must be what is permanent. And while human beings are always changing, human nature is not. In the *Wealth of Nations* he seems to have applied this idea to study how we achieve prosperity. With the strict assumption of constant and unchangeable human nature, a human nature that includes both reason and passions, he endeavors to find out what changes, examining how different customs, institutions, and levels of wealth emerge. He develops hypotheses and tests them with the data he finds in history. He analyzes his data carefully, questioning the veracity of what we perceive "at first sight" and "commonly believe" with reason and models, searching for the most rational direction of causation between different variables. His scientific method is what we recognize today, despite all the "crudeness" that Cannan identifies.

It may not be an accident that Adam Smith is looked at with interest and awe by contemporary economists who do experimental economics. Experimental economics is a relatively new branch of economics that uses laboratory and field experiments with human subjects. The 2002 Nobel Prize winner in economics, Vernon Smith, is a pioneer not only in experimental economics but also of incorporating the work of Adam Smith into this field. Today's experimental results, in part, force economists to question the validity of the assumption of *Homo Economicus* and the relevance of his behavior. As a close reading of the *Wealth of Nations* demonstrates, *Homo Economicus* cannot be found in it.

Instead, there is a human being with a variety of instincts, passions, and emotions, including of course self-interest, but also vanity, envy, and resentment.

Adam Smith, like Vernon Smith today, prefers to describe human actions as "conduct" rather than "behavior". *Behavior* implies a sort of mechanical response to specific incentives. *Conduct* implies more of an understanding of the different circumstances and motivations in which an action takes place, so the same set of incentives may generate different responses depending on the understanding of the context. Conduct also implies judgment, and judgment implies the perception of context and intentions. Our systematic perception biases may tilt judgment as both Smith and experimenters observe.

Adam Smith judged the policies in place in Britain at his time. His judgment was based not only on efficiency, as we would expect from an economist of today. Smith was quite comfortable, and quite explicit too, in expressing moral judgments. His loud condemnations of the mercantile system are based on efficiency, yes, but also, and particularly, on justice.

Another Nobel Prize winner in economics (1986), James Buchanan goes so far as to claim that:

> Adam Smith considered the *Wealth of Nations* to be a demonstration that the "system of natural liberty", which emerged from fundamentally normative criteria of justice, could also meet efficiency criteria. [We tend to] overlook the noneconomic, or more generally, the nonutilitarian, foundations of the "natural system of perfect liberty and justice". ... Smith may well have conceived his masterpiece to be an argument to the effect that the system which was acknowledged to embody justice could also be efficient.
>
> (Buchanan, 1978, pp. 70–77)

Buchanan may have put his finger on another reason for the long-lasting interest in the *Wealth of Nations*. The *Wealth of*

Nations is not just a book about specific policy prescriptions or specific economic concepts. The *Wealth of Nations* is also a book about big ideas and big questions, ideas and questions with which we still grapple today.

We too often forget that the book is titled *An Inquiry into the Nature and Causes of the Wealth of Nations*: an inquiry! And in a sense what we care about today are these inquiries, these questions, not necessarily the answers given. This is why even if we think the answers are wrong, we still want to hear them because we are asking the same questions.

Adam Smith asks: What would a *just* system that also promotes the *well-being* of humankind look like, given the imperfect and *nonperfectible nature* of humankind? How do we get there? How can we preserve it?

When we look at the *Wealth of Nations* in this way, we can start to see its long-lasting appeal. The questions Smith asks are questions that are of interest to us too and will be of interest in the future as well. His policy prescriptions may be particular to his time and may or may not be appropriate for ours, but by being hooked by his questions, we can and do overlook the specificity of his answers and we look for answers that are appropriate to our time. The curiosity that Smith still generates today can be witnessed in the extremely large body of literature on him and his work, as testified by my own (2015) survey and by the multitude of edited volumes on his works (e.g., Haakonssen, 2006; Young, 2009; Berry, Paganelli, and Smith, 2013; Hanley 2016).

Smith links the understanding of the nature and causes of the wealth of nations to understanding an undefined and unexplained "system of natural liberty", which for him may be what allows nations to grow wealthier. Smith's questions are so big and so appealing because they are not just technical questions. They are moral questions as well. They have a technical as well as a moral dimension. After all, Smith writes in a time in which strict disciplinary distinctions are still not present. He is a professor of Moral Philosophy. He writes *The Theory of Moral Sentiments* before the *Wealth of Nations*, and keeps editing both until his death, as he sees both as part of a bigger project that should have also included a part on jurisprudence that was not completed. His analysis can be rigorous and "scientific". His answers can be positive. But the choice of questions is a normative choice in the *Wealth of Nations* or, maybe, *especially* in the *Wealth of Nations* (Bittermann, 1940).

For Smith, wealth and justice are to grow hand in hand. A nation can grow wealthy only if its growth is accompanied by justice. This is why James Buchanan claimed that the *Wealth of Nations* can be read as a book about justice, about a just system that could also be an efficient system, a vision that I have endorsed and explained in this *Guidebook*.

Smith is concerned about understanding how countries grow wealthy, but one of the reasons, if not the main reason, for his concern is that in poor countries people unjustly die, while in rich countries people have more chances to live, to live longer, and to live better.

This is how Smith explains the motivation of his work, in the introduction of the *Wealth of Nations*:

> Some countries are so miserably poor, that, from mere want, they are frequently reduced, or, at least, think themselves reduced, to the necessity sometimes of directly destroying, and sometimes of abandoning their infants, their old people, and those afflicted with lingering diseases, to perish with hunger, or to be devoured by wild beasts.
>
> (WN Introduction, 4, p. 10)

Some countries can be so poor that people "dispose of children in the streets at night" or have them "drowned like puppies" (WN I.viii.24, p. 90). A woman in the poor parts of the Scottish Highlands usually bears 20 children, but she is lucky if only a couple survive (WN I.viii.23, p. 88). Poverty is the unjust cause of suffering of the weakest of society; it is the weakest of society who suffer the most, it is the weakest of society who die. Poverty prematurely kills infants, the old, the sick. Smith wants to investigate the nature and causes of wealth because for him a poor worker in a wealthy nation could live better than "an African king, the absolute master of the lives and liberties of ten thousand naked savages" (WN I.i.11, p. 24). We should care and understand wealth because wealth is what gives us the means to live, and to live relatively longer, better, and freer lives.

The combination of our natural propensity to truck, barter, and exchange, our natural desire to better our condition, the division of labor, capital accumulation, and some luck, allow for "the silent and insensible operations of foreign commerce" to break the chains of poverty and dependency. In Smith's view, commerce brings wealth, liberty, and justice.

Smith wants to understand a "system of natural liberty", which for him may be what allows nations to grow wealthier, and therefore with more "order and good government, and with them, the liberty and security of individuals" (WN III.iv.4, p. 412).

The dichotomy of the state versus the economy, or polity versus the economy, despite what Joseph Spengler may claim (Spengler, 1978), is therefore an alien imposition on Smith. A sharp division between the state and the economy is not going to help us understand the nature and the causes of wealth. For Smith, as a nation grows wealthier, its institutions grow more complex, and the protection of justice also grows more complex. A society of hunter-gatherers has a very limited government, but also has a very limited wealth. As wealth grows, the demand for government grows too. As Benjamin Constant, a good reader of Adam Smith, tells us, in antiquity it was easier to have more people directly involved in political decisions because few people worked (thanks to their slaves). Today, in commercial society, we are interested in our businesses and are more than happy to delegate many political decisions to others. So we rely more and more on government, and the government therefore grows with the growth of the economy. Again, we may or may not agree with Smith's answers, but questions of the relationships between the state and the economy are still ones we ask today.

But the same propensity to truck, barter, and exchange and the same presence of government can also create both conflicts between masters and workers as well as mercantile empires, both of which enrich a few at the expense of many. Smith does not pull his punches against the commercial privileges bought for a few big merchants and manufacturers with the "blood and treasure" of a country's citizens (WN IV.vii.c.63, p. 613). The *Wealth of Nations* can be read therefore as a great anticolonialist and antiimperialist tract. Smith sees his work as a "violent attack against the whole commercial system of Great Britain". He justifies his violent attack on a moral ground, which happens to also be efficient.

His question is relevant for us too: If we manage to achieve a wealthy society, how do we preserve it? His solution against what today we would call lobbyists and cronyism, whether we agree with it or not, is competition.

The singing of the sirens in Homer's *Odyssey* seduces and kills sailors. Despite knowing it, some sailors still go too close to them to resist their allurements. Similarly David Hume writes: "And though men are commonly more governed by what they have seen, than by what they foresee, with whatever certainty; yet promises, protestations, fair appearances, with the allurement of present interests, have such powerful influence as few are able to resist. Mankind are, in all ages, caught by the same baits: the same tricks, played over and over again, still trepan them" (363).

The mercantile baits are indeed played over and over again over the centuries, including in our days. Adam Smith's "violent attacks against the mercantile system" in the *Wealth of Nations* may offer us, today, tomorrow, as well as it did in the past, that rope that tied Ulysses to the mast of his ship. It is a rope that enabled his survival as he sailed through the siren-infested seas, protecting him from his human tendencies. As long as mercantile interests allure people into restricting the size of the market, the *Wealth of Nations* will have something to teach us. As long as we are interested in big questions about the human condition, the *Wealth of Nations* will have something that makes us think.

FURTHER READINGS

Berry, Christopher J., Maria Pia Paganelli, and Craig Smith, eds. 2013. *The Oxford Handbook of Adam Smith*. Oxford and New York: Oxford University Press.

Bittermann, Henry J. 1940. "Adam Smith's Empiricism and the Law of Nature: I". *Journal of Political Economy* 48. 4: 487–520.

Buchanan, James. 1978. "The Justice of Natural Liberty". in *Adam Smith and the Wealth of Nations: Bicentennial Essays 1776–1976*, by Fred Glahe, 61–82. Boulder: Colorado University Press.

Cannan, Edwin. 1926. "Adam Smith as an Economist". *Economica:* 123–134.

Haakonssen, Knud, ed. 2006. *The Cambridge Companion to Adam Smith*. Cambridge: Cambridge University Press.

Hanley, Ryan Patrick. 2016. *Adam Smith: His Life, Thought, and Legacy*. Princeton, NJ, and Oxford: Princeton University Press.

Paganelli, Maria Pia. 2017. "240 Years of Adam Smith's *Wealth of Nations*". *Nova Economia* 27.2: 7–19

Smith, Vernon and Wilson, Bart. 2018. *Humanomics*. New York: Cambridge University Press.

Spengler, Joseph. 1978. "Smith versus Hobbes: Economy versus Polity", in *Adam Smith and the Wealth of Nations: Bicentennial Essays 1776–1976*, by Fred R. Glahe, 35–60. Boulder: Colorado University Press.

Young, Jeffrey T., ed. 2009. *Elgar Companion to Adam Smith*. Cheltenham: Edward Elgar Publishing.

INDEX

ability to pay, taxation in proportion
    to 224
absolute government 172
administration of justice 193–196,
    222–223
affluence, periods of 51–52
aggregation fallacies 98
agio 152–153
agricultural societies 7–8, 190–191
agriculture: discouragement of 126;
    preference for investment in 125
Amsterdam 152, 154, 176, 222
annuities 246–247
apprenticeships 60, 64–65, 68, 150
Aristotle 32
artificers 191
asymmetry of information 105
authority, sources of 194–195,
    216–217
Ayr Bank 106

Bank of Amsterdam 152
Bank of England 104, 107, 165, 245
bank money 152–153
bank runs 103, 109–110, 152–153

banking 101–110; costs and benefits
    of 107; need for trustworthiness
    100–101; Scottish 102–108;
    Smith's proposed regulation of
    108–109
bankruptcy 115, 136
Banks, Joseph 9
bargaining power 49, 55
barter 28–29
Bastiat, Frederic 239
Beattie, James 11
Bengal 51–52, 179
Bentham, Jeremy 119
Berne 222
bills of exchange 102, 104, 152
Black, Joseph 3, 10
borrowing 244
botanical gardens 9
bounties 137, 156–159, 182, 239
Brazil 169–170
Britain 137, 162–163, 251
British colonies 170–174
Buccleuch, Duke of 2, 106, 111
Buchanan, James 55, 254, 256
Buenos Aires 72

bullion prices 37
burghers of towns 130–131
Butler, Joseph 22

Caledonians 8
Calvin, John 218
Cambridge University 208
canals 25, 199
Cannan, Edwin 252
capital stock 16, 39, 48, 54, 56, 63, 68, 88–89, 96, 112–113, 116–119; four uses of 119
capitalism 17
capitation taxes 235
carrying trade 101, 120–121, 145–146, 155–156, 162–163
cartels 49, 64–67
cash accounts 102–103, 106
Catholic Church 213, 217
causation *see* correlation
child labor 23
children and child mortality 53–54
China 9, 50–52, 57, 91, 120, 144, 181, 187, 200, 227
church lands 226
church-state relations 213–218
circulating capital 96–99, 105, 110
circulation, raising money by 105–106
clan system 6
clergymen 67, 111, 218
clubs 4
coal mines 77
coffers of banks, replenishing of 104, 165
coinage 29–30, 33–38, 78, 81–85, 99, 151–152; adulteration of 248–249; value of 37–38
Colbert, Jean-Baptiste 183
collective action theory 49
colonies 67, 125, 136, 166–178; in America 167–171, 174–175, 250; of ancient Greece and Rome 166–167, 170; benefits bestowed on home countries 173–175; causes of prosperity for 169–173; complete

union with 178, 249–251; extending taxation to 249; withdrawal from 177, 249
Columbus, Christopher 167–168
combinations 49–50, 68, 182
commerce, alternative instruments of 28–29
commercial societies 6–8, 17–20, 27, 33, 136
commodity money 100
comparative advantage 24
compensation of labor 58–59; in approbation 197; *real* 92; *see also* wages
competition 72, 110, 197, 204, 239, 258; excessive 67; limits to 59; reduction of 64–66
conduct as distinct from behavior 254
conspicuous consumption 146, 228
Constant, Benjamin 257
consumption 14–16
contract theory 194
conversion prices 82
Copenhagen 113
corn: cost of production in relation to meat 72–73; price of 36, 80, 157, 159, 162
Corn Laws 160, 163
corn merchants 160–161
"corporations" 46, 64–68
correlation as distinct from causation 9, 52, 81, 92, 149–150, 157, 163, 174
corruption 196–197
court cities 113
credit 95–96, 105
crown lands 223
crusades 132
Cullen, William 10
Culloden, Battle of (1746) 5
customs duties 238–240, 249

dancers, professional 61, 111
dancing, teaching of 205
debt burdens 247–248

defense spending 149, 159, 174–175, 189–193, 196, 222, 251
Denmark 170–171, 179
Dick, Robert 1
Dick, Sir Alexander 9
discounting of bills 102
"dismal science" 23
distance sale of manufactures 133
division of labor 17–25, 34, 40, 55, 76, 80, 92–93, 95–96, 116, 123–124, 132, 144, 186, 191, 198, 209–210, 257; limitations of 25, 27
Draco, laws of 183
"drawbacks" on reexportation 239
durables, consumption of 115–116

East India Companies 9, 140–141, 144, 179–180, 201, 203, 227, 245, 250
economic growth 123–124
Edinburgh 4, 10, 113
education 60, 67–68, 204–213, 216, 219
effectual demand 43–45
Egypt 120, 187
Elizabeth I, Queen 93
the Encyclopedie 18
entails 126–127
"enumerated commodities" 171
equalization through trade 22, 24
exchange, process of 21; rules of 31
excise duties and taxes 238–240
"exclusive companies" 179–181
experimental economics 253
experimental method 9–10
export encouragements 145
extraordinary expenses 74

fairness 52
famine 160
farmers' capital 120
"farming" of public revenue 242
feminization and effeminacy 7–8
Ferguson, Adam 8, 194
feudal system 91, 134–136, 191
fiat money 100
fiduciary money 101

firearms 192–193
fishing 40
fixed capital 96–100, 105, 110
Fletcher, Andrew 8
food for human consumption, central significance of 74–79
foreign trade 125; benefits from 144
France 2, 4, 46, 86, 107, 143, 154, 157, 162, 171–173, 186–187, 200, 205, 225, 236, 241, 246–247
free trade 130, 141, 150, 154, 162, 175, 185
frugality 113–116, 237
fruit gardens 74

Gama, Vasco da 167
Genoa 83–84, 132
Gerard, Alexander 10
Germany 8
Glasgow 2, 10, 113
gold: colonists searching for 168–170, 173; desire for accumulation of 142–145, 151, 158, 164; value of 35–36, 83, 87
governments, role of 30, 116–117, 147, 189–220, 257
Grand Tour 2, 111
gravitation of market prices towards natural prices 44–45
Greece, ancient 166, 170, 187, 191, 208–211
Greek language 206
Gregory, John 10
ground rents 228–229
gunpowder 193
gymnastics 208

Hamburg 222, 231
happiness 52–54, 136
Hayek, F. A. 161
Highlands of Scotland 6, 53, 256
historical analysis 126–132, 136–138
history, study of 10, 25
hoarding 97, 244
Holland 56, 83–84, 171, 179, 232

Homer 258
Homo Economicus 254
Hope, John 9–10
hospitality 116, 243
Hudson's Bay Company 203
human nature 11–12, 21, 62, 97, 181, 252
humankind seen as part of nature 10–11
Hume, David 5, 10–11, 109, 118, 132, 134, 137–138, 191, 194, 213–214, 238, 252, 258
Hungary 173
Hutcheson, Francis 1
Hutton, James 3, 10

imagination with respect to others' wants 28
import restrictions 144–145, 182, 238–239
improvement, ideology of 8–9; *see also* land, improvement of; society, improvemet of
India 9, 203
Indonesia 120
Indostan 144, 167, 187
inflation 103, 248
in-kind payments (of tax) 227
institutions 51, 58, 97, 124, 126, 132, 170
interest: definition of 41; fixed by law 118–119; prohibition of 58; rates of 56; of society 93–94, 148, 160, 175–176; *see also* special interest groups
inventories of finished goods 97
"invisible hand" metaphor, Smith's use of 77, 121, 135, 146–147, 161
Ireland 89
Italy 131–132, 162

Japan 144, 187
Jevons, William Stanley 31
joint stock companies 202–204

Kames, Lord 11
Knapp, Georg 29

labor: blocking the circulation of 68; embodied in a good 33–35, 38–41; productive power of 16, 19, 116, 186; "productive" and "unproductive" 111–115, 119–121, 184–186, 234, 248; as the true source of wealth 14, 95, 98; value of 34–35, 46, 52, 110
land: improvement of 71–73, 79, 88–91, 125–129, 170–171, 184, 186, 226; private ownership of 40, 49
land banks 33, 107, 245
land tax 200, 226–227, 249
Latin language 206, 211
Law, John 33, 107
law, rule of 7
law enforcement 58; *see also* administration of justice
lawyers 61, 111
legal tender 36, 110
license fees 231–232
limited liability 202
Linnaeus, Carl 11
Lisbon 113
living conditions 52
local knowledge 161
Locke, John 37, 118, 140
logic, teaching of 207
London 113
lotteries 62–63
Luther, Martin 217–218
luxuries 14, 81, 87, 124, 133, 135, 199, 236–237, 243

Maclaurin, Colin 10
Macpherson, James 8
Malthus, Thomas (and Malthusian theory) 54–55
manufacturing, development of 133
manufacturing towns 113
marginal utility theory 31, 34
marine insurance 63

markets and market prices 24, 43–46
Marx, Karl (and Marxian theory) 16, 49, 55, 252–253
McCloskey, Deidre 56
meat, price of 72–74
melting down of coins 164–165
"men of letters" 67, 111, 209, 218
Menger, Carl 31
mercantilists 14–15, 35, 51, 79, 94, 140, 164, 239
metayers 128
Mexico 85, 144, 169–170
middlemen 42
militias 191–192, 212
Millar, John 11, 194
mining 77–80, 83–87, 90–92, 96, 168
Mississippi Scheme 107
mistakes, making of 62
money 27–30, 32–33, 25, 38, 99–103, 107, 114; based on gold or silver 32–33; definition of 29; evolution of 29–30; as a "great wheel of circulation" and great instrument of commerce 99–101; as a measure of value 35, 38; not to be mistaken for wealth 140; seen by Smith as a highway 107; Smith's theory of 79; state theory of money 29; supply of 85–86; as a tool for fraud 30; as the unintentional consequence of human actions 29–30; value seen in terms of 35
monitoring costs 125
monopolies 46, 57, 71–72, 145, 148, 150, 154–156, 160, 171, 174–177, 182–183; temporary 201–202
Montesquieu, Baron de 11, 118
morality, systems of 207, 214–215, 254–255
Mun, Thomas 140–141
music, study of 208

"natural inclination of man" 124–125
natural philosophy 206–207
natural price 43–46

natural resources 97
nature-nurture debate 211
Navigation Act 149, 175
neat revenue 98–100
necessities, tax on 235–236, 241
new types of job 64
Newton, Sir Isaac (and Newtonianism) 1, 10, 33, 44–45, 207–208

Oeconomists 186
ontology, study of 207
opera singers 61–62, 111
option clause 109
Ossian 8
overconfidence as a human trait 61–63, 168, 246
overissuing by banks 104–110
Oxford University 205

paper money 100–103, 107–110
passions influencing economic growth 123–124, 128, 131, 137, 235
Pennsylvania 222
"perpetual funding" 245, 247
Peru 77–78, 85, 144, 169–170
perverse incentives 181, 205
Peter the Great 192
philosophers, role of 17–18
physics and metaphysics 207
physiocrats 2, 14, 16, 110, 119, 184–185
piece work 53
pin manufacture 18
Pisa 132
Plato 24
Playfair, William 110
Poker Club 191
Poland 83–84, 91, 173
"political economy": general use of the tern 13; Smith's definition of 139
Poor Laws 68, 150
population growth and decline 50–51, 54; related to food supply 75, 77; related to wages 48

Portugal 91, 140, 154, 158, 163, 170–174
potatoes, cultivation of 74
poverty 15, 41, 51–53, 126, 256–257
precious metals 77–79, 83–84, 91
precious stones 78
Presbyterian clergy 218
price elasticity of demand and supply 233
prices: of manufactures 92–93; of metals 90–91; *nominal* and *real* 80–92, 157, 159, 162
primogeniture 126–127, 136–137, 170, 223
prodigality 113–115, 118–119; public 115
productivity, theory of 19, 40
profit 39–45, 49, 56–58, 61–64; extraordinary levels of 45
promissory notes 101–103; in small denominations 108–110
property rights 78, 194
protection of trade 148, 150, 201; restraint of trade 249
Protestantism 217–218
Public Choice analysis 66, 68, 90, 93–94, 150, 172, 181
public works 198, 200, 219
purchasing power 34, 36, 99

Quakers 128
Quesnay, François 111, 183–187

reflux, law of 104
regulated companies 202
regulation of trade 89–90, 163
Reid, Thomas 11
relative prices *see* prices, *nominal* and *real*
relative wages 48
religious institutions and sects 213–216
rent 40–46, 70–77; determined by the amount of land producing human food 74–75; economic regulation of 74–75; on mines 77; related

to scarcity 76; as a residual after payment of costs 72; variations caused by prices 71
retailers, prejudice against 120
Ricardo, David 24
rice fields 74
risk: attitudes to 62–63; running of 41, 58
Robertson, William 10–11
Rome, ancient 126, 130, 166–167, 170, 187, 208–211
Rousseau, Jean-Jacques 7, 17
Royal African Company 203

Samuelson, Paul 31
saving 113, 115, 153, 244
scarcity 160–161
scholarships 67, 205
scientific method 252
Scotland 211, 236, 240; division into Lowlands and Highlands 6; politics in 5–6; trade and infrastructure of 4–7
Scottish banks 102–108, 152
Scottish Enlightenment 10–11
secrets 45–46
seigniorage 37–38, 164–165
self-love and self-interest 22, 28, 62
shepherds 190–192, 195
showing off one's wealth 78–79, 228
silver: desire for accumulation of 142–145, 151, 158, 164; value of 35–36, 79–92, 157–158, 168, 225–226
Simson, Robert 1
Sinclair, John 10
sinking funds 246, 249
slavery 23, 54–55, 128, 170–173; abolition of 128
Smith, Adam 1–4, 8–11; burning of manuscripts 3; career 2–3; emphasis on justice *and* efficiency 68, 78, 172, 254, 256; essentially "modern" economic analysis 54; *History of Astronomy* 146–147; *History of Metaphysics* 11; language skills 1;

literature on 255; parentage and education 1–2; *Principles Which Lead and Direct Philosophical Enquiries* 17; social life 4; *The Theory of Moral Sentiments* 2–3, 14, 22, 28, 61, 77–78, 93, 114, 135, 146–147, 180–181, 214, 255; theory of value 33, 35; works in general 2–4

Smith, Vernon 253–254

smuggling 63, 141, 151, 158, 177, 181, 224, 238–240

society, improvement of 75–76, 80, 89, 93

South Sea Company 107, 203

South Sea Fund 245

sovereigns: duties of 187; sources of revenue for 221–223

Spain 89, 91, 140, 158, 163, 167–174

special interest groups 90, 176, 212

specialization 22, 24

speculation 64

Spengler, Joseph 257

stamp duties 197, 233–234, 249

standards of living 250

standing armies 192–193; professional armies 191, 212

stationary economies 50–51, 54, 57, 136

Steuart, James 13

stock for immediate consumption 96–99, 110; *see also* capital stock

Stuart rebellions 5

subsidies 85–86, 145; *see also* bounties

subsistence 50–55

sugar production 75, 128, 172–173, 249

supply: changes in 45, 79–80; limitations of 74–75

Sweden 179

Swift, Jonathan 238

Switzerland 162, 231

taille tax 129, 232

tax revenue: mortgaging of 244–245; sovereigns' need for 223

taxation 129–131, 182, 196, 201, 242; on consumable commodities 235–242; direct and indirect taxation 233; head taxes 235; heart taxes 229; on house rents 228–230; on imports 239; on land rents 224–226; on luxuries and on necessities 236–237, 241; on malt, beer and ale 240; on particular activities 232; poll tax 232; on the produce of land 226–227; on profits 230–232; by requisition 177–178; Smith's four maxims for 223–224; on wages 234–235; window tax 229–230; *see also* capitation taxes

teaching 204–213; private 209

tobacco production 75, 128, 175, 249

tolls 198–200

town and country, differentials between 65–67, 72–73, 83, 124–125, 132–134, 183

trade, benefits from 154

trade balance 151–156, 164; positive 141–145

trade restrictions 3, 181; *see also* import restrictions

transit duties 241

transport costs 72–73, 84, 132–133, 148–149, 199

travel diaries 10–11

treasure troves 243

truck, barter and exchange, human propensity for 20–24, 257

trust required for certain jobs 60–61

Tucker, Josiah 22

Turgot, Anne Robert Jacques 48–49

tythes 227

universities 204–208, 218

unlimited liability 100, 106, 202

usury and usury laws 56, 118–119

utilitarianism 52

value in exchange 31–34; measured by embodied labor 33–34

value in use 31–32

Veblen, Thorstein 228
Venice 132, 167, 222
vent for surplus 144
violence in society, effects of 97, 161

wages 48–68; balanced against other
   compensation 58–59; inequalities in
   59–68; *see also* relative wages
Wallace, Robert 8
Walras, Leon 31
warehouses for imports 240
warfare 116; financing of 142–144,
   222, 247–248; opportunity cost of
   190

waste 76
water–diamond paradox 31
water transportation 25–26, 124–125,
   132
Watt, James 10
wealth, analysis of 12, 14–16, 256; seen
   as the ability to consume 98
"wearing" of coins, plate and metal
   tools 85
Westminster Hall 134
wholesale trade 120–121
William III, King 37
wine and vineyards 74–75, 148
wool and hides, marketing of 89–90